Plone 3 Theming

Create flexible, powerful, and professional themes for
your web site with Plone and basic CSS

Veda Williams

BIRMINGHAM - MUMBAI

Plone 3 Theming

First published: July 2009

Production Reference: 1100709

Published by Packt Publishing Ltd.
32 Lincoln Road
Olton
Birmingham, B27 6PA, UK.

ISBN 978-1-847193-87-2

www.packtpub.com

Cover Image by Parag Kadam (paragvkadam@gmail.com)

Credits

Author
Veda Williams

Reviewers
Steve McMahon

Denys Mishunov

Acquisition Editor
Rashmi Phadnis

Development Editor
Siddharth Mangarole

Technical Editor
Mithun Sehgal

Indexer
Hemangini Bari

Editorial Team Leader
Abhijeet Deobhakta

Project Team Leader
Lata Basantani

Project Coordinator
Neelkanth Mehta

Proofreader
Angie Butcher

Production Coordinator
Shantanu Zagade

Cover Work
Shantanu Zagade

About the Author

Veda Williams has worked in software development for more than eighteen years, and as a Plone themer for three of those years. She currently works for ONE/Northwest in Seattle, Washington. Veda is an editor for the documentation section for `plone.org`, and was an author and the managing editor for Practical Plone 3.

I would like to thank my colleagues, Andrew Burkhalter, Jon Baldivieso, David Glick, and Josh Boese for their help in answering my many questions. I'd also like to thank my reviewers, Steve McMahon and Denys Mishunov, for their time and attention to detail. Most of all, I'd like to thank Jamie Bishop and Mark Porcaro for getting me started with Plone in the first place.

About the Reviewers

Denys Mishunov is the Plone expert, specializing in Plone themes development since early 2004. During his Plone career, Denys worked as a freelancer with a lot of Plone consulting companies, distributed all over the world, and participated in more than 200 Plone projects by providing services in design and Plone themes development. Originally working as a freelancer in Ukraine, Denys has established one of the first Plone 3 projects in the world, Web Couturier, some days before the official release of Plone 3. The project doesn't exist in its original form any more, but has provided some, previously commercial, packages as open source products for the Plone Collective. In 2008, Denys moved to Norway to work with one of the leading Plone consulting companies Jarn (ex- Plone Solutions).

Steve McMahon is a Plone developer based in Davis, California. He's the creator of PloneFormGen, and is currently the maintainer for PloneHelpCenter and Plone's Unified Installer and the OS X Installer. He's serving his second term on the Plone Foundation Board of Directors.

Steve is a partner in Reid-McMahon, LLC, a Plone consultancy specializing in non-profits. He is one of the many authors of *Practical Plone 3* (http://www.packtpub.com/practical-plone-3-beginners-guide-to-building-powerful-websites/book).

Table of Contents

Preface

Themes are among the most powerful features that can be used to customize a web site, especially in Plone. Using custom themes can help you brand your site for a particular corporate image; it ensures standards compliance and creates easily-navigable layouts. But most Plone users still continue to use default themes, as developing and deploying themes that are flexible and easily maintainable is not always straightforward.

This book teaches best practices of Plone theme development, focusing on Plone 3. It provides you with all the information useful for creating a robust and flexible Plone theme. It also provides a sneak peek into the future of Plone's theming system.

In this book you will learn how to create flexible, powerful, and professional Plone themes. It is a step-by-step tutorial on how to work with Plone themes. It also provides a more holistic look at how a real-world theme is constructed. We look at the tools required for theming a web site. The book covers major topics such as configuring the development environment, creating a basic theme product, add-on tools and skinning tricks, integrating multimedia with Plone, and configuring your site's look and feel through the **Zope Management Interface** (**ZMI**). Finally, the book takes a close look at the thrilling and greatly-simplified future of theming Plone sites.

What this book covers

In *Chapter 1*, we will take a look at how theming has become more complex with the newest release of Plone and how this impacts themers. We will also compare other popular CMS platforms with Plone.

In *Chapter 2*, we will take a look at the recommended tools that are needed for theming. We will also take a look at the browser add-ons that are available for inspecting a web site's CSS, JavaScript, color palette, and more.

In *Chapter 3*, we will configure the development environment. We will also learn some of the jargon associated with Plone 3 development.

In *Chapter 4*, we will learn how to create a vanilla theme product and install it.

In *Chapter 5*, we will learn how to expose a theme product to a filesystem. We will take a look at the elements that compose the component architecture for a theme product. We will also learn how the skin layers and through-the-web configuration work. And finally, we will take a look at how to take many of these changes and incorporate them in a filesystem product.

In *Chapter 6*, we will focus on basic Zope 3 components that are involved in filesystem theme development. We will learn how to use ZCML code to tie together the Zope 3 components. We will also learn how to use images, stylesheets, and browser resources and how to write browser views.

In *Chapter 7*, we will focus on viewlets, viewlet managers, and how to manipulate them. We will take a look at portlets and how to customize them. Finally, we will learn how `portal_view_customizations` can be used to manipulate Zope 3 templates through the Web.

In *Chapter 8*, we will learn what a **Zope Page Templates (ZPT)** system is. We will also take a look at **Template Attribute Language (TAL)** and learn common TAL expressions that are used in Plone's templates.

In *Chapter 9*, we will learn how to create a custom theme product, how to modify the file structure, how to set up a Plone theme to use mostly skin layers for images and stylesheets, how to install the theme product, and how to customize the content of your site to support the design.

In *Chapter 10*, we will learn how to change the logo, how to modify the `portal_actions` on a site, how to modify various viewlets and portlets and the templates that are used to render a Plone site, and how to do basic CSS styling.

In *Chapter 11*, we will learn how to create custom home page views, how to do sectional styling, how to enable and create sectional banners, and how to test our site against multiple browsers.

In *Chapter 12*, we will take a look at the popular add-ons, the current state of sub-site theming, non-Plone products that can be used to alter the site's look and feel, and Plone-specific debugging tools.

In *Chapter 13*, we will learn how to embed multimedia into the content of a page and into a page template. We will also take a look at the Plone-specified add-ons that provide multimedia support.

In *Chapter 14*, we will take a look at the suggested development environments, theme deployment workflow, the quality assurance process, and how to contribute to the Plone theming community by creating publically available themes.

In *Chapter 15*, we will take a sneak peek into the future of rules-based theming for Plone. This chapter will feature a complete walk-through of theming a site using the `collective.xdv` add-on.

What you need for this book

To run a Plone 3-based web site you need:

Operating system requirements:

- Windows XP or later
- OSX 10.4.x or later
- Linux 2.6.x or later
- Python 2.4 (Plone 3.x series do *not* work with Python 2.5, 2.6, or 3.0)

On OSX and Linux you need to have development tools (GCC) installed for installing Plone.

Conventions

In this book, you will find a number of styles of text that distinguish between different kinds of information. Here are some examples of these styles, and an explanation of their meaning.

Code words in text are shown as follows: "Notice the `enabled` flag here, and also notice that it's not necessary to include the `.dtml` indication in the `id` field, even though we will be using DTML."

A block of code is set as follows. (Code and markup preceded and ended with ellipses, "...", are extracted from the full context of code and/or a larger body of code and markup. You will also see the occasional use of "[snip]" for the same purpose. Please reference the downloadable code packet to see the entire work.)

```xml
<?xml version="1.0"?>
<object name="portal_css">
<stylesheet title=""
    id="ace.css"
    media="screen" rel="stylesheet" rendering="import"
    cacheable="True" compression="safe" cookable="True"
    enabled="1" expression=""/>
</object>
```

When we wish to draw your attention to a particular part of a code block, the relevant lines or items are set in bold:

```
<?xml version="1.0"?>
<object name="portal_css">
<stylesheet title=""
    id="ace.css"
    media="screen" rel="stylesheet" rendering="import"
    cacheable="True" compression="safe" cookable="True"
    enabled="1" expression=""/>
</object>
```

Any command-line input or output is written as follows:

```
./bin/buildout -n
```

New terms and **important words** are shown in bold. Words that you see on the screen, in menus or dialog boxes for example, appear in the text like this: "Within the site_actions category you will find the menu options that correspond to the top navigation on a default Plone installation. By default, these include **Site Map**, **Accessibility**, **Contact**, and **Site Setup**."

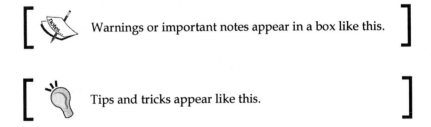

Warnings or important notes appear in a box like this.

Tips and tricks appear like this.

Reader feedback

Feedback from our readers is always welcome. Let us know what you think about this book—what you liked or may have disliked. Reader feedback is important for us to develop titles that you really get the most out of.

To send us general feedback, simply send an email to feedback@packtpub.com, and mention the book title via the subject of your message.

If there is a book that you need and would like to see us publish, please send us a note in the **SUGGEST A TITLE** form on www.packtpub.com or email to suggest@packtpub.com.

If there is a topic that you have expertise in and you are interested in either writing or contributing to a book, see our author guide on `www.packtpub.com/authors`.

Customer support

Now that you are the proud owner of a Packt book, we have a number of things to help you to get the most from your purchase.

Downloading the example code for the book

Visit `http://www.packtpub.com/files/code/3872_Code.zip` to directly download the example code.

The downloadable files contain instructions on how to use them.

Errata

Although we have taken every care to ensure the accuracy of our content, mistakes do happen. If you find a mistake in one of our books—maybe a mistake in the text or the code—we would be grateful if you would report this to us. By doing so, you can save other readers from frustration and help us improve the subsequent versions of this book. If you find any errata, please report them by visiting `http://www.packtpub.com/support`, selecting your book, clicking on the **let us know** link, and entering the details of your errata. Once your errata are verified, your submission will be accepted and the errata added to any list of existing errata. Any existing errata can be viewed by selecting your title from `http://www.packtpub.com/support`.

Piracy

Piracy of copyright material on the Internet is an ongoing problem across all media. At Packt, we take the protection of our copyright and licenses very seriously. If you come across any illegal copies of our works, in any form, on the Internet, please provide us with the location address or web site name immediately so that we can pursue a remedy.

Please contact us at `copyright@packtpub.com` with a link to the suspected pirated material.

We appreciate your help in protecting our authors, and our ability to bring you valuable content.

Questions

You can contact us at questions@packtpub.com if you are having a problem with any aspect of the book, and we will do our best to address it.

1
Theming Plone 3: An Overview

For those of you who are unfamiliar with Plone or this is your first introduction to it, Plone is a content management system (CMS). A CMS is a tool that enables webmasters to manage their web sites' content easily **through the web (TTW)**. Plone provides additional support by auto-generating navigation elements, making content searchable, allowing for multilingual content, handling permissions and security, and much, much more. In comparison to other CMS platforms, Plone is extremely stable, secure, and is actively working toward increased adoptability.

One of the most common needs with a CMS web site is the ability to change the look and feel. As with any framework, building a design around a CMS introduces special challenges. With Plone, the process of separating content from presentation is not entirely straightforward. By the end of this book, you will have the knowledge to create your own robust Plone themes and understand where the line is drawn between content and presentation. Specifically, this book is geared toward web designers with little or no knowledge of Plone who need to theme a Plone web site.

This chapter will explore the origins of Plone as well as analyze the current state of theming in Plone.

Background

The origin of Plone is one of community lore. In 1999, founders Alexander Limi and Alan Runyan had a fortuitous meeting on **#zope**, the IRC channel dedicated to **Zope** development. Zope is the framework upon which Plone is built. The two of them forged an online friendship based on a mutual love of Zope, Python, and music.

These two men, with too much time on their hands and the encouragement of Paul Everitt (one of the founders of Zope Corporation), built a CMS named after an electronica band with questionable musical talent. In the process, they also gathered a thriving community of people around them. They continue to work in the service of Plone today and to grow the ranks around them.

The last year or so has brought tremendous change to Plone, as we have moved from the Zope 2 architecture to the mixed implementation of Zope 2 and Zope 3. Don't worry too much yet about what this means; suffice it to say that when Plone 3 was released, the ground shifted underneath the feet of Plone users worldwide. This shift not only brought a lot of power to the table, but also introduced a lot of fear, particularly in the hearts of themers. Most of this fear is exaggerated, and this book aims to quell much of this fear. The theming process for Plone may be complex at the moment, but it's still possible to generate beautiful, high-impact themes.

Plone is useful for all kinds of web sites, from large enterprise sites to educational and government sites, and even small environmental sites. I work at an environmental non-profit named ONE/Northwest. (We hosted the 2006 Plone Conference in Seattle.) ONE/Northwest has produced almost 200 attractive, high quality, but generally small Plone sites that empower other environmental groups. These web sites give our clients the tools they need to reach their audiences and to hopefully preserve our natural environment. Every day brings new excitement, revelations, more complex sites, and plenty of ideas on how to improve Plone. As an open source CMS, it's especially thrilling to be able to contribute ideas and put efforts that incrementally improve Plone.

For many members of the Plone community, we stay with it because it's all about contributing and the community. We are a vast and far-flung crowd, yet surprisingly close-knit. At any given point in time on **#plone**, the IRC channel for Plone users on freenode.net, you can be talking simultaneously to the people in Belgium, South Africa, Australia, Israel, or the United States. Sometimes the community gets together in person to work, sometimes at conferences, but more often at sprints (small gatherings geared toward solving a particular problem). People have sprinted on projects in castles, on archipelagos, on beaches, in the swank offices of Google Corporation and online, all over the world. The community has proven to be extremely welcoming, bright, ambitious, and inclusive to those who are willing to contribute back to the community.

As a themer, I continue to use and improve Plone because it's a rewarding platform with which to work, and because I've witnessed the change in the world it can effect. My personal pet project with Plone is a small non-profit called Safe Passage that helps to educate, feed, and protect children who work in the garbage dumps of Guatemala City. With a very simple (and sadly outdated) theme, and a form-building product called PloneFormGen, Safe Passage has managed to get more than 900 children sponsored, fed, and in school. It's a small, unassuming site, but without Plone, we could not have achieved such a tremendous accomplishment. Plone is a wondrous tool, frustrating at times, but absolutely worth the time spent and valued by the organizations that use it to manage their content and spread their message. From the simple theme I built for Safe Passage to the intricate themes I build now, I've learned that Plone is a deep and sometimes swift river, but not impossible to cross. The best part is that even as you read this book, work is being done in the Plone community to ease the pain of theming. This book is one small step in that direction.

Before we move into the theming portion of this book, let's learn a little more about Plone and why it might be a good choice for your organization.

What is Plone, really?

The following is an overview of Plone:

- **Plone is an open source CMS**: Plone is a downloadable content management system that is built on the powerful and free Zope application server. Plone is easy to set up, extremely flexible, and provides tools for managing the content of large web sites, extranets, intranets, government and educational sites, and even social networking sites. Plone is licensed under the GNU General Public License, the same license used by Linux. This gives you the right to use Plone without a license fee, and to improve upon the product.

- **Plone has the tools you need**: Plone provides numerous out-of-the-box and add-on tools that make working with content easier. These include kupu, the powerful visual editor built into Plone, and PloneFormGen, a tool for creating quick and easy forms. Plone also includes the ability to integrate with other open source tools, databases, page compositors, e-commerce solutions, and more. Plone may not have as many add-ons as frameworks like Drupal, but you can feel secure in knowing that the popular add-ons for Plone are generally quite stable and thoroughly vetted by the community.

- **Plone is easy to install**: You can install Plone by going to `http://plone.org/products/plone` and downloading the Plone installer that is the right option for you. Simply run the installer, follow the `README.txt`, and you will have a working content management system in minutes. As of Plone 3.1.2, Plone is by default installed using a system called **buildout**, which we will cover later. It's more complex than WordPress's "Famous 5-Minute Install", but installing Plone and add-on products is simple once you get used to the process.

- **Plone is easy to use**: Plone's development team has usability experts who have made it simple for content managers to add, update, and maintain content. Plone's UI team is constantly looking for ways to simplify and improve the end user experience, and founder Alexander Limi is on the forefront of this charge. I've had the joy of having content managers from completely different continents grasp the concepts of how to manage content in Plone without problem, and the average web-savvy user will have the same experience.

- **Plone is secure**: While the Drupal platform may have much to offer to end users, as a PHP-based CMS, it has many security problems that Plone does not have. Plone has had only one security-related patch in the last two years, whereas Drupal has had several in the last few months. The difference is that Plone runs on Python, which is markedly safer. Having a secure CMS is critical, and Plone is clearly the frontrunner here.

- **Plone provides international support**: The Plone interface has more than 35 translations, right-to-left support, and tools such as LinguaPlone for managing multilingual content.

- **Plone is compliant**: Plone rigorously follows standards for usability and accessibility, including US Section 508, and the W3C's AAA rating for accessibility.

- **Plone is protected**: The nonprofit Plone Foundation (`http://plone.org/foundation`) was formed in 2004 to promote the use of Plone around the world and to protect the Plone Intellectual Property and trademarks.

- **Plone has planned development and supports contributors**: The Plone team development keeps a close eye on the future of Plone, gives considered thought to new features, and presents a unified front. This is different from a CMS such as Drupal, which has more sprawl in its development processes, especially in terms of add-on products. As of this writing, the biggest developments in Plone include dramatically lowering the bar on theming, making the page compositing experience much simpler, and enabling through-the-web creation of content types. Ultimately, the focus for Plone 4 and 5 is on integrators and themers, which is right where the focus needs to be in order to have an adoptable CMS.

- **Upgrades are easy**: Upgrades are less frequent, and releases are carefully coordinated to make the transition easier. For anyone who has suffered a painful upgrade, you'll appreciate this fact more than anything.

Technical overview

Plone sits on top of the Zope technology stack. Zope is an open source application server for building content management systems, intranets, portals, and custom applications. The Zope community consists of hundreds of companies and thousands of developers all over the world who work on building the platform and other Zope applications.

Zope and Plone are both written in Python, an easy-to-learn, widely used and supported open source programming language. The security benefits available with Python, as well as the cleanliness of code, are great advantages for Plone.

By default, Plone stores its contents in Zope's built-in transactional object database, the **ZODB**. There are products and techniques, however, that allow sharing of information with other sources, such as relational databases, LDAP, and more. WSGI support is also now available with Plone, which means even greater integration with other web applications. WSGI is the basis of what makes **Deliverance** (one of the possibilities in the future of theming for Plone) possible. Read the last chapter for more exciting information on Deliverance and `collective.xdv`.

Plone runs on Windows, Linux, BSD, Mac OS X, UNIX, Solaris, and other platforms. Double-click installers are available for all platforms. For full information and to download Plone, see `http://plone.org/products/plone`.

Books about Plone

Plone currently has approximately 8 books available, several of which are out of date, but a few of which are extremely helpful. None of the books are specifically geared towards themers, although sections of each are relevant.

- Released in February 2009 is a community-written book, *Practical Plone 3*, which is intended for integrators and individuals new to Plone. It contains several chapters geared towards themers, plus a wealth of other information for integrators.

- Martin Aspeli's developer's guide, *Professional Plone Development* (2007). While it is geared towards developers, some of the technical information in this book is pertinent to themers.

- The defacto Plone book, *The Definitive Guide to Plone* by Andy McKay. It is woefully out of date, but is relevant for giving a broad understanding of Plone and the templating language used by Plone. A rewrite to this book was released in 2009 and written by Redomino and Andy McKay.

- Philipp von Weitershausen published *Web Component Development with Zope 3* in 2007. It is a helpful book conceptually, but geared specifically towards pure Zope 3 development, not Plone.

- *Plone Live*, which had regular updates for years, but is now languishing since the Plone 3 release. The information it contains is still valid, however.

- *Content Management with Plone: Handbook for Authors and Editors* (available in English and German, updated for Plone 3). This book is intended for end users and not generally helpful to themers.

- James Cameron Cooper's *Building Websites with Plone* (2002). Mostly out of date, and not especially relevant to themers.

Theming and other CMS frameworks

To understand the current state of theming with Plone, it's helpful to examine a rival content management system's theming story. In this case, we will look at Drupal, a popular open source CMS that is written in PHP, and touch briefly on WordPress.

Both Plone and Drupal provide online theming manuals. Plone also has additional quick start documents that explain how to build a theme in Plone 3. These documents have been integrated into the Plone theming manual and include practical instructions on how to accomplish common tasks. It is on par with Drupal's theming manual. As of this writing, both projects have solid theming documentation, although Drupal's might be organized slightly better.

Drupal may have more theming books than the Plone community, but it's worth mentioning that the theming documentation for Plone is quite helpful and covers most use cases. Unlike Drupal, the book you are reading now is the first book specifically geared toward theming with Plone, but it is the beginning of a trend. Basically, what this means is that either CMS is a good choice, and Plone has the documentation ready for new themers.

Another telling point is the availability of open source themes. Interestingly, at one point, Drupal had the `themes.drupal.org` site that allowed users to test-drive the available themes for Drupal. As of Drupal 5.0, the site was abandoned due to the shortage of volunteers. WordPress also offers a number of add-on themes, though most of them are geared specifically toward bloggers. Similarly, Plone volunteers are rapidly putting out new themes on a daily basis, although there isn't a single location (other than `plone.org`) where Plone themes can be found.

This is the most active time for the Plone theming community to date, and the entire community has taken notice.

More than books, tutorials, and the availability of open source themes, the actual skinning process is where comparing Plone and Drupal is most critical. It's generally acknowledged that getting started with skinning in Drupal and WordPress is easier because users only have to worry about CSS, but once you get past the initial theme, you have to worry about PHP, which can be spidery and hard to understand. Conversely, Plone's theming framework is tough at the outset, but easier, more logical, and sophisticated over the long haul. Both situations present special challenges.

According to Larry Garfield in **#drupal**:

> *I'd say the hardest thing to get used to with Drupal is letting Drupal do things the Drupal Way rather than trying to force it into your mold. Drupal can bend in all sorts of weird and exciting ways, if you bend it where it's designed to bend. But if you try to shoe-horn it into the way you wish it worked rather than the way it does, you'll waste a lot time needlessly,* especially *at the theming layer.*

The same could be said about Plone, but Plone's problem is less about shoe-horning and more about having a lot of concepts that need to be understood before the real progress can be made. Additionally, Plone currently provides more than one method of accomplishing theming tasks, which can cause confusion. Those various methods are steadily being unified and simplified, and the goal of this book is to demystify the complexity of Plone with regards to theming.

Larry Garfield from #drupal followed his previous comment by saying that:

> *Drupal 6 includes a heavily rewritten theme layer that is a lot nicer to work with.*

Plone doesn't currently have an abstracted theming layer, though there are certain tools that are available to themers that will be discussed in this book. Moreover, the future of Plone is Deliverance and `collective.xdv`, non-Plone-specific tools that will turn the theming process into a nearly CSS-only experience. Deliverance and `collective.xdv` will position Plone over with the Drupals and WordPresses of this world, and with much greater power.

It's worth spending time with Plone, especially once you get a glimpse at the power under the hood. The real potential is in the value to the content manager. Heavyweight blogs such as WordPress, or lightweight CMS's such as Drupal, simply don't offer the necessary flexibility or ease of use, nor do they have the same level of extensibility. If you can build a Plone theme, you'll appreciate the real value inherent in Plone, and building a theme doesn't need to be intimidating once you know where to start.

While there's always going to be the question of which CMS is the most appropriate for the job, it's clear that Plone has a bright future, and is keeping pace with other CMS frameworks.

The evolution of skinning for Plone

Plone has always offered a robust base skin from which to start with solid CSS hooks, and it also has cleanly separated the CSS files that make skinning a fairly straightforward process. The actual process of working with the skin and CSS is what has changed dramatically over time and become more complex.

As of Plone 2.0, skinning was most commonly done through the web via the **ZMI** or **Zope Management Interface**. Working TTW via the ZMI resulted in a mixture of content and code that could not be easily pulled out of the ZMI. While tools exist that helped extract skin-related elements from the ZMI, it was still difficult to back up sites or to preserve the configuration in the event that a site needed to be moved to another Zope instance.

When Plone 2.1 was released, a tool known as **DIY Plone Style** was introduced that allowed users to quickly create a skeleton product so that users could work more easily on the filesystem. Additionally, a system known as **GenericSetup** was gaining momentum as a means of exporting settings to a skin product. TTW management was still possible, though pressure was mounting to move away from working through the ZMI.

Very little changed for themers in the transition from Plone 2.1 to Plone 2.5. Generally speaking, themers only had to know where to find certain knobs and switches in the ZMI, modify Plone's default templates, understand the TAL templating language, and work with CSS to make changes to their sites. While modification of basic templates is still a legitimate approach for writing templates and business logic, there is an extra layer of templating involved now, known loosely as "viewlets" and "portlets", that themers need to know about. Filesystem development is now the present state of theming. While it may sound daunting to work on the filesystem, once you get started, it's actually quite liberating.

As of Plone **3**, a system known as **buildout** was introduced as well, and new visual design and deployment schemes were revealed that enabled developers to create a repeatable, testable development environment that could be shared across teams. For themers, this meant learning how to manage a development environment without necessarily having the programmatic knowledge to do so. Thankfully, Plone's installers mostly take care of this now.

In addition, themers not only had to understand the previously mentioned technologies, but they also had to learn about Zope, including such programmatic jargon as "multi-adapters", "browser layers", "boilerplate", "ZCML", and "GenericSetup profiles". Worse, they needed to learn how to work with Python classes and understand the difference between Zope 2 and Zope 3 templates and how to use them in their skin products. The complexity involved in skinning a site doubled, if not tripled, and the theme development time increased.

The positive side of this was a dramatic increase in the robustness, reusability, and flexibility of theme components. Once learned, the Plone theming framework provides tremendous leverage for web-design professionals. And, much of the Plone theme framework is unit testable, which is amazing! While there is a lot to know, it's worth stating that theming for Plone is a challenging but exhilarating experience. Even better, it has encouraged the Plone community to spend some real time focusing on the theming needs of the Plone users, meaning that the road forward will be easier to tread.

It's also important to mention that community resources are available if you have questions or problems. In particular, themers should be aware of:

- The Plone-users email list that can be found at `http://plone.org/support/lists`
- The Plone forums found at `http://plone.org/support/forums`
- The IRC chat channel that can be accessed at `http://plone.org/support/chat`.

You should always feel that no question is too stupid to ask, and someday you might even be able to answer someone else's questions. It's how most of us have arrived in the community, and we're always happy to have more contributors.

In the meantime, this book attempts to break down the barriers to Plone 3 theming in a way that makes it easier for non-programmers to successfully change the look and feel of their sites. While themers who are accustomed to working with systems such as WordPress and Drupal may find the learning curve challenging, with some effort, it is still possible to generate attractive and robust themes. I hope you enjoy the ride.

Summary

In this chapter, we have learned that:

- The current theming story for Plone is challenging for new themers, and has become even more complex with the newest release of Plone
- Plone is on par with other CMS frameworks in terms of the theming story
- It is possible to create attractive themes in Plone 3, but it requires extra effort and some knowledge of programmatic concepts

Next, we will look at the tools necessary for any themer to be productive and then dive deeper into the actual theming process. Onward!

2
Skinner's Toolkit

Choosing the right tools for implementing a design in Plone is the most important step. Fortunately, there are a number of tools available that make the process much easier. We will cover graphic design tools, browser toolbars and extensions, CSS validators, text editors, and more.

Graphic design tools

Any serious skinner needs a graphic design tool with certain capabilities in order to take the design files and assemble them into a finished web site. In particular, layers and the ability to slice pieces of a design and export those pieces are essential. Layers allow a themer to hide pieces not needed in a finished CSS theme, such as text that will eventually become real HTML on a page. Slices, meanwhile, are the pieces of an overall design that are exported during the layer manipulation process. They are the images the end user eventually sees on the rendered page. This is different from cropping, which actually alters the size of the canvas; slices are just pieces of the overall design, cut with precision, exported, and then manipulated with CSS.

The most commonly used graphic design tools used for web design are Adobe® Photoshop®, Adobe® Fireworks® (formerly Macromedia) tool, and open source tools such as GIMP. It is not generally recommended to use tools such as Adobe® Illustrator®, Corel Draw and other vector-based packages. Web designs primarily use raster-based media, meaning that raster images are based on pixels and thus scale with loss of clarity. Conversely, vector-based images can be scaled infinitely without degrading, but are typically not appropriate for web design.

Adobe Photoshop

The most popular tool for processing image files is Adobe Photoshop. The files generated for designs are PSD, or Photoshop Document files. Adobe Photoshop meets the basic requirements of being able to manipulate the vector and raster images, layers, and slices, and offers a lot of additional functionality. The ability to control anti-aliasing and the quality and size of an exported image is essential in web design, and Adobe Photoshop (also, Adobe Fireworks) is quite powerful in this respect.

A quick look at the **Layers** panel illustrates how sections can be grouped together, moved, or be shown or hidden via the "eyeball" icon.

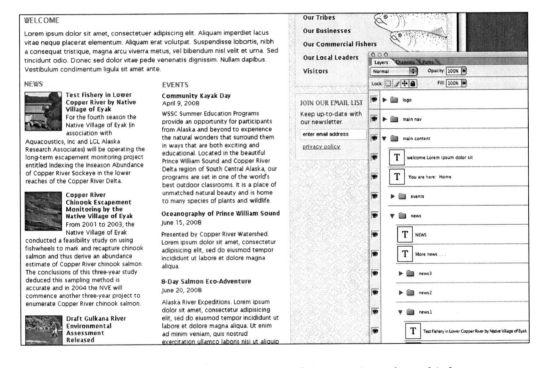

This *show/hide* functionality is very important. One situation where this becomes valuable is when you have a PSD file that indicates graphical buttons with text over them. For accessibility reasons, you may want to render the text as real HTML-rendered text, and not as an image. You need to be able to export the buttons in both their on and off states in order to get a proper rollover effect, and you need to hide the graphical text in order to do this.

One site that illustrates this concept is http://greenforall.org. Using Adobe Photoshop, the layers where the text appears on the top navigation were hidden, and just the background on/off images were imported. On the finished web site, the top menu used the background images and real rendered text.

The other core functionality that Adobe Photoshop offers is the ability to slice images and export them. The Copper River Watershed Project web site (http://www.copperriver.org) illustrates how slices might be used. The original Adobe Photoshop document is here:

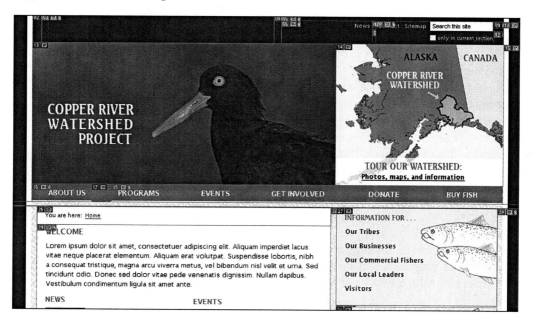

If you look closely, you can see a few key slices: the "Go" button next to the search field has been sliced, as has the **Tour Our Watershed** map and the gradation on the top navigation, which will be tiled horizontally. Below the orange navigation is a long slice that spans from the left-hand shadow over to the right-hand shadow. This image can be used to tile the length of the page. Additionally, the entire **Information For...** box has been sliced; in this case, for the final implementation, the text overlaying this slice was hidden and replaced with rendered text. If you look at the finished web site, you can see how these slices were applied.

Photoshop provides a great deal of power, but in general, you may only use about 20% of the power it offers. You can visit http://adobe.com to see the tutorials on how to use the Adobe Photoshop effectively. Additionally, you may want to investigate Photoshop Elements; it doesn't allow you to slice images for the Web, but for the current price of $139.99, it's still a great tool for many web design activities: http://www.adobe.com/products/photoshopelwin/.

Adobe Fireworks

I have not used Adobe Fireworks in many years, not since Macromedia was purchased by Adobe in 2005. At the time, I found the interface a little clumsy at times, but it did have a basic implementation of layers and slices. Over the past few years, based on the demos available, it appears that the interface has seen some great improvements, though it does not have the same power or market share as Adobe Photoshop has. However, at nearly $400 less than Adobe Photoshop, it's a great option.

According to the Adobe web site, "Adobe Fireworks CS4 software is used to rapidly prototype web sites and application interfaces and to create and optimize images for the Web more quickly and accurately. It is ideal for web designers, web developers, and visual designers." It differs from Photoshop in that "Adobe Photoshop software is the industry standard for digital imaging, with a broad array of features and functionality used by photographers, graphic designers, web designers, and many other creative professionals. Fireworks is a much more focused tool, with the features for prototyping vectors and bitmaps for the web and application interfaces." The real selling point here, though, is integration with Adobe Photoshop, as a design may be shared between multiple people, each using different graphical programs.

The ability to manipulate the vector and raster images is also important. Additionally, like Adobe Photoshop, Adobe Fireworks provides the ability to work with layers and slices, and preserves many of the settings in an Adobe Photoshop PSD file. It's not as good at compositing and photo manipulation as Photoshop, but is a lot stronger with text, shapes, and final optimization. Selective JPEG optimization is also very handy, and allows you to heavily compress the portions of a JPEG while keeping text legible. Additionally, it's great for generating image maps (not often used in Plone), rollovers, and other common tricks. Finally, it allows you to view your work with either Windows or Mac gamma. Gamma correction basically refers to the ability to correct for differences in how computers (and especially computer monitors) interpret color values. There are two factors here: the ability to predict what an image, say a photograph, will look like on another monitor and the ability to match the colors from different sources on a single page—Adobe Fireworks excels at both.

While Adobe Fireworks is not as feature-rich as Adobe Photoshop, it is still an extremely competent tool for slicing and exporting design elements at implementation time, not to mention more affordable.

GIMP

GIMP, also known as the GNU Image Manipulation Program, can be downloaded for free from `http://www.gimp.org`. It is a freely distributed program for such tasks as photo retouching, image composition and image authoring, and is covered by the GNU GPL license. According to the GIMP's web site, it can be used as a simple paint program, an expert quality photo retouching program, an online batch processing system, a mass production image renderer, an image format converter, and more.

From the perspective of how it compares to the key aspects of Adobe Photoshop® and Adobe Fireworks®, it has full support of layers and channels, plug-ins that allow for the easy addition of new file formats (that is, it can read Adobe Photoshop or Adobe Fireworks files), and best of all, it is open source.

You can visit `http://www.gimp.org/docs/` to download the user manual for the current release. GIMP also lists several user groups and resources at `http://www.gimp.org/links/` that may be helpful. Even so, the latest releases are still quite recent, so development is still happening.

For a free solution to the image processing needs, GIMP is an excellent choice, but weak in terms of the user interface and layer compatibility with Adobe Photoshop.

Browser add-ons and important notes

Now that you have sense of the tools that are available for manipulating design files and exporting the necessary images for building your web site, let's look at how browsers affect the web site building process, either through add-on tools or through sheer bugginess.

It's also worth mentioning that users should reference the A-List of popular browsers to see which browsers are still considered to be supported by web developers: `http://developer.yahoo.com/yui/articles/gbs/index.html`. This can help to ease the quality assurance load during web site testing.

Many of these A-List browsers come with browser-specific tools that allow you to inspect your web site to descry the CSS (Cascading Style Sheets) ID and class selectors, manipulate your CSS on-the-fly, optimize your site, explore color options, and more. We'll look at the available options for three major browsers: Internet Explorer, Firefox, and Safari, but you should always be conscious of general browser penetration statistics so that you know which browsers are still in popular use: `http://en.wikipedia.org/wiki/Usage_share_of_web_browsers`.

Now, let's get back to our key browsers.

Internet Explorer

From a themer's perspective, Internet Explorer is the most finicky browser against which to implement, as older versions of Internet Explorer followed the W3C's (World Wide Web Consortium's) standards differently than many other popular browsers.

According to `http://positioniseverything.net`, a leading collector of browser fixes, "All browsers have CSS bugs, and IE leads the pack in this area, but that is not the end of the story. Microsoft has seen fit to engineer their browser to deliberately violate the standards in several critical ways. It might just be a misguided attempt to 'make it simple' for newbie coders, or it might be a cynical ploy to crush the competition, but in any case it creates huge headaches for those of us who desire to employ CSS positioning on our pages." While this may be true, many fixes for Internet Explorer have been identified, and thankfully, IE6, one of the more problematic browsers in recent years, is finally becoming obsolete. It was replaced by IE7, which was a vast improvement, but still did not implement the W3C conventions for CSS faithfully. As of this writing, Internet Explorer 8 was released and showing signs of having finally made strides toward real compliance to W3C standards.

What this equates to is that web developers tend do their initial browser testing in browsers that are more compliant; that means doing most upfront testing in Firebug and Safari, and then rounding out the testing at the end against IE6, IE7, and IE8. Where possible, it's also important to test against other major browsers and handheld media.

For testing against Internet Explorer, IE provides a tool called the Web Developer Toolbar for debugging. It is available for both IE6 and IE7 as an add-on and can be downloaded here: `http://www.microsoft.com/downloads/details.aspx?FamilyId=E59C3964-672D-4511-BB3E-2D5E1DB91038&displaylang=en`. Web Developer Toolbar will no longer be the tool of choice for IE8, however; instead use the developer tools included with IE8.

[To use the developer tools in IE8, press *Shift+F12* or click the "Developer Tools" icon in the command bar to begin using the tool.]

For IE6 and IE7, Web Developer Toolbar provides several features for exploring and understanding web pages. These features enable you to:

- Explore and modify the **document object model (DOM)** of a web page.
- Locate and select the specific elements on a web page.
- Selectively disable the Internet Explorer settings.
- View HTML object class names, IDs, and details such as link paths, tab index values, and access keys.

- Outline tables, table cells, images, or selected tags.
- Validate HTML, CSS, WAI, and RSS web feed links.
- Display image dimensions, file sizes, path information, and alternate (ALT) text.
- Immediately resize the browser window to a new resolution.
- Selectively clear the browser cache and saved cookies. Choose from all objects or those associated with a given domain.
- Display a fully-featured design ruler to help accurately align and measure objects on your pages.
- Find the style rules used to set specific style values on an element. Right clicking on a style rule will allow you to trace the rules to a specific CSS file, if one is found.
- View the formatted and syntax colored source of HTML and CSS.

The Developer Toolbar can be popped up within the Internet Explorer browser window or opened as a separate window.

If you are using a PC to test your sites, VMware, parallels, or a Windows emulator, you should download the Toolbar from `http://go.microsoft.com/fwlink/?LinkId=125120`, install it, and restart IE. You can then click the Developer Toolbar icon in the command bar to display or hide the Developer Toolbar. Alternately, you can open the **View** menu and then use the **Explorer Bar** menu. In Internet Explorer 7, open the **Tools** menu and then use Toolbars/Explorer Bars to display or hide the Developer Toolbar.

There are a few caveats here:

- The Developer Toolbar icon may not be visible by default. If you do not see it after restarting Internet Explorer, click the right-facing arrows at the end of the IE7 command bar to view all the available Toolbar buttons.

- Some menu items are unavailable (grayed out) when running Internet Explorer in Protected Mode on Windows Vista. To use those options, temporarily turn off Protected Mode or right-click the Internet Explorer icon in the **Programs** menu and choose **Run as administrator**.

- In IE6 or in IE7 with tabbed browsing off, using the validation links will navigate the current window to the validation page. To launch the validation links in a new window, open the **Tools** menu, click **Internet Options**, and uncheck **Reuse windows for launching shortcuts** in the **Advanced** tab, or use IE7 with tabbed browsing enabled.

Generally, you can use this tool by expanding the left side of the panel displayed to navigate through your site's structure. It displays CSS IDs and classes in a hierarchical fashion. On the right-hand side, it displays the properties assigned to each of those IDs or classes. You can modify those by using the **+** icon in the center **Attributes** section to add a new property and using that to add to or alter the existing CSS.

As stated before, the left-hand pane allows you to expand and walk through the structure of your web site. When you refresh, unfortunately, the entire tree closes. To continue troubleshooting a specific element on the page, you must drill down to it again or use the "selector" tool. It's somewhat clumsy, but it works and is invaluable when debugging web pages in Internet Explorer.

Firefox

As of this writing, Firefox 2 and Firefox 3 browsers are both in use, and from a general perspective, both should be used during debugging, as there are very slight differences between them (particularly around the sizing of elements on the page). However, the versions seem to be pretty similar overall, and they both follow the W3C's web standards quite well.

In addition, Firefox also offers several excellent tools that are helpful to themers. The first plug-in is the Firefox Web Developer Extension, which is similar to the IE Toolbar, but a little more robust. We'll also cover Firebug, the coolest kid on the block for CSS debugging.

Firefox Web Developer extension

This open source toolbar can be downloaded from Mozilla's site `https://addons.`
`mozilla.org/en-US/firefox/addons/versions/60`, or the developer's personal
web site, `http://www.chrispederick.com`. For installation information and
support, visit Chris Pederick's web site. Note that all the work on `chrispederick.`
`com` is distributed for free under the terms of the GNU General Public License.

This extension adds a menu and a toolbar to the browser with various web developer
tools. It is designed for Firefox, Flock, and Seamonkey, and will run on any platform
that these browsers support, including Windows, Mac OS X, and Linux. The
downside of this toolbar is that it doesn't come with instructions, so to use it
requires some exploration.

After installation, the toolbar displays at the top, where you see the options **Disable**,
Cookies, **CSS**, and so on. Choosing **Edit CSS** from the **CSS** drop-down menu opens
up a panel that allows you to examine each individual stylesheet.

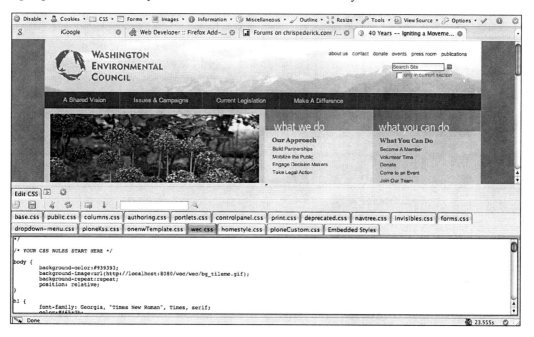

Key features of this toolbar include:

- **Disable Cache**: This can be done using the **Disable** drop-down list. It may
  slow down your web browser's performance, but you will get more realistic
  results. This is probably the most valuable feature of this add-on tool, as it
  allows you to make sure that your cache is always clear, and it can be used
  selectively from site to site.

- **Images | Display Image Dimensions**: This setting can help to diagnose the minor pixel errors where an image might be pushing against a padding setting elsewhere in your site.

- **Information | Display ID and Class Details**: This setting is extremely important, as it can help to quickly illustrate the name of the object you are trying to style. It can be hard to identify the object you want to work with, though, as this screenshot indicates:

- **Display Element Information**: This setting is another important setting. Enabling it allows you to click on any element on your page and gather details about that element. This is significantly more powerful than the basic **Display ID and Class Details** option. All of these details can help to determine if a current attribute on a tag is causing issues, or if an attribute assigned to an ancestor might be responsible.

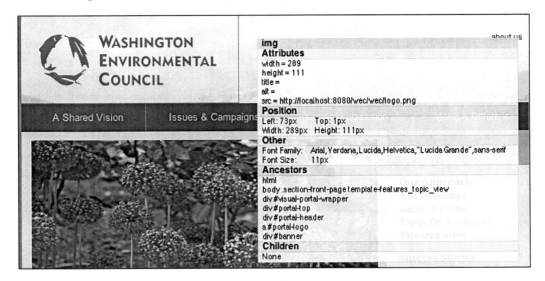

- **Validate CSS/Validate HTML:** When you are working with local Plone instance standard, **Validate HTML** and **Validate CSS** will not work, since the validators are not able to get to your localhost. Deploying to a test server allows you to validate against your code prior to going live with your web site, or you can (and should) use the **Validate Local CSS** and **Validate Local HTML** options.

- **Error and Warning Logs:** Clicking on the checkmark or **X** symbols to the right of the **Options** drop-down list gives you the ability to go into compliance mode, which gives you CSS and JavaScript warning logs when you click on them.

The Web Developer Extension is a powerful tool, worth using for many tasks (such as disabling stylesheets to check accessibility), and it's not uncommon to use it in tandem with the next excellent tool, Firebug.

Firebug extension

Firebug is another open source extension for Firefox that can be downloaded from Mozilla's web site `https://addons.mozilla.org/en-US/firefox/addon/1843`, or `http://getfirebug.com/`. There is a dedicated team of developers that maintains the extension, and the documentation is plentiful, so this is a tool that themers can hopefully count on in the future.

Firebug can be used for both Firefox 2 and Firefox 3, but different versions are required for each, so pay attention to the installation instructions.

It's worth mentioning that there is a bug in Firebug for Firefox 3 that causes Firebug to crash if you attempt to edit user stylesheets. For this reason alone, many individuals choose to do their initial debugging on Firefox 2. It's hoped that this bug gets fixed soon.

Firebug allows you to edit, debug, and monitor CSS, HTML, and JavaScript live in any web page. It is similar to the Web Developer Toolbar, but the way in which it surfaces the CSS on a page and allows you to browse the styling of ancestors is cleaner. For a list of keyboard shortcuts, you can visit this page: `http://getfirebug.com/keyboard.html`.

The interface for Firebug looks like this:

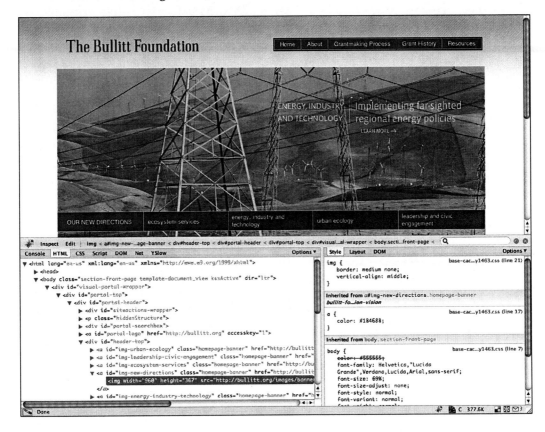

The bug icon in the bottom corner of your browser allows you to expand or minimize the Firebug pane. You can also enable it via the **Tools | Firebug | Open Firebug** option in your menu.

The HTML view of this tool is extremely helpful. The left-hand pane allows you to expand and walk through the structure of your web site, or you can use the **Inspect** option. The right-hand pane displays the available CSS, listed in order of precedence.

One great feature of this tool is that you can select an ID or class, and Firebug will highlight the item you wish to inspect, which can help to diagnose padding or sizing issues. It also offers a graphical representation of its box model rendering via the **Layout** tab.

In this case, we are inspecting the image on the home page, known here by the ID **features-slot**. When we click on this item, the right pane immediately shows the CSS that is used by that piece of content. In this case, the `wec.css` file has direct references to the **features-slot**, but after that, the nearest closest ancestor is `.documentContent`.

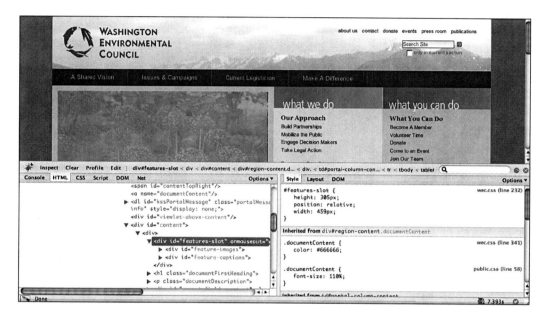

While an element is selected, you can click in the right side of the pane and change the CSS that is active (for example, change the position to absolute), or you can right-click to add a new property to that page element and type in the details. Right-clicking also gives you the option to add a new style in the right pane by choosing **New property**. The changes you insert will be immediately rendered on your page, but for these changes to make it into your skin product, you must either make the changes through the Web or in your filesystem product; Firebug will not add them to your site's CSS files for you.

Another great feature is that if you refresh your browser while you have selected an element on the page to clear out your on-the-fly CSS changes, when the page refreshes, Firebug will reopen to that exact ID or class.

Additionally, using the **Inspect/Script** combination setting will expose your site's JavaScript and allow you to step through your code.

Also helpful is the Network Monitoring tab, seen here, which lets you monitor how much time is spent when loading a web page. Use the **Net** tab to see the bar that shows when a file started and stopped loading relative to all the other files. Network Monitor breaks up the traffic on a file-by-file basis, so you can see how much time was spent loading images, JavaScript, HTML, and so forth. You can also see whether resources were loaded from the browser cache. Expanding each item listed shows additional HTTP header information. Debug mode in Plone (which we'll discuss in the future) needs to be OFF in order for this feature to work correctly.

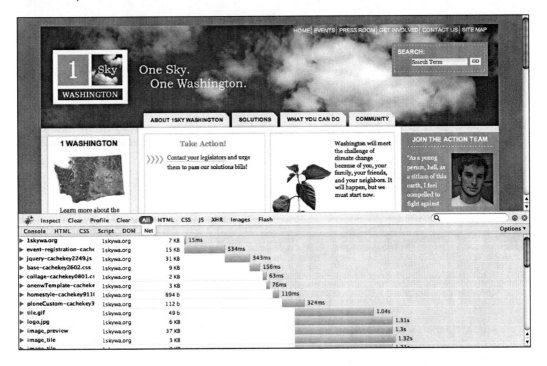

Finally, Firebug provides excellent error reporting, DOM explorer, and lots more.

Generally speaking, Firebug plus Web Developer Toolbar for Firefox are two tools that are essential for Plone web site development, and it's recommended that these two tools be in the toolkit of every Plone themer.

YSlow

Another essential add-on for Firefox is the wonderful YSlow. YSlow analyzes web pages and tells you why they're slow based on the rules for high performance web sites, and gives you the information you need to optimize your sites further. YSlow analyzes any web page and generates a grade for each rule and an overall grade. If a page can be improved, YSlow lists the specific changes to be made.

To activate it, click on the YSlow icon at the bottom of your browser.

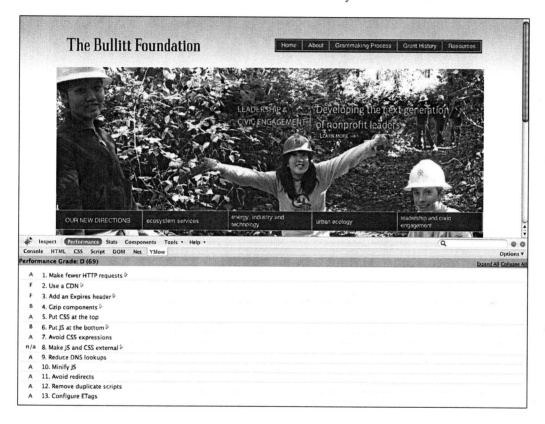

YSlow will then grade your web site based on its performance against several components. Clicking on any rule will take you to the page that contains suggestions on how to improve in that area. A lower grade on something like "Make fewer HTTP requests" could possibly be solved by using sprites instead of multiple images on a page, for example.

Clicking on the expand arrow next to any rule will give you more specific information about your web site, such as here, where we clicked on "Add an Expires Header":

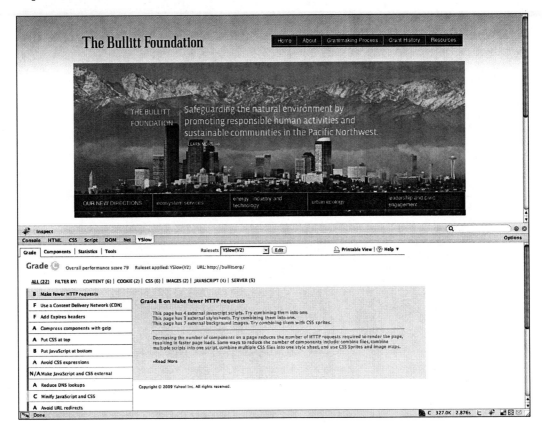

It's interesting to note that the rules are listed in order of priority, and so rules at the top of the list are weighted more heavily than rules at the bottom of the list when calculating the overall **Performance Grade**.

Clicking on the **Stats** button gives you an overall look at the statistics of the page; for example:

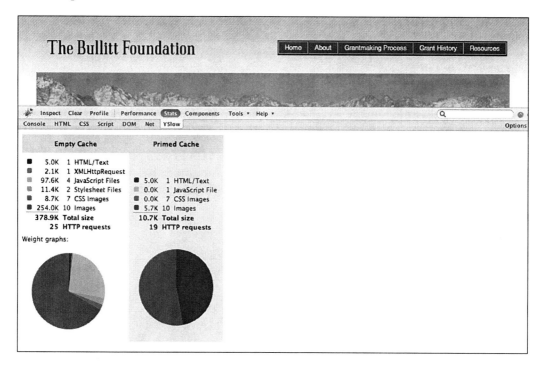

The tool can crawl the entire DOM stack and give you an idea of what a user visiting the site for the very first time would have to download. In this case, we're loading a lot of images, and those images are primarily responsible for slowing down this site on the first uncached visit to it.

Clicking on the **Components** tab shows us all of the items that are loaded when the page is requested, listed by type.

There is also an option for using a few built-in tools. Clicking on the **Tools** drop-down list provides an error log called **JSLint**, which allows all of the JavaScript to be analyzed all in one step, as well as a dump of all of the JavaScript and CSS that is loaded on the page. The **Printable View** option is used to send the overall **Performance Grade** to other members of the team in a more readable fashion.

YSlow is an essential tool, and should always be used during the site optimization process.

Colorzilla

Another handy add-on for Firefox is an advanced color picker named **ColorZilla**, found at https://addons.mozilla.org/en-US/firefox/addon/271. After installation, ColorZilla displays in the lower-left Firefox status bar. Clicking on the color picker icon will allow you to mouse over any pixel in your Firefox window and display the RGB and Hexadecimal value for that pixel.

R: 78, G: 118, B: 84 | #4E7654 | ΔX: 0, ΔY: 0 | img

You can then take those values and use them in your stylesheets, as necessary. If it is awkward to select the specific pixel you want, ColorZilla also provides the ability to zoom into a selection in your window. Right-click on the color picker to access the **Zoom** menu and the contents of your browser will enlarge or shrink based on your selection.

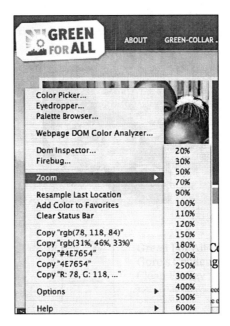

You can automate copying the selected color in either RGB or Hexadecimal format by turning on the **Auto Copy** option under the **Options** menu.

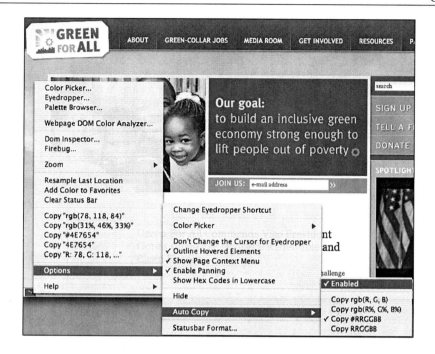

Additionally, you can capture the entire color palette of that site and save it for future reference. This can be especially helpful if you are creating a new web site based on a specific existing color palette. To capture the palette, right-click and select the **Webpage Dom Color Analyzer** option. The inspector will display the full palette, and choosing the **Save as colorzilla palette** option will save it for future reference.

To access the palette again, right-click to pull up the menu and choose
Palette Browser.

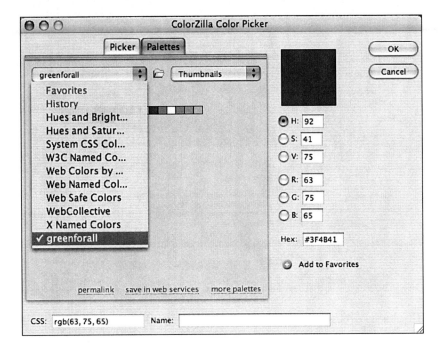

Selecting the palette will allow you to click on the individual colors in the palette and
get the color values for each of the colors.

For more information on how to use this tool, reference the online help available via
the **Help** menu option.

Safari tools

Safari doesn't have nearly the kinds of CSS debugging tools that Firefox and IE have,
but running Firefox in tandem with Safari allows skinners to simultaneously do
browser testing while still making use of Firefox's debugging tools.

Safari's greatest strength is that it has a solid, extremely fast rendering engine that
can point to problems with your CSS. For example, I've been able to look at a site
in Firefox and in IE, and both display beautifully, but in Safari, the result might
look like half-rendered garbage. The offending code? A missing semi-colon. Other
browsers might swallow such minor errors, but Safari is diligent enough to render
your code exactly as it is written.

There is, however, a tool that may allow you to do debugging with Safari: Safari Web Inspector/WebKit.

Safari Web Inspector

Without going into too much detail here, Safari WebKit is a nightly build of Safari that has a web inspector enabled by default. Safari 4 has the web inspector built in, but for Safari 3, it must be enabled via a command in terminal and a restart of Safari:

```
defaults write com.apple.Safari WebKitDeveloperExtras -bool true
```

If you choose to run the nightly build, you can get that here: http://nightly.webkit.org/, but for most themers, it's not necessary. Enabling the **WebKitDeveloperExtras**, as explained above, should be sufficient. For more information, you can read here: http://www.usingmac.com/2007/12/2/web-inspector-for-safari.

Activate the inspector by right-clicking on any object on a page. You will see an **inspect element** option that can open a web inspector window.

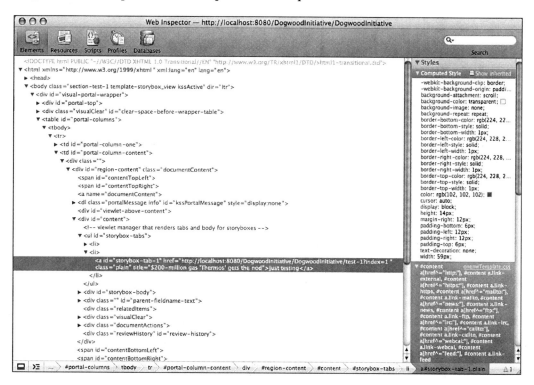

The left pane displays the code for your web site, while the pane on the right side displays the CSS applied to that particular selection, plus the styles applied to the ancestors of that item. What's also helpful is the bottom status bar that allows you to click from one element and upwards through each of the ancestors to inspect their styles. The inspector gives you all of the relevant CSS information, including your current place in the markup hierarchy, the final computed style, and a listing of the other cascading styles.

While it is not possible to modify the computed styles in the right-hand pane, it is possible to modify the styles in the hierarchy. Making a change and hitting *Enter* will automatically make the change in your browser. This is similar to when you make a change using Firebug works instantly. To reload and undo the changes, reload the browser (not the inspector window).

Safari provides additional tabs at the top that allow you to see load time, inspect JavaScripts, utilize a profiler, and work with a database. The first three tabs are likely the only three you would use for theming a web site.

Overall, it has a clean, stripped-down interface that is a pleasure to use. The only apparent downside is that it pops the inspector up in a separate window, which means it requires slightly more real estate.

Validation tools

Having a good graphical editor and a solid set of CSS browser add-ons is a step in the right direction, but as with any project, the proof is in the finished product.

At the end of every project, any good CSS themer needs to check his/her CSS and his/her HTML for cleanliness and adherence to the W3C standard. The best resource here is the official W3C validation web site, known as Jigsaw, which is used by the **Validate Local CSS** and **Validate Local HTML** options available with Firefox's Web Developer Toolbar.

We'll talk about this more in future chapters, but Plone gives us approximately 20 stylesheets out of the box that you can extend and override by using a stylesheet named `mytheme.css` or similar.

This means that when using the Jigsaw service, it's important to fix the inconsistencies located in `mytheme.css`, but there isn't much need to worry about issues in the original Plone stylesheets, which are fairly clean already and the errors Jigsaw points out are not that significant.

The only real downside of Jigsaw's validator (and pretty much every other validator) is that it only works on live web sites, and not on web sites being run on localhost. Hence, be sure to use the "Validate Local" options prior to deployment.

Text editors

The last key piece to successfully skinning a site is to choose a text editor or CSS editor that matches your needs and plays well with Plone. We are not talking about a word processor here, like Microsoft Word or Pages; rather, a text editor is a type of program used for editing plain text files. Text editors are often provided with operating systems or software development packages, and can be used to change configuration files and programming language source code.

We'll look at a few of the more popular text editors that are appropriate for Plone development and theming.

TextMate

TextMate is a combination of text editor and programming tool that is exclusively for the Mac, and can be found at `http://macromates.com`.

One of the key joys of working with TextMate is that it lets you open up an entire file structure at once to make navigation between related files easier. For Plone, this is essential. Your average file structure will look something like this:

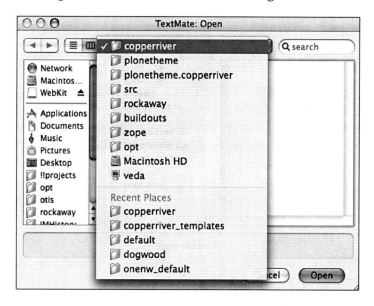

Rather than opening the entire `buildouts` folder, or even the `plonetheme.
copperriver` folder, generally you only want to open the structure closest to the files
you need in order to keep performance snappy—in this case, `mybuildout[rockaway]/
src/plonetheme.copperriver/plonetheme/copperriver/`:

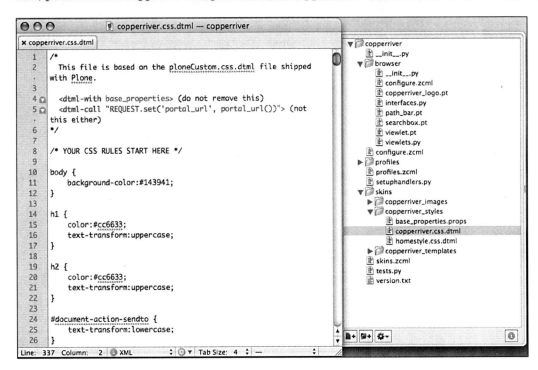

As you can see, it opens the entire project in a clean interface with an easily
navigable structure. Without this feature, skinning for Plone would be much
more time-consuming.

TextMate also offers numerous programmer-related tools:

- You can open two files at once (or more), and using the **diff** option you can
  compare the files easily
- **Subversion (svn)** support
- Ability to search and replace in a project
- Regular expression search and replace (**grep**)
- Auto-indent for common actions such as pasting text
- Auto-completion of brackets and other characters
- Clipboard history

- Foldable code blocks

- Support for more than 50 languages

- Numerous key combinations (for example, *Apple* + *T* opens a search window that makes it easy to locate a file)

- Themable syntax highlight colors

- Visual bookmarks to jump between places in a file

- Copy/paste of columns of text

- Bundles

- And much, much more

The **Bundle** feature is one of the more interesting aspects of the tool. If you look at the HTML bundle, for example, it shows a list of common actions that you might wish to perform in a given document, and on the right, the code that spawns that action, and the hot-key that activates it.

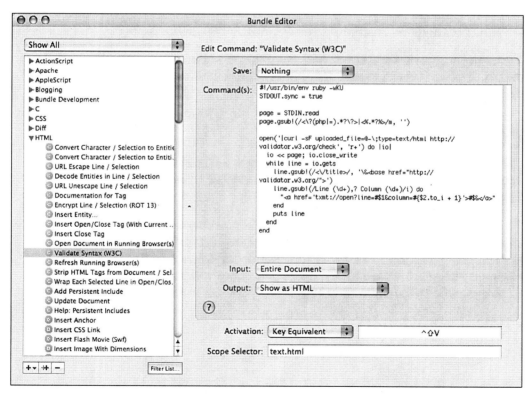

There's even a Zope/Plone TextMate support bundle found at `http://plone.org/products/textmate-support` that was developed by some of Plone's core developers. It enhances TextMate's already existing support for Python, XML, (X)HTML, CSS, and Restructured Text by adding features aimed specifically at the modern day Zope and Plone developer.

For the geeks in the audience, the bundle's features include: Doctest support (restructured text with inline Python syntax and auto-indent of python code), pdb support (for debugging), ZCML support (no more looking up directives with our handy and exhaustive snippets), and a ZPT syntax that marries the best of both worlds (XML strictness with the goodness of TextMate's HTML support). This bundle plus TextMate's other capabilities make switching to developing for Plone on a Mac a good idea any day!

As well as assigning a single key equivalent to a bundle item, it is possible to assign a tab trigger to the item. This is a sequence of text that you enter in the document and follow it by pressing the tab key. This will remove the sequence entered and then execute the bundle item. TextMate is full of hot-keys and features in general, yet it's surprisingly compact. Thankfully, the documentation is thorough.

TextMate is a dream for themers and programmers alike. For those who are still new at CSS, another tool might be a good place to start, but for power users, TextMate is the primary tool of choice.

CSS Edit

CSS Edit (not to be confused with CSS Manager, a Plone add-on), is a lovely, easy-to-use CSS tool for OS X. It can be purchased at `http://macrabbit.com/cssedit` for around $30.00.

To get started, click on the **Add Site URL** button. It allows you to navigate to either a localhost site or a live site. Next, click on the **Inspector** button. An inspector pane pops up that is updated as soon as you click on an element on your page. The element is also highlighted nicely and shows arrow indicators if you want to click to expand to the containing object and show the parent's CSS instead.

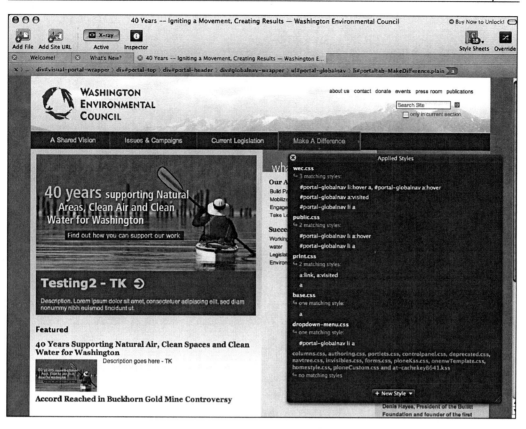

Expanding the arrow to the right of the **Make A Difference** button in the above screenshot selects the ID `globalnav-wrapper`, as indicated here and in the top hierarchy bar.

If you select one of the styles in the black **Applied Styles** window, it pops up a message that asks if you wish to override an existing stylesheet with a local stylesheet. Answering in the affirmative opens a small CSS editor window where you can make additional changes, see the immediate effects, and still access the **Applied Styles** window/navigator.

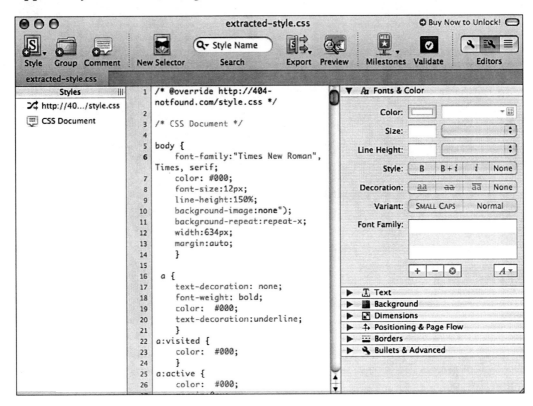

In this case, I opted to let it extract all of the CSS from my theme product's main stylesheet, wec.css. This prevents the issue of having to integrate your changes from a blank stylesheet into your core stylesheets, though you could optionally do that.

 In order to test the functionality of this product, it requires you to purchase the product if your site has over 2500 characters of code in it.

According to the developers of CSS Edit, it offers real-time styling of absolutely any web page. Even if your site is powered by a complex database or makes use of advanced AJAX, you can style and analyze it without the hassle of uploading or refreshing.

The **Selector Builder** lets you describe what elements to style in plain English. Advanced CSS selectors have a steep learning curve, but with this product there is help. In the case of some of the more convoluted areas of Plone to style, such as the navigational structures, this feature is helpful.

You can also take advantage of a feature called **CodeSense**. Instead of merely suggesting a list of predefined keywords, it analyzes your stylesheet and behavior to offer context-sensitive suggestions.

Additionally, you can use the **Validation** inspector to check your site against W3C conventions.

Finally, using a **Milestones** interface, you make big changes without any risk of losing your work, and still have the option to roll back.

All in all, this is a slick tool. It's a bit pricey, but for people who want a little extra assistance with their CSS, it's invaluable.

The downside of this tool is actually not the tool itself: it's Plone. For themers who will be working on the filesystem, you'll quickly learn that Plone's file structure is scattered, and it's important to be able to access the various pieces and parts quickly; this tool doesn't provide that flexibility. Ultimately, this tool is best for CSS-only tasks, not for filesystem development of themes. As Plone development evolves and the Deliverance and `collective.xdv` tools for theming (covered in the last chapter) becomes more of a reality, this tool may have more applicability.

E Text Editor

As a Windows alternative to TextMate, E Text Editor provides much of the same functionality (`http://www.e-texteditor.com/`) for a mere $34.95.

It can automate manual work via snippets, and it supports Text Mate bundles. It gives you access to the full range of UNIX shell tools and lets you extend "e" with your choice of languages such as Python and Ruby. Moreover, "e" users get the luxury of a personal revision control system. As with TextMate, you can even open up a directory full of files all at once, which can be invaluable in Plone development.

As a Windows-based text editor, "e" is an excellent first choice.

Notepad

As a text pad alternative for Windows users, the Windows default, Notepad will certainly suffice. Notepad does not support formatting of any kind. If rich text is copied from a web page and pasted into Notepad, then copied again from Notepad before being pasted into a destination program, Notepad will have stripped all of the formatting. This can be very handy when dealing with the HTML that is pasted into kupu (Plone's visual editor), but it doesn't help much in terms of working with code in Plone. It doesn't give you shortcuts, bundles, or helpful highlighting, but as a straight text editor, it does the trick.

As an interesting aside, Notepad does support both left-to-right and right-to-left based languages, and one can alternate between these viewing formats by pressing and releasing the arrow key followed by *Ctrl+Shift*, using the right or left arrow and shift keys to go to right-to-left format or left-to-right format, respectively.

Notepad can edit files of almost any format; however, it does not treat Unix- or Mac-style text files correctly, but another text editor, Wordpad, does.

WordPad

A slightly more sophisticated text editor for Windows, WordPad is also a fine choice, though still lacking in Plone-specific features. WordPad supports **Rich Text Format (RTF)**, which doesn't help us much, but it does allow files shared between OS X and Windows to be read correctly. If you're using it solely as a text editor, you'll be fine.

Dreamweaver

Sometimes regarded with a little snobbery, Dreamweaver could hypothetically be used if no other options exist for Windows or OS X users. Using the code layout view is really the only part that makes it usable in Plone development. Unfortunately, Dreamweaver tends to be a bit of a memory hog and can be a little slow. Additionally, you can't open up a directory containing multiple files, which means it will slow themers down significantly. In investigating it for this chapter, it was not possible to open .pt (page template) files using Dreamweaver, which is a deal breaker, as page templates are certainly part of the theming process. It's not known if this is merely a configuration error, but several attempts at configuring Dreamweaver to open .pt files failed.

All in all, Dreamweaver is intended for editing CSS and HTML files, and without page template support, it has limited use for Plone themers.

Summary

In this chapter, we have learned:

- What graphic design tools are appropriate for theming a web site and why
- What browser add-ons are available for helping to debug a web site's CSS, JavaScript, color palette, and more
- How to validate your CSS against W3C conventions
- What text editors are appropriate when developing for Plone and why

Now that you have the tools available to approach the skinning process, we will next address the dependencies needed to run Plone, create a development environment, generate a base theme product, and get an understanding of the overall file structure in preparation for making deeper modifications.

3
Setting up your Development Environment

The next steps for skinning effectively are getting your development environment configured and building the scaffolding for a theme product. It is also important to learn some of the jargon associated with Plone 3 development so that you can understand the development environment and how to use it.

Buildout and you

Prior to Plone 3, setting up Plone was fairly straightforward: you installed Plone and dropped all of your Plone add-on products into a `Products` directory. Making modifications meant that you simply edited a template and your changes showed instantly. While that sounds simple (and for themers, it was), it was not flexible or repeatable, and resulted in the development of monolithic products that were difficult to distribute or reuse and could only be used in the context of Plone.

Since Plone 3, the development environment has moved toward a more pluggable "egg-based" environment. **Eggs** are a way to package and distribute Python packages, with certain metadata intact. The Python library that powers the egg mechanism, **setuptools**, is able to automatically locate and download dependencies for eggs that you install. This technology means that it is easier to create shared, repeatable, and easily-configurable development or staging environments. The Plone community has also standardized on the **buildout** system for managing complex configurations so that they are flexible and repeatable.

While using buildout seems like a lot of overhead for themers (and in fact, it can seem downright scary), Plone has made it easy by distributing the Plone installers with buildout by default. Also, theme products are now egg-based, and can be easily installed just like any other Python package—generally, just by adding a few lines of code to a configuration file.

We will take advantage of the default buildout generated by Plone, although it is possible to create buildout environments specific to your own needs separate from the installer. It's not important to understand everything about buildout, but with a few key pointers, it's relatively simple for themers to get started. Much of buildout is documented on `plone.org`, but the goal in this chapter is to show themers only the pieces they need to care about.

Understanding the terminology

Before we begin, we need to get a general introduction to some of the terminology associated with Plone development. Don't worry if the terms sound overly technical; in many cases, themers do not need to know about these terms in much detail.

Buildout:

A buildout is a self-contained environment where you can manage the dependencies (including Zope and Plone and any third-party products or libraries you need) and custom code for your project. Even if you are not planning on writing any custom code, the buildout approach is an easy way to install Plone in a robust, well-tested manner. It is documented thoroughly on `plone.org` and by Jim Fulton of Zope Corporation at `http://buildout.zope.org/`. When you install Plone, you are automatically given a working buildout.

Zope installation:

This is what you get by downloading and compiling Zope, or using one of the binary Zope installers. Downloading Plone and installing it gives you a Zope installation with Plone sitting on top of that installation. Zope is the application-server framework upon which Plone is built. Again, when Plone is installed, Zope comes with it.

Zope instance:

One Zope installation can support multiple instances, or runnable Zope servers. Within each instance, you can have many Plone sites. We will let buildout create and configure a Zope instance for us.

Instance home:

The Instance home is the path to the current Zope instance, which houses the Zope's configuration and data files.

Python path:

Plone uses Python, and while Plone is running, the Python interpreter looks for modules in one or more folders, known as the `pythonpath`. It is essential that the interpreter uses the correct Python path. Buildout and Plone's installers set your `pythonpath` by default, so you will not normally have to adjust this. This can be an area of confusion if you have a non-standard setup. If in doubt, ask on the Plone user lists how to adjust your `pythonpath`. When Zope is running, it typically includes the global Python modules making up the standard library, the interpreter's `site-packages/` directory (where third party "global" modules and eggs are installed), and the Zope instance's home. Buildout generally controls which additional eggs are loaded.

Python package:

A Python package is a general term describing a redistributable Python module. At the most basic level, a package is a directory with an `__init__.py` file and some Python code.

Zope product:

A Zope product is a special kind of Python package used to extend Zope. In old versions of Zope, all products were directories inside the special `Products` directory of a Zope instance and would have a Python module name beginning with `Products`. For example, the core of Plone is a product called **CMFPlone**, known in Python as `Products.CMFPlone`. We will use some of the files in the CMFPlone product during the skinning process.

Python egg:

As stated before, eggs are a way to package and distribute Python packages. Eggs contain metadata such as the author's name, email address, and licensing information, as well as information about dependencies. Plone themes created using current technology are considered eggs.

Setuptools:

Setuptools is the Python library that powers the egg mechanism. It is able to automatically sniff out and download dependencies for eggs that you wish to install. You can read more about eggs at the PEAK web site: `http://peak.telecommunity.com/DevCenter/PythonEggs`.

PyPI or the Python Package Index (also known as The Cheese Shop):

Named after a *Monty Python* sketch, PyPI is a repository that hosts thousands of Python packages: `http://pypi.python.org/pypi`. You can browse this if you are looking for a particular package, and developers can also add their own packages to this repository. More importantly, buildout and the `easy_install` script can query this index to download and install eggs automatically. Many eggs are now also stored in the Plone Subversion respository, which is set up as a PyPi server.

easy_install:

Easy_install is a console script that can be used to search the `PyPi` and other repositories, and then install those packages into the global Python environment. Generally speaking, we will only rarely use `easy_install` to install eggs, as `easy_install` doesn't give us adequate control over which eggs are active; our buildout will take care of egg installation.

Namespace package:

Namespaces are a mechanism used by advanced programming languages, such as Python, to help programmers control complexity and avoid name collisions. A namespace package is a feature of setuptools that makes it possible to distribute multiple, separate packages sharing a single top-level namespace. For example, the packages `plone.theme` and `plone.portlets` both share the top-level "plone" namespace, but they are distributed as separate eggs. When installed, each egg lives in its own directory (or possibly a compressed archive of that directory). Without namespace packages, we would have had to distribute one giant Plone package, with a top-level plone directory containing all possible children, for instance `plone/theme` and `plone/portlets`. Instead, we can break these into manageable eggs.

The following is a screenshot of a Plone buildout that holds eggs, as illustration. Notice in particular the eggs named `plone.app.content`, `plone.app.layout`, and `plone.app.portlets`. For themers, these are the three most important parts of the Plone tree to be concerned with, in addition to the before-mentioned CMFPlone product.

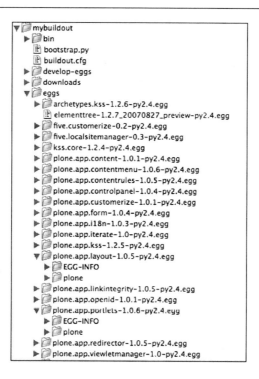

PasteScript:

PasteScript is a pluggable command-line front-end that includes commands to set up package file layouts. Specifically, it allows you to create file layouts for packages. It is not necessary to install PasteScript, but it is necessary to install ZopeSkel if your Plone installer does not do this for you (and it does if you are using the newer installers).

ZopeSkel:

ZopeSkel is a powerful set of PasteScript templates that allows you to use the `paster` command to generate common Plone boilerplate and skeleton products. Don't confuse paster templates with page templates, which we'll talk about later. Paster templates are not templates you edit, but rather templates that allow you to create a Python product, such as a theme product.

Paster:

Installing ZopeSkel automatically installs the paster command that uses PasteScript to create setuptools-based packages, including a skeleton theme product. Using a simple command, you can create a new theme product in less than a minute.

Now that we've had some introduction to the basic terminology for Plone, let's build our development environment.

Setting up your development environment

In order to get set up and start theming, we first must get the development environment set up. This generally consists of installing Subversion (optional, but highly recommended), and of course, installing Plone and all of its dependencies.

Subversion for version control

The importance of version control cannot be underestimated in the development process, especially where teams are concerned. It can also be valuable for a team of one person, if only to keep your product safe and up-to-date in a central location, known as a repository. It's not required, but serious themers will find it invaluable. Subversion is not included by default with a Plone installation.

Subversion is a free/open source version control system originally started by Collabnet: `http://www.collab.net/`. It manages files and directories and the changes made to them, over time. Subversion, often referred to as "svn", allows you to recover older versions of your data, or examine the history of how your code changed. In this regard, you can think of a version control system as a sort of "time machine".

Over the course of a project, it's especially important to check in your product's changes in stages. In Plone, you generally want to check in your theme product immediately when you create it, after significant coding is done that does not adversely affect other Plone products, and at the tail end of your project. You will likely make numerous small check-ins until all of your code is safe in Subversion.

Hardy command-line users control their svn repositories with `svn . . .` command lines. But, there are excellent graphical interfaces available for Subversion on every major platform. Many of these integrate with Explorer (on Windows) or Finder (on OS X). The Subversion bundle that ties into TextMate makes it extra helpful to keep your projects in sync.

Generally, if you are not using Leopard (OS X), you will need to install the Subversion client: `http://subversion.tigris.org/getting.html`.

Macintosh users who have MacPorts can also install it by typing the following into a terminal window:

```
sudo port install subversion
```

MacPorts is an optional tool for Mac OS X that makes installing UNIX software easy, and can be found here: http://www.macports.org/. It's wonderful, but should not be needed by most theme-development level OS X users. We can use it to install GCC, Python, Python modules, Subversion, and other UNIX-based tools. The MacPorts Plone kit is extremely out of date, however, and should not be used.

Alternately, Subversion support for OS X users is provided by the XCode tools. However, it only provides support for Version 1.5 and above, and you need to have a local version of Subversion that matches the version of your Subversion repository.

Up-to-date copies of XCode are available for free on Apple's developer site: http://developer.apple.com/tools/xcode/. Downloading XCode may take several hours, and since it's included on the Tiger and Leopard distribution disks, it is much faster to just run the installer from the disks. You're generally going to need XCode no matter what, so it's best to just go ahead and install it.

Macintosh users who want a tool with a graphical interface may prefer Cornerstone (http://www.zennaware.com/cornerstone/), a client which is especially helpful for Subversion newbies. A full version of Subversion is actually baked into the application, which means that you don't need to install Subversion on Tiger.

If you are running Debian or Ubuntu Linux, use this command to install Subversion:

```
aptitude install subversion
```

Windows users, meanwhile, may find the graphical TortoiseSVN client useful: http://tortoisesvn.tigris.org/.

If you use Fink, then you should install the svn client package: http://fink.sourceforge.net/pdb/package.php/svn-client.

For information on how to use Subversion and how to create a repository, you can refer to any number of web sites. You should also keep handy the commonly used Subversion Reference Card http://svnbook.red-bean.com/en/1.2/index.html.

If you are creating multiple Plone sites, it's absolutely crucial to use Subversion, and it's a relief to know that even if your hard drive dies, your code is safe.

Download Plone

The first real step in getting set up is to download and run a Plone binary installer: `http://www.plone.org/products/plone`. If you have a newer installation, all dependencies should be installed by default, your buildout is already bootstrapped (bootstrapping is a command that makes your buildout usable), and you're ready to start!

 As of Plone 3.2, all of the installers are generally consistent, and will install most of the dependencies required for each operating system. That means that much of what you read next about the dependencies can be largely ignored, but we've included the information here for your edification.

If you are using an older Plone installation, or you wish to create a standalone buildout, you will need to create one via the command line, bootstrap it, and possibly install a few dependencies. You can find instructions on this here: `http://plone.org/documentation/tutorial/buildout/creating-a-buildout-for-your-project`.

All of the Plone installers come with buildout since Plone 3.2, while the Unified Installer for Linux has included buildout since Plone 3.1.

The binary installers have no dependencies at all. They install everything you need. With 3.2, this includes `easy_install`, setuptools, ZopeSkel, and all their dependencies.

The Unified Installer, though, has several dependencies. All of those dependencies are GNU build tools that are typically present on any Linux, BSD, or Solaris development box. The dependencies are also fulfilled on OS X by the XCode toolkit.

Anyone using an OS X box for theme or product development should use the OS X binary installer. You'll benefit from a GUI installer and launcher. For themers, this is generally what you want.

Anyone installing on an OS X server should probably install XCode and use the Unified Installer for greater flexibility. You'll also need a custom buildout when working off of a server.

Macintosh dependencies for the Unified Installer

There is one important dependency when using the Unified Installer that must be resolved for Macintosh users, but thankfully, this dependency is now handled by the newer installers, and by XCode:

GCC (GNU Compiler Collection):

GCC is an integrated distribution of compilers available for several major programming languages.

Windows dependencies for the Unified Installer

The newer Plone binary installers take care of all of the Windows dependencies, and you can just install it and go. Note that nobody but a very serious developer should even consider installing their own GCC, Python, and so on. What they get from the Plone Windows binary installer is more than adequate for theme- and product-level development.

However, if you really want to install Plone on Windows without using the binary installer, there are a few additional things you need to do to satisfy Plone's dependencies. (Additional information can be found here: `http://plone.org/documentation/how-to/buildout-using-windows-installer`.)

If you're using the unified installer, you'll need to get and install the Python Win32 extensions for Python 2.4: `http://downloads.sourceforge.net/pywin32/pywin32-210.win32-py2.4.exe?modtime=1159009237&big_mirror=0`.

If you intend to compile Zope yourself, rather than using a binary installer, or if you ever need to compile an egg with C extensions, you will need the mingw32 or Visual C compilers. If you use the freely available mingw32, make sure you choose the "base" and "make" modules at a minimum when the installer asks. By default, this installs into `C:\MingW32`. Inside the installation directory, there will be a `bin` directory; for example, `C:\MingW32\bin`. Add this to your system `PATH`.

Finally, you need to configure Python's `distutils` package to use the mingw32 compiler. Create a file called `distutils.cfg` in the directory `C:\Python24\Lib\distutils` (presuming Python was installed in `C:\Python24`, as is the default). Edit this with Notepad, or "e" (the Windows TextMate clone), and add the following:

```
[build]
compiler=mingw32
```

Operating system agnostic dependencies

For most of the following items, you will not need to worry but links and instructions on how to use them are included, just in case you are using an older installer.

Python 2.4:

Plone depends on Python 2.4.x. Other versions are *not* compatible. More recent Plone installers include the correct version of Plone by default. Using the wrong version of Python is one of the more common mistakes made by new themers, especially in the case of Macintosh users, as OS X provides Python 2.5 as the system Python.

PIL (Python Imaging Library):

PIL can be downloaded from PythonWare's site: `http://www.pythonware.com/products/pil/`. The most recent version should be compatible. Plone gives us this for free.

Wget:

GNU Wget is a free software package for retrieving files using HTTP, HTTPS, and FTP—the most widely-used Internet protocols. For the next step, you'll need to download Wget here: `http://www.gnu.org/prep/ftp.html`.

easy_install:

To install ZopeSkel, you first need to have `easy_install` on your system. If you don't, download and run `ez_setup.py` (`http://peak.telecommunity.com/dist/ez_setup.py`); for example:

```
$ wget peak.telecommunity.com/dist/ez_setup.py
$ python ez_setup.py
```

ZopeSkel:

To install the ZopeSkel egg and its dependencies (including PasteScript), run:

```
$ easy_install -U ZopeSkel
```

This will install the `paster` command in the place where your Python binaries go. Keep an eye on the output of `easy_install` if you can't find it afterwards. If it's not in your `$PATH`, you may want to symlink it in there.

Buildout: The Plone filestructure

Now what, you ask? Assuming you've installed Plone using a binary installer, you now have a buildout-configured version of Plone sitting on your operating system and you're ready to generate a theme add-on product.

First, though, let's examine the buildout filestructure to see what makes development environment so special. If you open your buildout, you will see a tree structure similar to the following. As time goes on, the structure may change slightly:

```
Plone
   Python-2.4
   buildout-cache
      eggs
      downloads
   mybuildout/
      bin/
      buildout.cfg
      develop-eggs/
      parts/
      products/
      readme.txt
      src/
      var/
         logs/
         filestorage/
   Zope-2.10.7-final-py2.4
```

 Windows users, please note that we'll be using a forward slash to separate the parts of a file path. Please mentally replace these with backslashes.

This structure has evolved a bit, in that the eggs/ and downloads/ subdirectories are moving to a buildout-cache where they may be shared among several instances. Let's look at the directories provided by buildout:

bin/:

Contains various executables, including the buildout command, and the instance Zope control script for starting Zope (./bin/instance fg runs your Zope instance in the foreground for debugging purposes).

parts/:

Contains code and data managed by buildout. In our case, it will include the local Zope installation, a buildout-managed Zope instance, and Plone's source code. In general, you should not modify anything in this directory, as buildout may overwrite your changes.

buildout-cache/eggs/:

Contains eggs that buildout has downloaded. These will be explicitly activated by the control scripts in the bin/ directory (./bin/buildout, for example). On occasion, you may wish to add a new egg here, but the average theme-level developer will never have a need to do so. This folder should be regarded just like parts/, which will be managed by buildout.

buildout-cache/downloads/:

Contains non-egg downloads, such as the Zope source code archive. You will rarely use this directory. This folder should be regarded just like `parts/`, which will be managed by buildout.

develop-eggs/:

This folder is useful for programmers wishing to do development on eggs. It differs from the `eggs` directory, in that it keeps the egg separate until development is complete. It's generally maintained by buildout.

var/:

Contains the log files (in `var/log/`) and the file storage ZODB data (in `var/filestorage/Data.fs`). This is also where you would put existing `data.fs` files if you are skinning around an existing site, migrating a database, moving an entire site to a new server or instance, or for creating multiple mount points. We'll cover mount points in a moment. Buildout will never overwrite these files.

src/:

Initially empty. You can place your own development eggs here and reference them in `buildout.cfg`. For theme development, your theme products will go in the `src/` directory.

products/:

This directory is analogous to a Zope instance's `Products/` directory (note the difference in capitalization). Old-style (non-egg-based) Zope 2 products belong here, not newer theme products. Note that themers will rarely need to use this directory, but some publicly available themes on `plone.org` were not built with paster and might belong in this directory.

The important takeaway here is that:

- You will use a terminal window to execute commands in the `bin/` directory to start and stop your Zope instance
- You will use the `src/` directory as the primary directory in which to work
- You may need to make changes to your `buildout.cfg` file to recognize `data.fs` files located in the `var/` directory and any new theme products that you may have added to the `src/` directory

Other than that, you really don't need to know a lot about how buildout works. You just need to know a few basics, which we'll get to in the next chapter.

Summary

In this chapter, we have learned:

- How buildout fits into the Plone development process
- What terminology is commonly used in Plone development
- How you can use Subversion to safely store your code in a central, versioned repository
- How to set up your development environment
- What the buildout filestructure looks like, and what parts of it are important to themers

Now that we have our development environment set up, let's create and install a theme product and get started!

4
Create and Install a Theme Product

The next steps are to learn how to create a vanilla theme product and install it so that we can begin customizing it.

Generating your theme product using paster

Now that we have a working **buildout** and working instance of Plone, we will generate our skeleton theme product using paster. As mentioned in the previous chapter, installing Plone gives us paster by default. If you don't get paster by default, follow the instructions in the previous chapter to install `easy_install` and ZopeSkel on your system.

Newer installers will be getting paster under the control of buildout so that `paster` is always available at `bin/paster` (from your instance directory). ZopeSkel will also be under the control of buildout so that it is updated when buildout is run in "newest" mode. This means you'll always be able to get the most recent updates to paster and ZopeSkel.

Available templates

A number of paster templates (not the same as page templates) are available to Plone developers for developing different types of Plone products, including themes. To see the available templates, you can run:

```
$ paster create --list-templates
```

This command will give you an output like the following:

```
[bash: ~] paster create --list-templates
Available templates:
  archetype:          A Plone project that uses Archetypes
  basic_namespace:    A project with a namespace package
  basic_package:      A basic setuptools-enabled package
  basic_zope:         A Zope project
  nested_namespace:   A project with two nested namespaces.
  paste_deploy:       A web application deployed through paste.deploy
  plone:              A Plone project
  plone2.5_buildout:  A buildout for Plone 2.5 projects
  plone2.5_theme:     A Theme for Plone 2.5
  plone2_theme:       A Theme Product for Plone 2.1 & Plone 2.5
  plone3_buildout:    A buildout for Plone 3 projects
  plone3_portlet:     A Plone 3 portlet
  plone3_theme:       A Theme for Plone 3.0
  plone3_theme_ootb:  A Theme for Plone 3.0, modified to implement OOTB best practices
  plone_app:          A Plone App project
  plone_hosting:      Plone hosting: buildout with ZEO and any Plone version
  recipe:             A recipe project for zc.buildout
  silva_buildout:     A buildout for Silva projects
[bash: ~] █
```

Your output may show different templates than you see here, as new recipes are created all the time. (The `plone3_theme_ootb` is a recipe I use internally, as it tweaks folder names and some of the boilerplate to suit my personal preferences.) Most themers will want to use the `plone3_theme` recipe, which is the official Plone theming recipe.

Generating your product

Navigate to your Plone product via your terminal tool, and drill down to the directory called `src/`. Then, type this text into your terminal window:

```
$ paster create -t plone3_theme
```

The `paster` recipe will then ask you a series of questions. You usually want to accept the defaults here (just hit the *Enter* key), but not always. We'll see the reason in a moment.

```
[bash: /opt] paster create -t plone3_theme
Selected and implied templates:
  ZopeSkel#basic_namespace  A project with a namespace package
  ZopeSkel#plone            A Plone project
  ZopeSkel#plone3_theme     A Theme for Plone 3
Enter project name: My Theme
Variables:
  egg:        My_Theme
```

```
package:  mytheme
project:  My Theme
Enter namespace_package (Namespace package (like plonetheme))
                                              ['plonetheme']:
Enter package (The package contained namespace package (like example))
                                              ['example']: mytheme
Enter skinname (The skin selection to be added to 'portal_skins' (like
                                              'My Theme')) ['']:
Enter skinbase (Name of the skin selection from which the new one will
                                      be copied) ['Plone Default']:
Enter empty_styles (Override default public stylesheets with empty
                                          ones?) [True]: False
Enter include_doc (Include in-line documentation in generated code?)
                                              [False]:
Enter zope2product (Are you creating a Zope 2 Product?) [True]:
Enter version (Version) ['0.1']:
Enter description (One-line description of the package) ['An installable
                                          theme for Plone 3']:
Enter long_description (Multi-line description (in reST)) ['']:
Enter author (Author name) ['Plone Collective']: Veda Williams
Enter author_email (Author email) ['product-developers
                  @lists.plone.org']: veda@onenw.org
Enter keywords (Space-separated keywords/tags) ['web zope plone theme']:
Enter url (URL of homepage) ['http://svn.plone.org/svn/collective/']:
Enter license_name (License name) ['GPL']:
Enter zip_safe (True/False: if the package can be distributed as a .zip
                                          file) [False]:
```

A few key points on these questions:

- The text in the square brackets is the default answer, and pressing *Enter* allows that default to be accepted. Or, you can type the preferred answer if it is different from the default.

- project name corresponds with the name of your theme. This might be your client's name or the name of the web site for which you are building a theme.

- namespace package is usually plonetheme, but you could name it after your company, if you wish to brand your theme.

- package name is usually a short name for your theme, and one word is generally advisable here, as packages with spaces in their names do not get correctly picked up by buildout.

- skinname is frequently several words, with case sensitivity. This is the name of the theme that you will see when installing it, so make it meaningful.

- For version, zope2product, and zip_safe, you should accept the defaults.

- One question that requires consideration is empty styles, which determines whether you wish to override default public styles with blank stylesheets.

  While this is a quick way of suppressing stylesheets, it can feel a little less elegant, a little unusual too. However, it's worth noting that this is the cleanest way of suppressing stylesheets. If you attempt to suppress stylesheets by altering the boilerplate code using **GenericSetup**, it suppresses them across your entire Plone site, not just within your own theme product. This means that you can't easily layer themes on top of each other if one theme product out of them uses the stylesheets mentioned above and one does not. Again, don't worry too much about this. For new users to Plone and CSS, you likely want to say False. Or, if you always prefer to build on top of the stylesheets that Plone provides you, rather than starting from scratch, you might want to say False. This is purely a personal preference, though it's worth stating that the Plone's stylesheets are quite robust.

- include_doc determines whether certain documentation will be included with your product. This can be helpful, especially when you're first getting used to the theming process.

- It's important to type True or False with case sensitivity, otherwise the default option will be selected.

If you've followed the above instructions, you should now have a vanilla theme product in your src/ directory that can be installed and customized.

Filestructure of a plone3_theme product

Next is a screenshot of a typical Plone 3 theme, outputted using the plone3_theme recipe. We'll examine first the filestructure, then look at a few of the relevant files that define the filestructure.

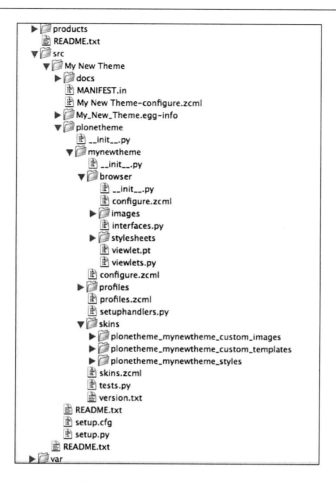

Generally speaking, you only need to worry about what is in the folder here called
`mynewtheme`. The code above is just a standard boilerplate.

There are two folders that have similar purposes here: `browser/` and `skins/`.
The distinction between these two folders is that Zope 3 items go in the `browser/`
directory, whereas old-school and non-Zope 3 templates go in the `skins/` directory.
For a novice themer, that may just sound like a lot of jargon, but to clarify, the
`browser/` folder will hold all templates and viewlets that are derived from the
`plone.app.layout` and `plone.app.portlets` eggs, as well as any other packages
you may wish to override. We'll talk about this more soon. Items that are derived
from the **CMFPlone** product will go in the `skins/` folder.

Optionally, if there's a reason to expose images or stylesheets to other products, you might want to put those items in the `browser/` folder. An example might be this: you have a shopping cart installed, and users want to be able to modify the buttons or styles to match those buttons and styles to an underlying product's look and feel each time. However, this is a fairly rare use case. Your images and stylesheets will normally live in the `skins/` directory unless you have a clear reason why they should not.

The `skins/` directory will hold not only images and stylesheets, but also Python, JavaScripts, and any portlet code that doesn't rely on the **component architecture**.

> In a nutshell, the **Zope Component Architecture (ZCA)** is a Python framework for supporting component-based design and programming. ZCA is about how to create reusable components, but it does not provide components by itself.
>
> It's not important to know more about this right now, but you can read *"Professional Plone Development"*, *Martin Aspeli, Packt Publishing* or some of the tutorials on `plone.org` for more information. We'll be focusing more on the patterns that we'll follow than on the "WHYs" behind them.

In the event that you need to modify `main_template.pt` from CMFPlone (occasionally needed these days), you would place your modified `main_template` in the `skins/` directory too. Any templates that come from CMFPlone will also go in this directory.

Another directory that is useful here is the `profiles/` directory. This directory will hold GenericSetup files (XML files that describe the underlying behavior of a skin product, or site configuration). In other words, this directory holds files that allow you to register stylesheets, JavaScripts, add/remove tabs, menu items, and more. It can also hold files that aid in uninstalling a product by describing what the end result should look like. We'll cover GenericSetup in detail later.

It's important to realize that the structure of your theme product isn't set in stone, and that's ultimately where the power of Plone becomes evident. When you get used to modifying ZCML and XML (we'll see more of this later), you'll have the ability to alter names of folders, remove code from the `browser/` directory, rename your theme, and more.

Do not be afraid to make changes, but always start your Zope in the foreground when you are making changes to your theme product, to spot any problems in your boilerplate code. In the case of changes to XML files, you'll also have to remember to import those files, which we will cover in a bit.

Let's look now at how to add our theme product to our buildout, so that we can install it.

Adding your theme product to your buildout

Our theme is a Python package by default, which means that it is ready to be "eggified" for easy distribution, but it's not an actual egg yet. An egg is a sort of hard-boiled Python package. Eggs don't include setup.py or various other parts of the package. Our theme product, however, does contain these parts.

Since we are still in development, we want to put our new skeleton theme product into the src/ directory, which is where we originally generated it. Open your buildout.cfg file located in the root of your buildout.

 If you are working with a production buildout, you can optionally create a new configuration file, called development.cfg, and make your modifications there. This can help to provide slightly different setups while in development mode versus production mode. For example, you wouldn't want PDB (debugger) to be available in a buildout on a production server, but you might very well want that to be part of your development buildout.

Open your buildout.cfg file, and make the following modifications in the develop and eggs and zcml parameters of the [buildout] and [instance] sections respectively, based on how you answered the questions when you ran the paster recipe:

```
[buildout]
develop =
    ... [other eggs here] ...
    src/plonetheme.mytheme
    # this tells buildout that it's a development egg, and that
    # it should find it in the src directory rather than fetching
    # from a repository.
... [other code here] ...

[instance]
eggs =
    ... [other eggs here] ...
    plonetheme.mytheme
    # this tells buildout that you'll be using your theme
    # with Plone.
```

```
zcml =
     ... [other zcml slugs here] ...
     plonetheme.mytheme
     # this tells zope that your product exists
```

These sections may not follow exactly each other in the `buildout.cfg` file, so be careful to add your code in the right place.

Since we have made changes to your buildout, you now need to rebuild your buildout with the following command for these changes to be read by Zope. You should be in your buildout's directory when you run this command. It might be named `zinstance` or similar, depending on how your buildout is set up. Just make sure you're above the `bin/` directory.:

`./bin/buildout`

You may use the following command to run buildout offline, if you don't need any new, external components—it's a good bit faster:

`./bin/buildout -o`

Advanced users may optionally want to look into the **eggtractor** egg (`http://pypi.python.org/pypi/buildout.eggtractor`) to cut down on some of the boilerplate needed in `buildout.cfg` when adding new eggs to the `src/` directory.

Similarly, in cases where you have modified your ZCML (adding an egg), you can often avoid rerunning your buildout by including an egg called **plone.reload** (`http://pypi.python.org/pypi/plone.reload`) in your buildout and going to `http://localhost:8080/reload` and choosing the "Reload Code and ZCML" option.

A third egg that helps to developers by consolidating the buildout tree structure (and thus making code easier to locate) is **omelette** (`http://pypi.python.org/pypi/collective.recipe.omelette`). Follow the ReadMe files for these eggs to understand how to install them.

Starting Zope and installing your product on a Plone site

After running your buildout, start your Zope in the foreground (extremely helpful during development, as it displays errors in your terminal window). All the installer buildouts will start with `bin/plonectl start`. It (`bin/plonectl fg`) will run a standalone install in foreground, which is useful for debugging.

Type:

`./bin/plonectl fg`

You'll know your Zope is working when you see the phrase, "INFO Zope Ready to handle requests".

Once Zope is up and running, you can connect to its management interface from any web browser. We'll assume in this chapter that Zope is running on port 8080, which is the default. In your browser, go to `http://localhost:8080/manage_main` and log in using **admin/admin** as your username and password. Optionally, at this point, you can create a new user in the `acl_users` area of the **ZMI (Zope Management Interface)**, create a secure password for that username, and assign manager permissions.

Creating a Plone site

As of Version 3.2, all the installers will create a Plone site by default. If one is not created, or you wish to create a different one, from the ZMI choose **Plone Site** from the **Add** pop-up list. You should not need to select a profile at this time, although you could do so if you know that you will be building on top of a policy product that will control generic settings that you want to repeat from project to project.

Once you add a site, you will be able to navigate to your new site by selecting the new site and clicking on the **View** tab. You should see the following result (notice that default Plone styles are applied):

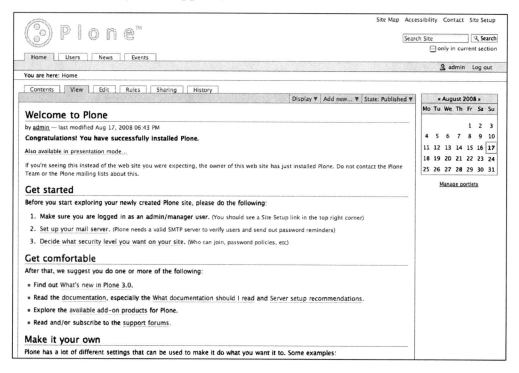

Advanced users may wish to skin against a data.fs file from an existing site. If so, you will want to create a mount point at the root of your Zope instance, instead of a standard Plone site. For more information, read this documentation:

http://www.plope.com/Members/chrism/whatsnew_27.

Installing your Plone theme

To install your theme on a Plone site, go to **Site Setup** | **Add-on Products** and select your theme product, or go to your site in the ZMI, and navigate to **portal_quickinstaller** via http://localhost:8080/newsite/portal_quickinstaller/manage_installProductsForm.

Choose your product from the list of installable products. If you do not see your theme present, you have not correctly registered it in your buildout.cfg file.

Click on the checkbox next to your theme product and choose **Install**.

Note that the ZMI **quick installer** is functionally the same as the **Add-on Products** option in the Plone **Site Setup** panel. The ZMI interface just gives you some additional options. Choosing an extension profile when creating a new Plone site is also functionally the same.

Putting your site into debug mode

Before going any further, we will put our site's stylesheets into **debug mode**. This allows us to see the changes that you will apply to stylesheets immediately after reloading a page, without having to restart the Zope server.

 This is one of the most common points where new skinners stumble. Remember to put your site's portal_css into debug mode, but only while in development, as it will slow down your site.

In order to set portal_css in debug mode, go to the portal_css tool in the ZMI by pointing your browser to an address that should look like http://localhost:8080/mysite/portal/css/manage_cssForm.

Then check the **Debug** | **development mode** and click the **Save** button. You can also access this by drilling down into portal_css through the ZMI.

You can optionally put your entire Zope in debug mode. This must be configured programmatically in a file usually located in the `etc/` folder of the Zope instance on the file system. If you are using buildout, debug mode can be set from the instance part of a buildout configuration file. (Zope debug mode is automatic when you're running in foreground mode.) It is also probable that you will need to put your entire Zope instance into debug mode just to theme a web site, and you may occasionally also need to put your `portal_javascripts` and `portal_kss` into debug mode.

In the future, debug modes may be consolidated and possibly enabled by default, so stay tuned.

Summary

In this chapter, we have learned:

- How to create a theme product
- What a theme product's filestructure looks like
- How to add a theme product to a buildout
- How to start Zope, create a Plone site, and install your theme product
- How to enable debug mode to ease theme development

Now that you have a theme installed on your Plone site, we are almost ready to start skinning it. First, we'll cover some aspects of Plone's inner workings that will shape the skinning process.

5

Making Manual (TTW) Changes or What Not to Do

You can customize Plone by changing settings **through the web (TTW)** in the ZMI (**Zope Management Interface**), or by making changes to an installable filesystem product. TTW changes are hard to back up, hard to share, hard to repeat, and generally tough to work with. In Plone 3, the recommended method of theme development is on the filesystem, but we'll look at how you can make some quick-and-dirty changes TTW if needed, and also cover briefly how to bring those changes back out to the filesystem.

In this chapter, we step through how to make our Zope instance recognize our theme product, then make minor manual adjustments to a Plone site through the ZMI. Next, we learn how to get the same changes into our filesystem product by using **GenericSetup** profiles and other tools.

Specifically, this chapter involves a tour of how to activate a theme and how to use **skin layers** and non-Zope 3 elements to affect the look and feel of your site. The lessons learned in this chapter should help transition you to filesystem development.

Prerequisites

In order to perform most of the customizations mentioned above, you need managerial rights to your site, light programming skills, and a little common sense. For some of the changes, you will need to be comfortable with the concept of Plone filesystem theme products, as discussed in the previous chapter. Please follow the steps in the previous chapter to generate a theme product and install it on your Plone site.

It will be helpful in some cases to have an understanding of **TAL** (the Zope **Template Attribute Language**) and **TALES** (**Template Attribute Language Expression Syntax**—it's expression syntax, but not critical yet). You can find a good description on them in *The Definitive Guide to Plone* (`http://plone.org/documentation/books/definitive_guide_to_plone.pdf`), and also in Zope's documentation (`http://www.zope.org/Documentation/Books/ZopeBook/2_6Edition/AppendixC.stx`).

We'll also briefly mention ZCML, XML, and Python, but will dig deeper into that later.

What this chapter will not cover

Beyond the realm of theming, there are a number of minor tweaks that integrators can make to a Plone site, and will likely need to make during the course of theming a site, but these tasks do not constitute theming, per se. These configurations enable the theming process, however.

For example, when you add a portlet, the portlet may give you a few options that allow you to control the look and feel of your portlets (such as including borders, including a header or a hyperlink, and so on). If you add a navigation portlet and modify it, or you modify the one that is installed by default, it gives you options to control whether that navigation displays at the root level, whether it shows all parents and children, whether to add borders, provide hyperlinks, and so on. Every portlet is different, of course, and may not provide all of these options.

Additionally, in **Site Setup**, configuration screens called configlets exist for various pieces of the Plone UI. These can be adjusted and may affect what displays on your web site. However, it's rare that most of these configuration changes will ever be incorporated in a theme product, though certainly it is possible. These tasks are for integrators, not themers. For more information, refer to *Practical Plone 3* (`http://www.packtpub.com/practical-plone-3-beginners-guide-to-building-powerful-websites/book`) to find out how to manage these changes, or refer to the *Plone 3 User Manual* (`http://plone.org/documentation/manual/plone-3-user-manual`).

Hence, this chapter is geared towards changes that are not readily available to integrators.

Registering and installing a new theme

To see some of these TTW changes, we first need to understand how to get our theme exposed to our Zope instance as a filesystem product so that it can be installed on a Plone site.

Creating a product that overrides a resource in a skin layer requires:

1. Installing paster and ZopeSkel (done in the previous chapter).
2. Running the appropriate paster recipe to generate a filesystem product (done in the previous chapter using the `plone3_theme` recipe).
3. Registering it in your buildout (done in the previous chapter).
4. Registering a new **filesystem directory view** for that product (done by default).
5. Placing this view in the list of available skin layers by installing your product (done in the previous chapter).
6. Copying the relevant resources (templates, stylesheets, images, flash files, and so on) into the new skin layers contained within your filesystem product.
7. Customizing the resource.

Since we have already created a theme product in the previous chapter, added it to our buildout, and installed it, we will start with Step 4. Note that most of these steps are taken care of by the boilerplate that is generated for you, but it's worth looking at the code that handles these steps. Don't worry if you don't understand everything we cover here; we're going through it to give you an idea of the architecture of your theme product. Most themers won't need to make changes to these parts of the generated code.

Register the filesystem directory view

To register this product as a filesystem directory view, or basically provide a hook into the folders contained within your filesystem product, the `__init__.py` file in the root of your filesystem product must be modified so that Plone can see it. This happens automatically, as long as you answered "yes" to creating a Zope 2 product when you ran the `plone3_theme` recipe (and you should).

```
def initialize(context):
    """Initializer called when used as a Zope 2 product."""
```

We must ensure that this package is a Zope 2 product. If it is in the magical `Products.*` namespace (for example, a traditional product placed in the `Products` directory of a Zope instance), then this happens automatically.

If we are using an egg-based product in a different namespace (which is what the `plone3_theme` recipe does), we add the following code to the package's `configure.zcml` file. This boilerplate is created by default.

```
<configure
    xmlns="http://namespaces.zope.org/zope"
    xmlns:five="http://namespaces.zope.org/five"
```

```
xmlns:cmf="http://namespaces.zope.org/cmf"
i18n_domain="plonetheme.mytheme">

<five:registerPackage package="." initialize=".initialize" />

<include package=".browser" />

<include file="skins.zcml" />

<include file="profiles.zcml" />
```
```
</configure>
```

Make the directory view available to portal_skins

We then need to create the directory view, which maps a portion of the filesystem into the skin layer for the current theme. We do this using a GenericSetup profile, which we will cover in depth later in this chapter. For now, all you need to know is that it is human-readable code (XML) that allows you to create steps that are activated when a product is installed or uninstalled and describes certain configuration settings.

In this case, installing your product will expose your theme product's configuration settings to your Zope instance via an **extension profile**. This is provided via the default boilerplate in your `profiles.zcml` file, as follows:

```
<configure
    xmlns="http://namespaces.zope.org/zope"
    xmlns:genericsetup="http://namespaces.zope.org/genericsetup"
    i18n_domain="plonetheme.mytheme">

  <genericsetup:registerProfile
      name="default"
      title="My Theme"
      directory="profiles/default"
      description='Extension profile for the "My Theme" Plone theme.'
      provides="Products.GenericSetup.interfaces.EXTENSION"
      />
```
```
</configure>
```

Next, we configure the `skins.xml` file located in the `profiles/` directory to create skin layers, again provided by default when you use the `plone3_theme` recipe.

```
<?xml version="1.0"?>
<object name="portal_skins" allow_any="False" cookie_persistence=
                              "False" default_skin="My Theme">

  <object name="plonetheme_mytheme_custom_images"
```

```
          meta_type="Filesystem Directory View"
          directory="plonetheme.mytheme:skins/plonetheme_
                              mytheme_custom_images"
          />
      <object name="plonetheme_mytheme_custom_templates"
          meta_type="Filesystem Directory View"
          directory="plonetheme.mytheme:skins/plonetheme_
                              mytheme_custom_templates"
          />
      <object name="plonetheme_mytheme_styles"
          meta_type="Filesystem Directory View"
          directory="plonetheme.mytheme:skins/plonetheme_mytheme_styles"
          />

      <skin-path name="My Theme" based-on="Plone Default">
       <layer name="plonetheme_mytheme_custom_images"
                              insert-after="custom"/>
       <layer name="plonetheme_mytheme_custom_templates" insert-after=
                              "plonetheme_mytheme_custom_images"/>
       <layer name="plonetheme_mytheme_styles" insert-after=
                  "plonetheme_mytheme_custom_templates"/>
      </skin-path>

     </object>
```

You can register as many directory views (skin layers) as you wish, and you can alter the boilerplate to use shortened folder names if you're feeling adventurous and comfortable with the code located in the filesystem product.

Essentially, what is happening here is that you are creating folders (skin layers) in a filesystem product and exposing them to Plone via the **CMF (Content Management Framework)**. Working with the CMF means that you are allowed to customize the resources within a CMF skin layer in real time on the filesystem or TTW. These resources are available everywhere, as opposed to within a specific context.

CMF is a set of add-on products for Zope used to build content management systems. It provides some basic tools for handling metadata, members, and so on, but is not a content management system itself. Plone is an example of a sophisticated CMS built using CMF. The new Zope 3 component architecture is layered on top of the CMF and provides greater extensibility and reusability of resources.

Zope 3 resources, meanwhile, are only fully available to you via the filesystem, and can be manipulated or reused in various contexts. It's worth stating up front that if you are dealing with a CMF skin layer item, it is treated differently than a Zope 3 item, and the items live in different places and are treated differently during the theming process as well.

Rather than focusing on the logistics of what all of this means, we'll introduce some patterns that you can follow to get used to the concepts. There are a lot of moving parts, and it's a wild ride, so hang on.

Install your theme product

Assuming you have followed the instructions from the previous chapter, you have already installed your Plone theme on your Plone site and put your stylesheets in debug mode.

If, at this point, your theme product is installed and you can view your site at `http://localhost;8080/mysite` (where `mysite` is the name of the Plone site you have just created), you are ready to start customizing your theme.

It may help to make a small change to your stylesheets before installing the product so that you can verify that your theme product did indeed get installed. This can be accomplished by editing the `mytheme.css` file found in the `skins/plonetheme_mynewtheme_styles` folder in your filesystem product. For example, you may wish to change the body background color:

```
body {
background-color:#000;
}
```

General guidelines during development

At this point, we need to look at the steps needed to make sure changes to your site can be seen.

Theming a Plone site requires modifying ZCML, XML, TAL, and Python code, in addition to simple CSS changes, and each change requires a different set of steps to activate. Specifically, the rules for restarts / reinstalls / imports / refreshes are as follows:

- To be able to see your changes immediately, you should rerun your site in foreground mode using the `./bin/plonectl fg` command, or your `buildout.cfg` has to explicitly enable debug mode in the `[instance]` section. Without this, you will not see CSS changes immediately even with `portal_css` in debug mode.

- If you change your CSS, refresh your browser as long as `portal_css` is in debug mode (located in the ZMI under `http://localhost:8080/mysite/portal_css/manage_cssForm`) and your cache is cleared. Firefox's Web Developer Toolbar may come in handy here, as it has a "disable cache" flag that can be set.

- If you change ZCML, you must restart Zope. You can use the `plone.reload` egg to get around full Zope restarts.
- If you change GenericSetup (XML), you must reinstall your product or reimport the necessary step. Importing is safer and gives you more control. We'll discuss GenericSetup later in this chapter.
- If you change Python files in your filesystem product (as opposed to TTW), you must restart Plone.
- If you change Python scripts TTW, you can simply refresh if you are running your Zope in foreground mode.

Be warned that uninstalling a theme product is generally not an option, and it can be messy. Uninstallation requires that a theme to have an uninstall profile written for it, and if the profile is incomplete (most will be), you will wind up with "leftovers" from your theme that can be difficult to remove. Similarly, you should be cautious about reinstalling your product over and over again, as it can have unexpected consequences and GenericSetup clashes that may be difficult to resolve.

About a theme product's architecture

Next, let's take a look at the pieces that comprise a theme product. The areas in the shaded boxes are the concepts we will cover in this chapter. In the case of configuration settings and skin layers (CMF elements), you can make changes manually TTW or through a filesystem product. In the case of Zope 3 components and programming languages, changes can generally only be achieved through filesystem development, with some exceptions that we'll cover in the next chapter.

To make things easier, we're going to look at the items that can be changed easily in both places first.

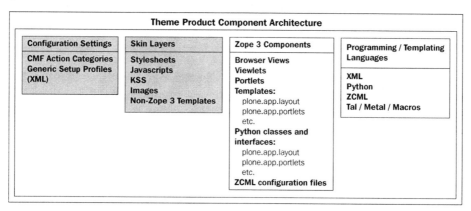

Changing your site via CMF action categories

On your Plone site's home page, you will notice various areas where there are menu options or buttons. As you can see from the next screenshot, the default Plone site shows a top navigation area, various links for printing or emailing a page, as well as menu actions that allow you to cut, paste, or otherwise manipulate the objects within a folder.

You may also see tabs or widgets that allow you to access the contents of a given folder, a **History** area, a **Sharing** tab, and various tabs on the top for **Home, Users, News**, and **Events**. It may help to log into your new Plone site as we walk through these items.

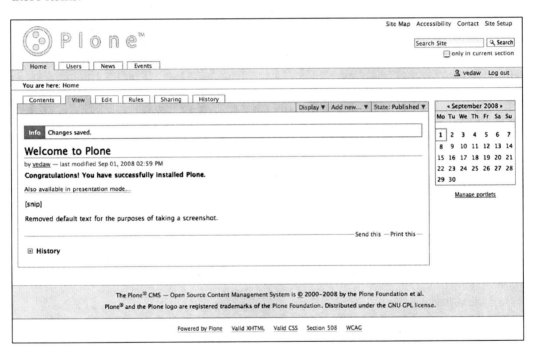

Many of these tabs, buttons, and menu objects correspond to actions defined in `http://localhost:8080/mysite/portal_actions/manage` (where `mysite` is the name of your Plone site) in the ZMI. You must log into your site's ZMI in order to see the available `portal_action` categories.

By default, there are seven CMF action categories. For practical purposes, CMF action categories are merely categories within which you can alter numerous buttons, tabs, and menu options on your site. These include the following items:

- `document_actions`
- `site_actions`
- `folder_buttons`
- `object`
- `object_buttons`
- `portal_tabs`
- `user`

To add a new `action_category`, choose **Add CMF Category** from the drop-down list found on the top-right area of the ZMI. Advanced users can add a new action category to drive something like a portlet with drop-down lists, but generally you will be adding or altering action items within the existing categories.

Often, all you may want to do is uncheck the **Visible?** checkbox to hide the items you do not wish to see or change the logic slightly. To edit an existing CMF action, simply click on it and alter the necessary properties.

To add a new action within a category, click on the category, and choose **Add CMF Action** from the drop-down menu.

 Note that you should not delete any of the categories or the actions. It is safer to simply mark the actions as not visible by un-checking the **Visible?** checkbox.

Document actions category

Default document actions include:

- **rss** — displays an RSS button with a link to the aggregated page.
- **sendto** — displays an email button with the logic needed to email the link of the page to a specified email address.
- **print** — adds a print button and the logic needed to print the page.
- **addtofavorites** — flags an item as a favorite. This option only appears and works if you have **user folders** enabled in the security control panel; actual support for this feature is unknown.

- **full_screen**—expands the content area to take up the full screen.
- **extedit**—enables external editing if an editor is specified.

Only the first three are visible, by default.

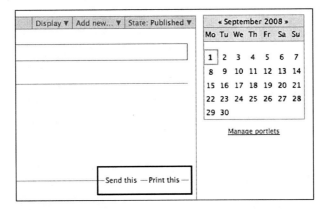

Site actions category

Within the `site_actions` category you will find the menu options that correspond to the top navigation on a default Plone installation. By default, these include **Site Map**, **Accessibility**, **Contact**, and **Site Setup**.

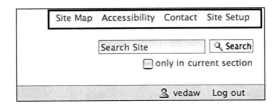

If you want to add an additional menu option here, or in another category (for example, **Site Help**, which may be available to persons with managerial rights), you can add a new CMF action. You would specify the **Title**, **Description**, i18n (internationalization) **Domain** if you wish to use Plone's translation services, and the **URL** to which the link would point via a TALES expression.

Next you would specify the URL for an icon to correspond with the action (if one exists), any specific conditions using a TALES expression, and then select the permissions required for that action. In this case, a new **Site Help** action would be specified as follows:

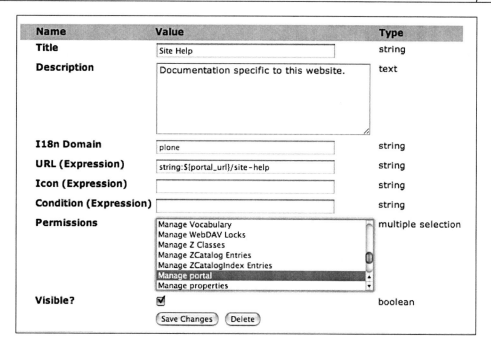

Name	Value	Type
Title	Site Help	string
Description	Documentation specific to this website.	text
I18n Domain	plone	string
URL (Expression)	string:${portal_url}/site-help	string
Icon (Expression)		string
Condition (Expression)		string
Permissions	Manage Vocabulary Manage WebDAV Locks Manage Z Classes Manage ZCatalog Entries Manage ZCatalogIndex Entries Manage portal Manage properties	multiple selection
Visible?	☑	boolean

Save Changes   Delete

Folder buttons category

Within the `folder_buttons` category you will find a listing of all of the buttons that are available when a user is on the **Contents** tab of any folder on the site. These include actions that can be taken against a piece of content, such as **Copy**, **Cut**, **Rename**, **Paste**, **Delete**, and **Change State**. You will rarely need to customize these items.

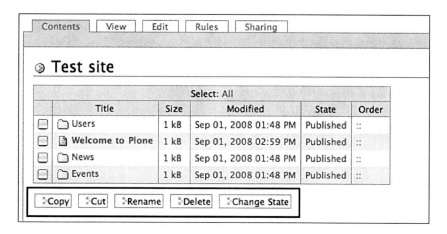

Object category

This category contains actions that appear as the tabs above the content area when you are logged into your web site.

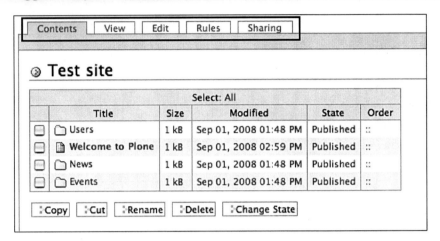

This includes the following:

- **folderContents** — provides the logic for displaying the **Contents** tab itself, not the view you get when you click on it. For this item and the items next, the actual views can be either skin layer templates or browser views, and those are configured elsewhere.

- **syndication** — provides the logic for determining if an object is able to be syndicated.

- **content rules** — provides the logic for displaying the view for the **Rules** tab.

- **local_roles** — provides the logic for accessing the **Sharing** tab.

- **history** — provides the logic for displaying an object's history that you get when clicking on the **History** tab.

You will rarely need to modify these category actions.

Object buttons category

Within this category there are actions that define the buttons that are shown in the **Actions** drop-down list on the `contentActions` bar for each content object in the site. These include **Cut**, **Copy**, **Paste**, **Delete**, and **Rename** actions.

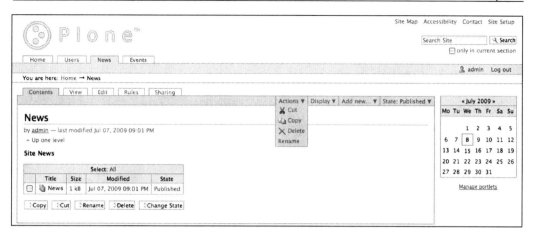

Again, you will rarely need to modify these actions.

Portal tabs category

This category contains a single action that causes a **Home** tab to display at the top of a default Plone site. You might see additional items showing next to the **Home** tab, but those items can also be controlled by the navigation settings. If you alter the navigation settings in `plone_control_panel` to disable **Automatically Generate Tabs**, only the tabs defined in the `portal_tabs` category will display.

In this screenshot, the only true `portal_tab` action is the **Home** tab, whereas the **Users**, **News**, and **Events** tabs are navigational items (content) made available by a default Plone installation, which are controlled by the **Navigation configlet** located in the **Site Setup** area.

User category

This category contains all of the actions that display in the personal tools area of your site.

Many of these items, generally, only display when the user is logged into the site. Logged out users will also see a **login** option in this area. Many of these are not enabled by default.

These actions include:

- A link to the logged in user's `Member` folder (`http://localhost:8080/mysite/dashboard`, where `mysite` is the name of your Plone site)
- A "preferences" link (`http://localhost:8080/mysite/plone_memberprefs_panel`)
- A "login" link (`http://localhost:8080/mysite/login_form`; disappears once the user is logged in)
- A "logout" link (`http://localhost:8080/mysite/logout`)
- A "join" link (`http://localhost:8080/mysite/join_form`)
- An "undo" link (`http://localhost:8080/mysite/undo_form`)
- An "Add to Favorites" link
- A "My Favorites" link

Many of these options are not visible by default. Additional items that might be useful to add to this area include:

- Link to a **Site Help** section specific to a client
- Link to Plone documentation
- Link to a **Support** page

For more information on each of these CMF action categories, read the *Plone Theme Reference* manual (`http://plone.org/documentation/manual/theme-reference`) or *Chapter 7* of *"The Definitive Guide to Plone"*, First Edition, Andy McKay, Apress.

We'll look next at a tool called GenericSetup, extract our `portal_actions` from the ZMI using the tool, and then insert those `portal_actions` into your theme product.

About GenericSetup

GenericSetup is a major step forward in managing Plone site configuration, and is a core part of how Plone handles its own site creation process. It is easy to get GenericSetup conflicts because it is sometimes unintuitive (unless XML is your first language), but it is also very powerful. It's also important to use care to protect yourself against settings that might have been made through the web.

Within the ZMI for your site, click on `portal_setup`, which is the control panel for managing your GenericSetup. There are three tabs that are important to point out here: **Import**, **Export**, and **Snapshot**. We'll look at each of these in turn, but first, let's get a sense of what GenericSetup is.

GenericSetup introduces the idea of the **configuration profile**. A profile is essentially a set of steps defined using XML. Each `.xml` file defines what happens in one of those steps. Note the fundamental difference between a profile and an install method: install methods define a set of steps that must be run to get a result, whereas a profile actually describes the result itself. If you export all the steps from `portal_setup`, you end up with XML defining the steps to get back to a defined state of the site, so it can feel like it describes an end result. But that's not true in general, particularly not in the partial profiles that get run when a product is installed.

Practically, all of the various knobs and twiddling that occur in the ZMI can be exported to the filesystem via XML files. Additionally, this XML can be tweaked by hand to create an import profile such that when the product is installed or the GenericSetup profile is imported by hand, the settings will take effect. An example here is that you might wish to turn on a new `portal_tab` for your site and have it display when your filesystem product is installed. If you find that you are doing a lot of tweaks in the ZMI, GenericSetup may save you some time in terms of getting lots of settings the way you want them quickly and easily. And, it's not just a timesaver; it makes it much less likely that you will forget some important part of the site configuration if you ever have to rebuild the site.

An important point to note about profiles is that there are two types of profiles that GenericSetup understands.

Base profile

The first type is called a base profile. Base profiles provide the base-level information that a site needs to be created. Plone's default setup is itself a GenericSetup base profile. Base profiles contain configuration information such as tools, workflows, types, and registered plug-ins for some packages. Most people building custom sites will not need to ever create a base profile, and you should not create or alter your base profile until you have some practice.

Extension profiles

Extension profiles are intended to be applied after base profiles. Any number of extension profiles can be applied to a site, whereas only a single base profile will ever be applied. Extension profiles are meant to describe new content types, custom skins, custom workflows, custom tools, and to add configuration to what has already been set up in a base profile. All of these are additive actions that do not make any changes to currently existing products. This is an important concept.

Changing configuration in existing tools, modifying content types to respond to a different workflow, or any other modifications of base profiles, are less safe actions, and only should be undertaken when you have a solid understanding of GenericSetup.

An example extension profile

The great thing about GenericSetup is that it's written in a human-readable format to make edits quick and easy. The profiles typically live in a `profiles/` folder in a filesystem product. Note that your product might have different files listed here:

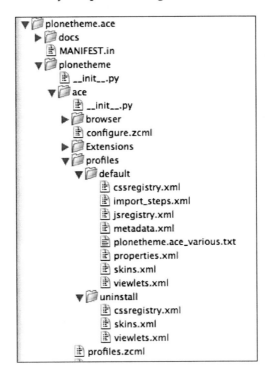

The `default` folder contains all of the information on what knobs and switches need to be twisted when the product is installed, and the `uninstall` folder obviously contains the information on what knobs should be un-twisted when the product is removed. Remember that the `quick_installer` takes care of this un-twisting for a number of things that a product installation normally does, but not everything.

The common examples of files you might see include:

- `skins.xml`: A list of all of the skin paths that should be added to the skins tool when your site is configured
- `cssregistry.xml`: Contains the information needed to install stylesheets for a filesystem product
- `jsregistry.xml`: Contains the information needed to install JavaScripts for a filesystem product
- `viewlets.xml`: Contains ordering / hiding / moving information on viewlets for a product
- `portlets.xml`: Contains information that defines new portlets or portlet managers, or modifies existing portlets for a product

If we open the `cssregistry.xml` file for the above example, a project called `ace`, we see the following code:

```
<?xml version="1.0"?>
<object name="portal_css">
<stylesheet title=""
    id="ace.css"
    media="screen" rel="stylesheet" rendering="import"
    cacheable="True" compression="safe" cookable="True"
    enabled="1" expression=""/>
</object>
```

In this case, the file states that upon install, a stylesheet called `ace.css` will be imported into the CSS registry as a `screen` type, meaning that it will be accessed when the site is rendered. The additional information is not necessary to understand here, but it might be helpful to investigate this topic more deeply as your themes become more advanced. Essentially, these variables are related to how your stylesheets are constructed for delivery.

CMFPlone, the default Plone product (now located in your buildout in the `buildout-cache`, or within the `eggs` directory with a version designation such as `Plone-3.3b1-py2.4.egg`), also contains a `profiles/` directory. Within its `cssregistry.xml` file is a much larger listing of XML that defines exactly what CSS files will be loaded when a base Plone site is installed. This means that since your site uses base Plone, and has its own profiles, the profiles are additive. This is where snapshots come in handy.

Taking snapshots

When working with GenericSetup, it's important to know what your site's profile looks like before you start making changes. This is especially important if you are trying to resolve a GenericSetup conflict.

Before making any changes to your site's profile, you should always make a snapshot of your site that will give you an opportunity to evaluate the XML at various points in time, using the `diff` command. It is very important to take a snapshot before making changes, so that you can backtrack to the original profile if you need to. Click on the **Create a Snapshot** button. The site will appear to spin for a while, and will actually never stop spinning, due to an annoying, but harmless, flaw in this area. (It's possible that this might be fixed by the time you're reading this.) Wait for about 30 seconds, then click on the **Snapshots** tab again, and you will see a snapshot. You may have better luck doing this with Firefox, due to the fact that Firefox does not timeout as often. This is due primarily to how your Apache may be configured. (Firefox is also helpful when re-cataloging your site for this same reason.)

The snapshot that is generated is given a title that is likely not very helpful. Click on the **Snapshots** tab again, select the checkbox next to the snapshot, and give it a more meaningful name. If you make additional changes to your GenericSetup, either through the filesystem or the ZMI, you can create a second snapshot, export both profiles to your desktop using the **Import/Export** button, and then use the **Comparison** tab in `portal_setup` to examine the differences.

Export profile

Occasionally, you just want to know what your current profile looks like for a select set of items. For example, you might want to know what the profile for your `portal_tabs` is. In this case, click on the **Export** tab. Select the checkbox next to **Action Providers**, and click on the **Export Selected Steps** button. Extract the `.tar` file, and you will see a file called `actions.xml`, which outlines the current state of affairs for your site. This file may be quite lengthy, so generally, if you want to make a small change within your profile, remove all of the pieces you don't want, and insert the pieces you do want in your theme product's `actions.xml` file, being careful to escape the lines correctly. Your next step would then be to import your new changes into your site.

Import profile

Click on the **Import** tab.. Select your theme product as the default profile (very important). Then, import the selected steps.

Once the profile is imported or the product is reinstalled, the new profile steps will be processed.

The key is to only insert the pieces that are different from the base profile, not rewrite the entire profile. Be vigilant here, as including more information than you actually want can cause unexpected behavior when your profile is installed, or more likely can force you to duplicate and maintain too much of Plone's own base profile.

The point is that it's easy to insert the wrong XML code, and thus to create problems with your GenericSetup, so be thoughtful as you write this code, and watch for traceback errors in your terminal window when you import your steps.

Moving portal_actions configurations into a filesystem product

The best way to understand how to use GenericSetup in practice is to have a practical example. In this case, assume that through the ZMI we have added some portal_tabs to our site:

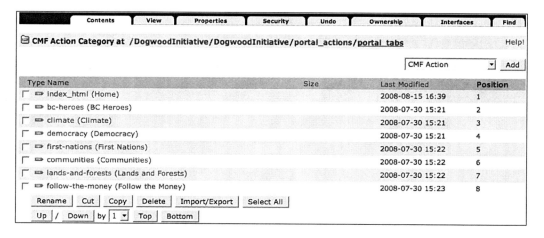

To extract those to the filesystem, it helps to see the necessary syntax first. Go to portal_setup in the ZMI, click on the **Export** tab, select the actions option, and export that selected step. It will export a large file that contains all of the portal_actions information, not just the information pertaining to the portal_tabs. In this case, we want to add the following CMF actions to the portal_tabs area:

- BC Heroes
- Climate

You want to extract only the relevant information from that file into a new file named `actions.xml`, to be placed in the `profiles/default` folder of your theme product:

```xml
<?xml version="1.0"?>
<object name="portal_actions" meta_type="Plone Actions Tool"
          xmlns:i18n="http://xml.zope.org/namespaces/i18n">
 <action-provider name="portal_actions"/>
 <object name="portal_tabs" meta_type="CMF Action Category">
  <property name="title"></property>
  <object name="bc-heroes" meta_type="CMF Action">
   <property name="title">BC Heroes</property>
   <property name="description"></property>
   <property name="url_expr"></property>
   <property name="icon_expr"></property>
   <property name="available_expr"></property>
   <property name="permissions"/>
   <property name="visible">True</property>
  </object>
  <object name="climate" meta_type="CMF Action">
   <property name="title">Climate</property>
   <property name="description"></property>
   <property name="url_expr"></property>
   <property name="icon_expr"></property>
   <property name="available_expr"></property>
   <property name="permissions"/>
   <property name="visible">True</property>
  </object>
 </object>
</object>
```

That's it! Next time you install your product, those items will be added to your web site.

However, to minimize the risk involved in installing a product and having your GenericSetup clash with other GenericSetup steps, it's usually best to go into `portal_setup/manage_snapshots` tool and create a snapshot. Then select the theme product that you're working on, choose the actions option, and import it into your web site.

The process is the same for all of the other XML files in your theme product.

Skin layer customization, the old-fashioned way

In addition to being able to alter many of the basic settings on a site via `portal_actions`, users can also modify certain page templates, images, stylesheets, JavaScripts, and so on through the ZMI. How Plone interprets these changes depends on the order of what are called "skin layers".

Prior to Plone 3, most customizations performed in the ZMI relied on the concept of a single, global namespace such that resources for a given product could not easily be shared between products. The global namespace was also a problem because it resulted in name conflicts in products. Authors were forced to use convoluted names in their products, such as `pfg_base_edit`, which was very "un-Pythonic". This was a fairly limiting idea but made modifying items fast and easy through the web.

Before Plone 3, Plone used Zope's concept of acquisition (and still does, but not always). This means that when looking up an identifier, Plone finds the closest object, property, or method that matches. For example, when looking for a logo specific to a given section, Plone looks first in the directory for that section, and if it does not find it, it moves up through the directory hierarchy until it does find one. You might think of acquisition as providing behaviors by context.

A Zope object can acquire any object or property from any of its parents. That is, if you have a folder called A, containing two resources (a document called homepage and another folder called B), then an URL pointing at `http://.../A/B/homepage` would work even though B is empty. This is because Zope starts to look for homepage in B, doesn't find it, and goes back up to A, where it's found. The reality, inevitably, is more complex than this, but it explains the basis of how skin layers are read. For more information, read the chapter on *acquisition* in *The Zope Book* found at `http://docs.zope.org/zope2/zope2book/source/Acquisition.html`.

Using the portal_skins tool

A tool called `portal_skins` was created to help manage the resources within Plone, and to control the order of acquisition. If you create a new Plone site and enter the `portal_skins` tool located in the ZMI just below the root and click on the Properties tab, you will see a skin called **Plone Default**, and next to it a listing of skin layers. A "skin", often referred to as a "theme", is just an ordered list of skin layers. (Don't worry about the distinction between skins and themes; there isn't much of one.)

The skin layers listed on the **Properties** tab in the ZMI correspond to folders inside the `portal_skins` tool. A skin's appearance depends heavily on the order in which these skin layers are listed. A new Plone site, with the **Plone Default** theme installed (done automatically), is illustrated next:

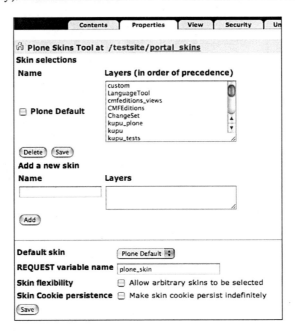

Plone uses something similar to acquisition to look through this list of skin layers, giving precedence to the skin layers at the top of a list. If Plone requests a resource such as `logo.jpg`, it will look for it in skin layers, starting at the top of the list and going down until it finds one.

In this example, it will start with the **custom** skin layer, then move to **LanguageTool**, **cmfeditions_views**, and so on.

The **Find** tab in this section provides an opportunity to search for a resource within a selected skin, if desired.

Notice that there is a drop-down list below the skin layers called **Default skin**. This area allows you to switch to a different theme product. When you install your theme, it becomes the default theme.

A first rule of thumb is if your site is ever not finding a resource that you're expecting to see, confirm that the layer it is contained within is found in the above list.

The **custom** skin layer should always appear at the top of the list of skin layers, generally followed by skin layers for a theme or product's images, stylesheets, and templates. This configuration might change in the event that you have a product installed that you want to override the installed products beneath it; in this case, the product with the most precedence should be listed at the top.

 Skin layers often get out of order when a new product is installed, and as a result, can cause some confusing behavior to occur, so it is helpful to monitor this area during product development and especially prior to going live with a Plone site.

In the next screenshot, a theme product named `plonetheme.mytheme` has been installed. Observe the order of the skin layers and the new layers that display:

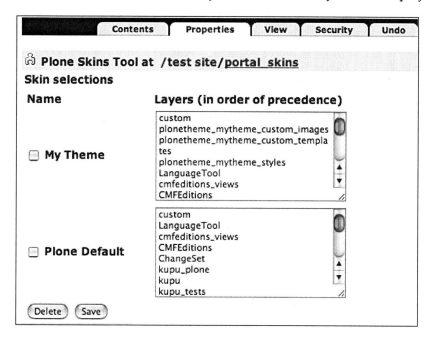

This theme looks first at the **custom** skin layer, then at `plonetheme_mytheme_custom_images`, `plonetheme_mytheme_custom_templates`, `plonetheme_mytheme_styles`, and then down the list. Items in the **custom** layer take precedence over all other resources in the skin layers below it, as long as **custom** is at the top of the list. In other words, if you have a `logo.jpg` that lives within your `plonetheme_mytheme_custom_images` folder, and you have a different `logo.jpg` in the `custom` folder, the one in the `custom` folder will take precedence.

Most skin layers are provided by filesystem files that are mapped into `portal_skins`. The advantage of the `custom` folder is that it is a normal Zope folder and its contents may be changed through the web. This can be helpful for integrators to make quick changes (for example, you want to swap out the logo with a different colored logo, and want to make that change immediately visible without having to worry about backing up your theme in Subversion, updating your server's version of the theme product, restarting your server, and so on). To make quick changes, all you have to do is to edit that item by first finding the image in an existing skin layer and then modifying it in the `custom` folder.

Click on `portal_skins` again to get to the main page that displays all of the available filesystem views, which in turn contain pages, templates, and other resources. To modify one of these resources, locate an item listed there (for example, `plone_images/logo.jpg` or `plone_templates/main_template`), and click on it. You will then be given the opportunity to customize that item in the `custom` folder. This makes a copy of the original in the `custom` folder, filesystem item provided by Plone. Removing that item from the `custom` folder after customizing it means that a site will use the original, not customized version.

You cannot customize items within their own folders, as they are not folders in the traditional sense—they are filesystem directory views, or folders that provide a window into a particular folder on the filesystem. The `custom` folder, in contrast, lives in Plone's database, and its contents cannot be found on the filesystem.

The most commonly modified files available from `portal_skins` include `plone_images/logo.jpg` and `plone_templates/main_template.pt`. These are considered non-Zope 3 templates. If you don't see the item you want to customize located in `portal_skins`, it's likely a Zope 3 style browser layer element that will most often need to be altered on the filesystem. We will cover that in the next chapter.

During skin development, the `custom` folder can be an area of great frustration, especially if more than one person is working on a given site TTW, instead of on the filesystem. If you don't see your changes taking place, make sure you are running your Zope in foreground mode, and check to make sure your `portal_css` is in debug mode and that your `custom` folder is cleaned out (or not conflicting). And, at the end of a project, you should always clean out your `custom` folder and extract files found there into your theme product to keep all components safe on the filesystem and in Subversion. In the world of Plone 3, this is especially important. To save yourself pain, it's best to avoid TTW changes in the `custom` folder completely and work entirely on the filesystem.

Changing base_properties

Good web designs typically use a limited color palette and design elements such as border styles and font styles may appear in several places in a page. In implementation, this means that a limited set of CSS attributes often appear many times in a site's stylesheets. However, separately entering those attributes over and over again in a set of stylesheets would be error prone and make for difficult maintenance. It would also make it impossible for style elements furnished in different add-on products to share these attributes.

The CMF's solution to this problem is to share information on commonly-used attributes in named properties in a Zope **property sheet**. A property sheet is basically just a collection of named properties in a single object.

Using a shared property sheet with properties such as `borderStyle`, stylesheets can include references by name to those properties, rather than fixed specifications.

Also, any third-party product that needs to use a site's common border style can do the same thing, dramatically increasing the likelihood that a third-party's add-on will fit in with your site.

The actual name of the base property sheet on the filesystem is `base_properties.props`, and it can be found in `parts/plone/CMFPlone/skins/plone_styles`. It can also be found in the ZMI in `portal_skins/plone_styles`. A quick examination of this file shows that it contains information like this:

```
plone_skin:string=Plone Default

logoName:string=logo.jpg

fontFamily:string="Lucida Grande", Verdana, Lucida, Helvetica, Arial,
                                                         sans-serif

fontBaseSize:string=69%
fontColor:string=Black
fontSmallSize:string=90%

backgroundColor:string=White

linkColor:string=#436976
linkActiveColor:string=Red
linkVisitedColor:string=Purple

borderWidth:string=1px
borderStyle:string=solid
borderStyleAnnotations:string=solid

globalBorderColor:string=#8cacbb
globalBackgroundColor:string=#dee7ec
globalFontColor:string=#436976

[snip]
```

The goal of this file is to provide default settings that can then be accessed by stylesheets at large by using variables. For example, the `public.css` stylesheet contains certain declarations, such as:

```
.documentContent p a:visited {
    color: &dtml-linkVisitedColor;;
    background-color: transparent;
}
```

This means that the color of the anchor tag within the paragraph after being visited will correspond to the `&dtml-linkVisitedColor;` value defined in the `base_properties` file.

Properties are inserted using an HTML-named entity format that you've seen before in code, such as the ` ` specification for a non-breaking space. The `dtml-` part means that such attributes are to be expanded by the **DTML (Dynamic Template Markup Language)** engine. The `base_properties` are enabled in two ways. First, the stylesheet you are using must have a second extension of `.dtml`; for example, `mystylesheet.css.dtml`—this marks it for DTML processing. Second, it must additionally contain DTML code that connects it to the property sheet:

```
/*
  <dtml-with base_properties> (do not remove this)
  <dtml-call "REQUEST.set('portal_url', portal_url())"> (not this
                                                         either)
*/
/* YOUR CSS RULES START HERE */
/* YOUR CSS RULES STOP HERE */
/* </dtml-with> */
```

The real advantage of using `base_properties` is that it's easy to make global changes to your site.

The important point to note here is that when extracting the `base_properties` file from the `custom` folder, make sure the file is named correctly (`base_properties.props`) and that you cut-paste the relevant values into place, one at a time. The `base_properties.props` file should be placed in your theme product in `skins/plonetheme_mytheme_styles`.

Modifying images using the custom folder

You can modify Plone-provided images (such as the `logo.jpg` provided with Plone) by going to the `portal_skins` folder, choosing the appropriate `images` skin layer (often `plone_images`), locating the desired image, and then selecting the **Customize** option.

You can also add new images to the `custom` folder and use CSS to style with those images. Eventually, those images will need to be extracted (using **File | Save As**) to your theme product's `images` folder. These images are not the same thing as content that will eventually end up on your site; they are specifically images that are used to build your theme.

One image that is considered "special" in Plone is the `logo.jpg` image. The viewlet that controls the logo references the `base_properties` code that looks for a file named `logo.jpg`. If you want to use a `logo.gif` image, you have to modify `base_properties` to look for a file with the `.gif` extension. If you wish, you can modify the viewlet for the logo to use different logic. We'll look at our options here in *Chapters 6* and *7*, and explore how to modify page templates to make the logo viewlet work differently, if you wish.

For now, try to override the standard Plone logo through the web. To do this through the ZMI, go to the `custom` folder and choose **Add image** from the drop-down list. Now upload the image named `logo.jpg`. Refresh your site to see the new logo, and clear your cache if necessary.

This isn't a good practice, but you could, in fact, upload a `.gif` or `.png` file, name it `logo.jpg`, and it would work. That's because Zope and Plone don't determine the MIME type of a ZODB object from its filename extension. When you upload an image, Zope determines its MIME type and stores that as a property of the object. That information is used to determine the MIME headers, which are sent to the browser when the image is requested.

On the other hand, the skin layer resources that we put on the filesystem as part of a theme product do need to have the conventional filename extensions. The file system is not an object database, and there's no good way to determine the type of a binary file, except via its filename extension (`.jpg`, `.gif`, `.png`, `.pdf`, and so on).

Extracting items from the custom folder

Remember that anything located in the `skins/` directory can be modified through the web via `portal_skins` and that any of these items ultimately belong in your `skins/` directory in your filesystem product. This includes images, stylesheets, JavaScript files, page templates from CMFPlone (found in `portal_skins`), and Python scripts.

Assuming you have customized items inside of your Plone site, you can extract these items and add them to your theme product in a couple of different ways. Optionally, you can go to the `custom` folder, open each individual file, and cut-paste it into your theme product's `skins` folder.

To move images into your theme product, copy them from your `custom` folder (or right-click and choose **Save As**) and put them in `plonetheme/mytheme/skins/plonetheme_mytheme_custom_images`. If you test this with a file named `logo.jpg` (with the `custom` folder cleaned out) and refresh your site, you should see your new logo.

In addition to moving images into your filesystem product, you will often be moving standard page templates. Give them a filename with an extension of `.pt` so that Zope will recognize them as templates. In this case, you only need to copy the file into your `skins/plonetheme_mytheme_custom_templates` folder and save it with the appropriate extension. These items will appear in the `portal_skins` without the `.pt` extension.

In some cases, there may need to be a `.metadata` file associated with that page template. This is not usually necessary with simple templates, CSS, JavaScript, or image resources. It usually becomes crucial to supply extra information when working with `.cpt` (**controller page template**) files, which are used when validation on a page template is required. An example here would be a page template for a form that can be submitted, where the page template needs to know if success or failure was achieved when the form is submitted. The `.metadata` file contains important information that ensures that the form can submit completely, and thus should be preserved in your filesystem product.

Similarly, you may be working with standard Python scripts, or you may be working with `.cpy` (**controller Python scripts**), that involve validation. Again, the `.metadata` file should be captured in addition to the Python script itself. In the case of Python scripts, you should also be careful to extract the information that generally precedes the Python script: this includes the name of file, the context, and so on. An example is the following script:

```
## Script (Python) "getDateConstraintsForSearchResults"
##bind container=container
##bind context=context
##bind namespace=
##bind script=script
##bind subpath=traverse_subpath
##parameters=
##title=
##
if not hasattr(request, "start") or not hasattr(request, "end"):
    return []
else:
    start = request.start['query'][0]
    end   = request.end['query'][0]
    format= "%a, %b %d, %Y"
    start = start.strftime(format)
    end   = end.strftime(format)
    if start == end:
        return {
            'start': start,
            'end': ''
            }
    else:
        return {
            'start': start,
            'end':   end,
            }
```

If you don't know the format in which Python scripts and other scripts should be extracted, you can optionally extract files from your `custom` folder by using the FS Dump Plone product (`http://plone.org/products/fsdump`). This tool is helpful for exporting any contents from the `custom` folder to your own machine, not just from Python scripts. It can be especially useful if you are exporting a lot of items, but not images.

Using stylesheets and the CSS resource registry tool

Now that we know how to manipulate the menus and tabs on our site, and to modify images and page templates in our `custom` folder, we will look at how to add extra stylesheets or JavaScripts. The principles here also apply to KSS files, which we will not cover here. Advanced users may also have need of KSS stylesheets (Kinetic Style Sheets) for managing AJAX-like behavior, but we will not cover this or jQuery in this book.

A special tool was created to manage CSS stylesheets, JavaScripts, and KSS stylesheets called **Resource Registries** (`http://plone.org/documentation/tutorial/working-with-resourceregistries`), which consists of `portal_css`, `portal_javascripts`, and `portal_kss` in the ZMI. These registries give the option of consolidating multiple style or JavaScript files into a single cached file, which causes them to load faster when a site is in production. Putting your `portal_css` or `portal_javascripts` into debug mode turns off this merging.

Resource Registries solve an important problem: how do we develop our style and JavaScript sources in a granular way (in which each source does only what it needs to do) without creating a proliferation of downloads to the browser, which has a terrible performance impact? In addition to merging sources, so that the browser sees fewer downloads, these registries also provide cache control and compression services.

Resource Registries also allow you to add, reorder, and enable or disable CSS or JavaScript files at the click of a button. Reordering of resource files is important in determining how your product renders, in much the same way that skin layer orders are important.

You can optionally provide conditional statements for these files; for example, "only use this stylesheet if you are in the home page section" or "only use this stylesheet if the user has certain permissions."

For advanced information on what these registries do, refer to the `ReadMe` file provided with the Resource Registries product that ships with Plone: `http://plone.org/products/resourceregistries`.

Common conventions for using stylesheets in Plone

Note that some of the information in this section is somewhat subjective, but also greatly debated by the Plone theming community. As a result, there may be a bit of flux in this area in the future, and room for interpretation.

When a new Plone theme product is created using paster, you are given the option to override Plone stylesheets if desired.

Overriding base Plone stylesheets

When a new Plone theme product is created using paster, you are given the option to override Plone stylesheets if desired.

As someone who has themed more than 100 Plone sites, I recommend that you always choose "False" and not override the Plone stylesheets. This is a personal preference, but it means that some of the CSS that controls layouts deep in the guts of Plone are styled adequately and you don't need to restyle those more delicate bits.

If you do prefer to rewrite your CSS from scratch, instead of building on top of Plone's default stylesheets, stick with the empty stylesheets. It may not seem elegant, but it is the most correct way to override stylesheets. You may have noticed that you can disable stylesheets in the CSS registry or via the "enable" flag in `cssregistry.xml` (found in your stylesheet). If you intend to layer more than one product on top of a Plone site, you likely do not want to disable your stylesheets through the registries, as those registries will affect all of the products layered on top. If you know that you will not be laying stylesheets from multiple products on top of a Plone site, it's probably safe to disable the stylesheets through the registries.

DTML support

The `plone3_theme` (at the time of this writing) also generates a `main.css` stylesheet located in the `browser` folder of your theme product. While this may technically work, it's not the most practical way to handle stylesheets. The stylesheet should be named `main.css.dtml` or, preferably, `mytheme.css.dtml` It's important to provide support for DTML, though it's optional for advanced users. It's also a best practice to name your stylesheet after your theme product, to distinguish it from other theme products and reduce the possibility of name-collision errors.

Location of files and controlling bloat

The theme recipe's placement of a stylesheet file in the `browser` folder was meant to fit it into the Zope 3 component architecture, enabling plug-in replacement. Speaking for myself, those benefits don't justify the complexity of use, and I remove the stylesheets and `images` folders from the `browser` folder, remove the boilerplate that supports this, and store all of my stylesheets, images, and so on in my `skins` folder. The only pieces that I keep in my `browser` folder are Zope 3-related components (viewlets, portlets, and so on), which we'll cover later.

However, if you do want your stylesheets in your `browser` layer, they should be directly in the `browser/` folder and not in a subfolder beneath that. This is because if you want to customize one item within a folder, you must customize them all. It's best to register your resources one at a time, not in a nested hierarchy.

The behavior of the plone3_theme recipe may change in the future, but has not occurred because the community wanted to make sure that existing documentation did not fall out of date. The key here is that you can modify your boilerplate if need be, and feel confident that the documentation will reflect the truth of what the plone3_theme recipe generates.

Ultimately, your options here are to:

- Use the functionality from the plone3_theme (not a problem, but complicates some of the code you'll need to write and means that you'll have to pull the stylesheets and images out of their subfolders and fix some of the boilerplate to reflect this)
- Ignore it and work in the skins/ directory anyways (leaves bloat)
- Remove it (takes a while, but slims down your theme)
- Write your own recipe that gives you a theme customized to your specifications

Adding new stylesheets

If you look at a default Plone site's portal_css registry, you can see some of the more important features:

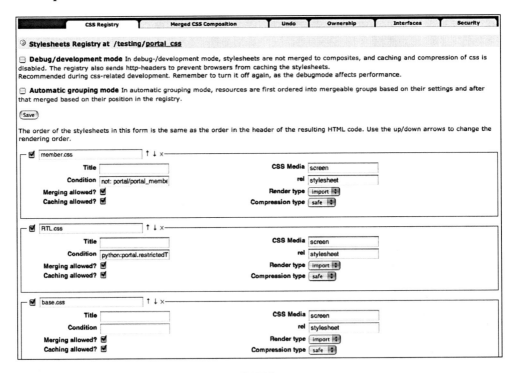

Note the checkbox on the left that allows you to turn the stylesheet on or off, the conditional field that accepts a Python statement, and the **CSS Media** field that tells you the media for which the stylesheet should apply, which is usually **empty** or **all**. Other possible values are **screen, print**, and so on. If you scroll down the list, you should see all of the default Plone stylesheets listed. You also see up/down arrows that allow you to order the items in the list. The stylesheet that takes the most precedence should appear at the bottom of the list, generally `ploneCustom.css`, which is typically used when you want to modify items TTW without delving into the main stylesheet being used for your theme. This is typically the file that you use to add temporary styles that will later be integrated into a site-specific stylesheet (such as `mytheme.css`). By default, it is empty. It can be found in **portal_skins/plone_styles**.

Starting with CSS in the ZMI

After you add a stylesheet to your site via the `custom` folder, you must then tell Plone that it exists. In this example, we'll add a stylesheet named `sections.css`, and add some code to tell Plone that we are looking at the home page, so that we can style it differently than the other sections of the site. This is a slightly advanced topic, but a common use case.

1. First of all, we want to open a stylesheet from CMFPlone, the product that is "base Plone", so that we can get the appropriate formatting, specifically DTML support. Go to your buildout, drill down to `parts/plone/CMFPlone/skins/plone_styles/`, and open `ploneCustom.css`.

2. Copy the formatting that provides DTML support. Then, go to the `custom` folder, and add a **DTML Method** to this folder, using the drop-down list (not a file, and so on).

3. Name it `sections.css`, choose **add and edit**, and add the following code.

   The key portion you'll need is this:

```
/* <dtml-with base_properties> (do not remove this :) */
/* <dtml-call "REQUEST.set('portal_url', portal_url())"> (not this
                                                    either :) */

/* DELETE THIS LINE AND PUT YOUR CUSTOM STUFF HERE */

.section-front-page #visual-portal-wrapper {
   background-color:#000;
}
/* </dtml-with> */
```

   Just so you can tell if your stylesheet is getting picked up, we're adding a temporary style here that looks at the shortname of the home page. (This corresponds to the URL `http://www.mysite.com/front-page`.)

4. Next, we have to add the stylesheet to the registry itself. Go to `portal_css`, and add a new stylesheet:

```
┌─Add a new stylesheet──────────────────────────────────────┐
│                        ID  │ sections.css              │   │
│                     Title  │                           │   │
│                 Condition  │                           │   │
│                 CSS Media  │ screen                │       │
│                       rel  │ stylesheet            │       │
│               Render type  [ import ▼]                     │
│          Compression type  [ safe ▼]                       │
│                  Enabled?  ☑                               │
│          Merging allowed?  ☑                               │
│          Caching allowed?  ☑  ( Add )                      │
└────────────────────────────────────────────────────────────┘
```

If you now visit the home page of your site and refresh the page, you should see the background color of the home page changes to black. Navigating elsewhere in the site will set the background color back to white. If you do not see your changes, remember to turn on debug mode in `portal_css`. You wouldn't ordinarily add a stylesheet through the web, but clearly it is possible.

The corollary to doing this is to create a stylesheet in your filesystem product, which we'll do next.

Creating a theme-specific stylesheet in your filesystem product

Since the `plone3_theme` recipe does not generate a stylesheet for your `skins/plonetheme_mytheme_custom_styles` folder, you should create one in that location and enable DTML support as indicated by the previous code. You should also name your stylesheet in a meaningful way; that is, `mytheme.css.dtml`. It helps to name your CSS after your theme product or client name, to avoid confusion.

Next, open your `profiles/cssregistry.xml` file. We will add support for this new file by including the following code:

```xml
<?xml version="1.0"?>
<object name="portal_css">
<stylesheet title=""
    id="mytheme.css"
    media="screen" rel="stylesheet" rendering="import"
    cacheable="True" compression="safe" cookable="True"
    enabled="1" expression=""/>
</object>
```

Notice the `enabled` flag here, and also notice that it's not necessary to include the `.dtml` indication in the `id` field, even though we will be using DTML.

If you wish to disable the use of the stylesheets and the `images` folders in the `browser` folder, remove the following code from `cssregistry.xml`. (You can tell that you are dealing with a browser layer file by the `++resource++` designation.)

```
<stylesheet title=""
    id="++resource++plonetheme.testtheme.stylesheets/main.css"
    media="screen" rel="stylesheet" rendering="import"
    cacheable="True" compression="safe" cookable="True"
    enabled="1" expression=""/>
```

You will also want to remove the `images` and `stylesheets` folders from the `browser` folder if you're disabling browser layer support for these items.

Next, open the `browser/configure.zcml` file, and remove the following code:

```
<!-- Zope 3 browser resources -->
    <!-- Resource directory for images -->
    <browser:resourceDirectory
        name="plonetheme.mytheme.images"
        directory="images"
        layer=".interfaces.IThemeSpecific"
        />
    <!-- Resource directory for stylesheets -->
    <browser:resourceDirectory
        name="plonetheme.mytheme.stylesheets"
        directory="stylesheets"
        layer=".interfaces.IThemeSpecific"
        />
```

When you install your product or you import settings pertaining to the CSS registry, it will automatically add any new stylesheets to the CSS registry in the ZMI and disable any, if desired. You'll also need to restart your Zope instance, as we have changed our ZCML code.

Working with JavaScripts in your theme product

JavaScripts work similar to CSS stylesheets, with a few key differences. If you add a file to the `custom` folder, it must be of type "file". To add it to your registry through the web, go to `portal_javascripts` and add it there. Again, you may need to enable debug mode to see your JavaScript changes. Once again, this is not the advisable way of adding JavaScripts, and you will typically do this on the filesystem instead.

To add a JavaScript to your filesystem product, add code like this to your `profiles/jsregistry.xml` file:

```
<?xml version="1.0"?>
<object name="portal_javascripts">
 <javascript cacheable="True" compression="none" cookable="True"
       enabled="True" expression="" id="sifr.js" inline="False"/>
</object>
```

You can either add this script file to your `skins/plonetheme_mytheme_custom_templates` folder, or you can create a folder that specifically holds JavaScripts and modify the boilerplate as needed. The boilerplate code available for supporting images and stylesheets in the browser space is not provided for JavaScripts, so there is no need to modify additional code.

Again, you can start by adding JavaScript to the ZMI first, or you can start by adding it to your theme product from the start. It is generally easier to start with a filesystem product from the very beginning, and is by far the recommended path.

Summary

In this chapter, we have learned:

- What elements comprise the component architecture for a theme product
- How to make minor adjustments to a Plone site through the ZMI and `portal_actions` and extract those changes into a filesystem product using Generic Setup
- How skin layers work and how acquisition affects images and page templates
- How to work with images and page templates in the `custom` folder and on the filesystem
- How to work with stylesheets and JavaScripts in the `custom` folder and on the filesystem

The real message of this chapter I am trying to communicate is that through-the-web development is evil, and it should not be used if you can help it. If you do TTW development of any kind, you should always bring your changes out to the filesystem, and wash your hands twice when you're done.

Now, using what you have learned in this chapter, you should next be able to learn about Zope 3 components and how they differ from skin layer objects. At this point, you are ready to move away from changes made through the web and focus only on filesystem development.

6

Working with Zope 3 Components

This chapter is probably the most technically challenging chapter that you'll read in this book, but read it with the objective of getting a basic understanding of Zope 3 and the moving parts you'll need to know about. You'll generally need to only understand where to find the pieces you require, where to put them, and how to tie them together, and that will come after this introduction to the general concepts.

As part of this chapter, we'll cover how images, stylesheets, and templates can be exposed as Zope 3 browser resources, instead of being used as "old school" skin layers, as discussed in the previous chapter. We'll also cover some of the jargon-y terms that you'll need to know about but not understand in depth.

About the architecture

Prior to Plone 2.5, Plone was built on top of the powerful, but relatively inflexible, Zope 2 architecture. As Plone evolved, more flexible Zope 3 technologies became necessary, but a full transition was impractical. In order to remain compatible with earlier versions of Plone and provide a migration path, it was important to provide a bridge between these two versions. You might have heard the name "Five", which is a product that helped bridge the gap between Zope 2 and Zope 3 (2+3=5) by backporting Zope 3 capabilities to Zope 2. Five is now baked into Plone, and is the basis of the Plone 3 architecture. What this means is that Plone runs on Zope 2, but uses some of the features provided by Zope 3, and thus is not a pure Zope 3 implementation.

Zope 2 plus **CMF** (the **Content Management Framework**) is best described as a framework that uses skin layers and acquisition to produce results. If you know some of the concepts of object-oriented programming, you might think of acquisition as a framework in which behavior can be inherited from context as well as class ancestry. Pure Zope 3 uses explicit acquisition plus the concept of adapters or reusable components.

The name "Zope 3" is unfortunate, because it implies that Zope 3 is the successor to Zope 2. While this may have been the original intention, Zope 3 has become more of a component toolkit than a standalone application server. All of this component toolkit is built into the latest versions of Zope 2. It is very uncommon for applications to be built on a 100% Zope 3 architecture.

Let's now take a look at the most common Zope 2 and Zope 3 components and programming languages (highlighted in gray) that come into play when theming a web site:

Theme Product Component Architecture			
Configuration Settings	**Skin Layers**	**Zope 3 Components**	**Programming / Templating Languages**
Generic Setup Profiles (XML)	CMF Action Categories Javascripts KSS Stylesheets Images Page Templates	Browser Pages Viewlets Portlets Page Templates Adapters and interfaces Images Stylesheets	Python ZCML XML Tal / Metal / Macros

The components we're primarily concerned with when theming are **viewlets**, **templates**, **browser pages**, **adapters**, and **interfaces**. In the case of images, stylesheets, and page templates, these can be either Zope 3 elements or skin layer elements. Specifically, we are going to focus on the Zope 3 components, since we covered skin layers in the last chapter.

Let's talk briefly about what these items are. Viewlets are typically regarded as the "furniture" on a page—breadcrumbs, logo, footer, and so on. Portlets, meanwhile, are the pieces that render in either the right or left column of your site; for instance a login box, news, events, or the calendar. They're similar to viewlets, but handled slightly differently behind the scenes. You can add more viewlet or portlet managers (containers) if you need to, which allows you to move items into areas of the page that you wouldn't ordinarily be able to do. Viewlets and portlets will be covered in more detail in the next chapter.

Page templates are the pieces of code with the extension `.pt` that generate HTML that is then outputted to the browser when the page is rendered. Page templates are typically driven by a combination of Python and TAL.

Next, a browser page can be defined as a component that can be found during URL traversal and that can usually render itself. For example, it might be something like a home page view that is accessible via the following URL: `http://localhost:8080/mysite/@@homepage-view` or `http://localhost:8080/mysite/homepage-view`. Typically, it contains a page template that is backed by a Python class. Since you generally don't want to be running un-trusted code over the Internet, you should instead use a browser page to work with classes that may be protected or have other security issues. The code within the browser page is not subject to the same restrictions as restricted Python in a template or a Python script.

Interfaces describe the methods and attributes that an object provides. They describe what a component can do, but not how. Adapters provide ways to adapt the behavior of an object to a new interface. A **browser layer**, meanwhile, is just a **marker interface** that is applied to the request upon traversal. A Zope 3 browser resource is a multi-adapter on the context and the request, and when the request is marked with a particular interface, the component architecture may find a more specific adapter in a view registered for that particular layer. A marker interface is simply a flag that says, "I have a special purpose". Views, and so on, attach to that flagged item and respond appropriately when they are called. Marker interfaces don't explicitly provide any functionality; they just provide a hook to functionality defined elsewhere.

What this means is that you can customize items in a Plone theme and override other items that would normally take precedence by assigning them to your theme product. Moreover, you can be very specific about how these items are applied in your theme. This is referred to as exposing items to the browser layer, but you can think of it as a different way of overriding or using resources in Plone other than as skin layer items.

In Plone, there are two main ways of enabling a custom browser layer interface. The first is to use the mechanism of `plone.theme`, often referred to as `IThemeSpecific`. This package, which ships with Plone by default, allows us to link a browser layer with a particular theme (skin) in `portal_skins` (not to be confused with a skin layer). When a theme is installed in `portal_skins` as the default theme, the layer is in effect. This is useful for products that install a whole new theme in Plone. It's sort of like applying a name tag to your theme product.

Other types of Plone products make use of a `plone.browserlayer` package, which is similar to `plone.theme` and allows layer installation to be additive. Themes do not have this functionality.

The IThemeSpecific interface mentioned above is provided with a Plone theme product by default through plone.theme and located in your interfaces.py file found in plonetheme.mytheme/browser/:

```
from plone.theme.interfaces import IDefaultPloneLayer

class IThemeSpecific(IDefaultPloneLayer):
    """Marker interface that defines a Zope 3 browser layer.
    """
```

What the previous code says is that the interface IThemeSpecific is based on an interface named IDefaultPloneLayer (defined in another section of the Zope/Plone stack), and is able to use all of the functionality that IDefaultPloneLayer provides.

In practice, what this means is that when you tell your theme product to use IThemeSpecific for a given component, that component's code only affects your current theme product. This is a very important step, as not including this interface definition could cause your theme product to step on other themes registered in your Zope instance. It's important to always use the IThemeSpecific directive when specifying browser resources, except when you are writing a package that needs to be used by more than one web site, such as a diagnostic utility. We'll see how this works momentarily.

All of the components mentioned above are glued together using a combination of Python, XML, ZCML, and TAL (Plone's templating language). We will get a brief introduction to ZCML here, and a formal introduction to XML and TAL in upcoming chapters.

Introduction to ZCML

Zope 3 knows how to find an adapter only if you tell it about the available adapters. In our case, adapters are components, such as viewlets, portlets, and other resources, that we wish to customize. We do this using **ZCML**, the **Zope Configuration Markup Language**.

ZCML is an XML dialect that is used to configure many aspects of Zope 3 code, such as permissions and component registration. You can do what ZCML does in Python code as well, but typically it's more convenient to use ZCML because it allows you to separate your logic from your configuration.

Many ZCML directives are stored in files named configure.zcml, which may themselves include other files. Three configure.zcml files are provided by default in a given theme product, one in the root of your plonetheme.mytheme/ folder, one in your mytheme/ folder, and one in your browser/ folder.

The `configure.zcml` file found in your theme product's root contains only the following code:

```
<include package="plonetheme.mytheme" />
```

In other words, it is telling Zope that a package named `plonetheme.mytheme` exists and can be "picked up" and used.

An example `configure.zcml` file in the `plonetheme.mytheme/plonetheme/mytheme` folder for a Plone theme looks like this:

```
<configure
    xmlns="http://namespaces.zope.org/zope"
    xmlns:five="http://namespaces.zope.org/five"
    xmlns:cmf="http://namespaces.zope.org/cmf"
    i18n_domain="plonetheme.mytheme">

    <five:registerPackage package="." initialize=".initialize" />

    <include package=".browser" />

    <include file="skins.zcml" />
    <include file="profiles.zcml" />

</configure>
```

All this code means is that your theme product uses a few different XML namespaces (`zope`, `five`, `cmf`), defines a domain for applying internationalization (i18n translation hooks), registers your package with Zope (Five), connects to your `browser/` folder and two files named `skins.zcml` and `profiles.zcml`. You'll rarely need to modify this file.

Meanwhile, the default `configure.zcml` file found in your theme product's `browser/` folder looks something like the following:

```
<configure
    xmlns="http://namespaces.zope.org/zope"
    xmlns:browser="http://namespaces.zope.org/browser"
    i18n_domain="plonetheme.test">

    <!-- 'test theme' Zope 3 browser layer -->
    <interface
        interface=".interfaces.IThemeSpecific"
        type="zope.publisher.interfaces.browser.IBrowserSkinType"
        name="test theme"
        />
    <!-- Viewlets registration -->
    <!-- Zope 3 browser resources -->
    <!-- Resource directory for images -->
```

```
<browser:resourceDirectory
    name="plonetheme.test.images"
    directory="images"
    layer=".interfaces.IThemeSpecific"
    />
<!-- Resource directory for stylesheets -->
<browser:resourceDirectory
    name="plonetheme.test.stylesheets"
    directory="stylesheets"
    layer=".interfaces.IThemeSpecific"
    />

</configure>
```

This code basically just tells Plone that it knows its identity (IThemeSpecific), and that it knows that images and stylesheets are browser resources and thus live in directories within the browser/ folder. This particular configure.zcml file is where most of the magic will happen when you customize Zope 3-styled resources. For example, if you want to move the various bits (viewlets and portlets) that comprise your theme around on the page, you would do that through ZCML in this particular file.

A default plonetheme product also contains ZCML in files such as profiles.zcml and skins.zcml. The profiles.zcml file provides the hooks Zope needs to read the **GenericSetup** files located in the profiles/default/ folder.

The skins.zcml file, meanwhile, is the file where you define the names of the filesystem folders that will hold your CSS, images, JavaScripts, and templates. These folders are skin layer folders, which means the items contained within these folders will be customizable through the **ZMI (Zope Management Interface)** via the portal_skins tool and the custom folder.

If you are generating your theme product in the Products namespace, a configure.zcml file in your product directory (Products/myproduct/configure.zcml) will be picked up automatically. However, packages in other namespaces (such as the plonetheme namespace) need to have a **ZCML slug** added as well. A slug is merely a ZCML line that includes another file. Plone 3.3 is scheduled to remove this requirement by allowing Python packages to signal that they have Zope 3 component configuration, but we'll include the following code in case you're running a slightly older version of Plone. In terms of theme and other product development, it means writing one less annoying line of code.

If you recall from *Chapter 3* where we configured our buildout.cfg so that we could install our skin product, you'll remember that we added code similar to what you see next. In this code, the "slug" is the line below the ZCML directive:

```
# Reference any eggs you are developing here, one per line
# e.g.: develop = src/my.package
develop =
    src/plonetheme.mytheme

# If you want Zope to know about any additional eggs, list them here.
# This should include any development eggs you listed in develop-eggs
above.
# e.g. eggs = ${buildout:eggs} ${plone:eggs} my.package
eggs =
    ${buildout:eggs}
    ${plone:eggs}
    plonetheme.mytheme

# If you want to register ZCML slugs for any packages, list them here.
# e.g. zcml = my.package my.other.package
zcml =
    plonetheme.mytheme
```

Assuming these lines are in place in your `buildout.cfg` file, when you next run your buildout (and you must for these changes to be recognized) and restart Zope, it should automatically make your theme product available for installation in `portal_quickinstaller`, located in the ZMI in your Plone site. And for lucky individuals working with Plone 3.3 and above, or for anyone using `buildout.eggtractor`, you won't have to worry about this slug at all.

As you can see, ZCML is a human-readable language that merely registers items so that Zope can see them. There's no magic involved here, just a lot of hand-shaking.

Zope 3 browser layers and resources

The idea of a single, global namespace with customization possible by ID only has been supplanted in Zope 3 by the notion of named resources being registered for a context type. This means that the HTML that renders when a view called `@@view` is invoked on a page may be different from the HTML that is rendered when the same view is invoked on a folder or other content object. (The `@@` designation looks like a pair of eyeballs, hence a view.) You do not have to use the `@@view` designation if you do not wish to—it's really just a visual cue. This same view may also be registered for a browser layer.

A Zope 3 browser layer is similar in purpose to a CMF skin layer, but is implemented differently. Technically speaking, a skin layer is a simple container of templates and resources, whereas a browser layer is a marker interface that is applied to the request upon traversal through the object database. In a sense, a browser layer "contains" browser resources, though it's not really a container. Views (and templates, browser resources, viewlets, and portlet renderers, which are all special types of views) can be registered to this layer as browser resources. An example of a browser resource is a special page view that can be used on the home page and optionally in important sections of your Plone site. A browser resource could also be a CSS file, or even an image, that can be used in various areas of your site depending on the context.

The browser layer technology allows you to use bits and pieces of your code in more than one context and keeps your ZCML registrations from applying to all of the Plone sites on a given instance via IThemeSpecific declarations. If not for browser layer support, a logo image that is registered as a browser resource might show up for all of the sites on a given Zope instance, which would be a bad thing.

Using images as browser resources

For the purposes of most themes, images will not be browser resources, but instead will be used as standard skin layer components as described previously. However, we will cover this in the interest of explaining that it is possible to expose images to the browser layer, if desired.

Zope 3 allows browser resources, notably images and stylesheets, to be registered under a special namespace. For example, if you register an image resource in your browser/ folder with the name myimage.gif, the browser resource would be addressable as http://yoursite.com/++resource++myimage.gif. This serves to get the resource out of the flat, global namespace.

Like all Zope 3 browser components, browser resources are registered with a ZCML directive in the browser namespace that, among other things, takes a layer attribute. The layer should resolve to an interface. The browser/images/ folder is a Zope 3 resource directory acting as a repository for images, and its declaration is located in browser/configure.zcml.cfg:

```
<!-- Resource directory for images -->
<browser:resourceDirectory
    name="plonetheme.mytheme.images"
    directory="images"
    layer=".interfaces.IThemeSpecific"
    />
```

An image placed in this directory (for example, logo.png) can be accessed from this relative URL:

++resource++plonetheme.mytheme.images/logo.png

It is best to register each of these resources separately, not in a folder, if you want to override them via ZCML directives. The only way to override a resource in a resource directory is to override the entire directory (all elements have to be copied over). Instead, you could simply register them like this:

```
<browser:resource
        name="myimage.png"
        image="myimage.png"
        />
```

Notice that it is referred to as a `resource` and not a `resourceDirectory`.

Then you could address your image as `http://yoursite.com/ ++resource++myimage.png`. Assuming this image was defined as a browser resource somewhere other than within our theme product (such as in another Python package), if we wanted to modify this image, we could customize it for the `IThemeSpecific` layer. With a custom image called `new_myimage.png` in our own `browser/` directory, we would add the following in `browser/configure.zcml`:

```
<configure
     xmlns="http://namespaces.zope.org/zope"
     xmlns:browser="http://namespaces.zope.org/browser"
     i18n_domain="example.customization">

     <browser:resource
         name="myimage.png"
         image="new_myimage.png"
         layer=".interfaces.IThemeSpecific"
         />

</configure>
```

Without the layer attribute, we would get a configuration conflict with the original `++resource++myimage.png` definition.

Similarly, a new Zope 3 browser resource is declared like this in `browser/ configure.zcml`:

```
<browser:resource
        name="logo.png"
        file="logo.png"
        layer=".interfaces.IThemeSpecific"
        />
```

This image can be accessed from this relative URL:

`++resource++logo.png`

Note also that images registered as Zope 3 browser resources don't have all the attributes that Zope 2 image objects have (that is, the `title` property and the `tag()` and `get_size()` methods), which is unfortunate.

This means that if you want the `html` tag of your image to be auto-generated (this is the case by default for the logo), you should store it in a directory that is located in the `skins/` folder of your package. Customizing or overriding images that are originally accessed from the `portal_skins` tool (for example, Plone default logo and icons) can be done inside of the ZMI via the `portal_skins` (Zope 2 way) tool, or in your theme product's `skins/` folder, which is the preferred way. There is no known way to alter images declared as Zope 3 browser resources via the ZMI.

In other words, images listed in the `browser/images/` folder cannot be customized via `portal_skins`, as these images are not considered skin layer elements. To override them, the images must be added to your `browser/images/` folder and be given a new name and `IThemeSpecific` designation in `configure.zcml` file.

The takeaway here is that for the purposes of this book, we will be treating images as skin layer elements, but there is a more Zope 3 way of working with them, if desired. The limitations involved in using them as Zope 3 resources outweigh the benefit, in my opinion.

Using stylesheets as browser resources

Like images, for most themes, stylesheets will not be browser resources, but instead will be used as standard skin layer components as described previously. However, we will cover this in the interest of explaining that it is possible to expose stylesheets to the browser layer if desired.

A stylesheet that is listed in the `browser/stylesheets/` folder, (for example, `main.css`) can be accessed from this relative URL:

`++resource++plonetheme.mytheme.stylesheets/main.css`

It might be better to register each of these stylesheet resources separately if you want to override them via ZCML directives, rather than registering the folder containing the resources. Again, the only way to override a resource in a resource directory is to override the entire directory (all elements have to be copied over).

A stylesheet is declared as a Zope 3 browser resource like this in `browser/configure.zcml`:

```
<browser:resource
    name="main.css"
    file="stylesheets/main.css"
    layer=".interfaces.IThemeSpecific"
    />
```

The stylesheet can be accessed from this relative URL:

```
++resource++main.css
```

Stylesheets registered as Zope 3 resources might be flagged as not found in the `portal_css` tool in the ZMI, if the layer they are registered for doesn't match the default skin set in `portal_skins`. This can be confusing, but it must be considered as a minor bug in the CSS registry, instead of a lack in the way Zope 3 resources are handled in Zope 2.

It is possible to interpret DTML from a Zope 3 resource view. However, if you need to use DTML for setting values in a stylesheet (the same way as default Plone stylesheets, where values are read from `base_properties.props`), it is much easier to store it in a directory that is located in the `skins/` folder of your package as a skin layer.

Customizing/overriding stylesheets that are originally accessed from the `portal_skins` tool in the ZMI (for example, Plone default stylesheets) can be done inside that tool. There is no known way to do it with Zope 3 browser resources using the `portal_skins` tool.

The takeaway here is that for the purposes of this book, we will be treating stylesheets as skin layer elements, rather than treating them as Zope 3 browser resources.

Browser pages

Creating custom views for a web site is a common request. In Plone 2.x, this was handled primarily via skin layers, but in Plone 3, we often create these as browser layer resources. In fact, the browser layer has been available and in use since Plone 2.5. The key change is that more of the templates have been moved to the browser layer in Plone 3 and thus can't be overridden on the skin layer. Also, all of the CMF skins, including templates such as `main_template.pt`, are still usable in Plone 3.

It is possible to customize browser pages either through the ZMI or through the filesystem, but you are limited to what you can change through the web. Additionally, you can't add new browser views through the web, so overall it's advisable to make changes to browser views via the filesystem and steer clear of the ZMI.

Next, we will create a simple browser view in a filesystem theme product called "test" that creates a new navigational structure that outputs the contents of a new `portal_actions` CMF category. To create a simple browser view, we will need:

- A Python class to hold the code for our View component (optional)
- A page template file that will hold the HTML and TAL

- ZCML code to register our browser page with Zope
- An interface
- Some GenericSetup code to create the new action category

Create a Python class for our browser page

The purpose of a template language like TAL is to handle presentation of content. Ideally, any serious logic is handled separately, via a real programming language. Python is the perfect programming language!

Let's start with our Python class. We'll create a new file named `audiences.py` in our `browser/` folder, and will insert the following code, which outputs text from our `portal_actions` and uses a page template called `audiences.pt`.

```python
from zope.component import getMultiAdapter
from zope import schema
from zope.formlib import form
from zope.interface import implements
from plone.portlets.interfaces import IPortletDataProvider
from Products.Five.browser.pagetemplatefile import
                                ViewPageTemplateFile
class IAudienceNavigationPortlet(IPortletDataProvider):
    portlet_title = schema.TextLine(title=u"Title for the portlet",
                    default=u"Information for:", required=True)
def audiences(self):
    """Return obj with attributes:
        - id
        - url
        - title
        - description
        - selected (str: 'selected' or 'unselected')
    """
    audiences = []
    current_url = self.context.absolute_url()
    for action in self._data():
        audiences.append({
            "id":     action['id'],
            "url":    action['url'],
            "title": action['title'],
            "selected": current_url.startswith(action['url']) and
                                    'selected' or 'unselected',
            "description": action['description'],
            })
    return audiences
def header(self):
```

```
    return self.data.portlet_title
class Renderer(base.Renderer):
    render = ViewPageTemplateFile('audiences.pt')
```

Add the interface for our browser page

In our theme product in `browser/interfaces.py`, we need to insert the following code:

```
from plone.theme.interfaces import IDefaultPloneLayer
class IThemeSpecific(IDefaultPloneLayer):
    """Marker interface that defines a Zope 3 browser layer.
    """

class IAudienceNavigationLayer(IDefaultPloneLayer):
    """Marker interface that defines a Zope 3 browser layer.
    """
```

Registering our browser page

Next, we register our browser page in our `browser/configure.zcml` file:

```
<configure
    xmlns="http://namespaces.zope.org/zope"
    xmlns:browser=http://namespaces.zope.org/browser
    xmlns:plone="http://namespaces.plone.org/plone"
    i18n_domain="plonetheme.test">
    <!-- 'test theme' Zope 3 browser layer -->
    <interface
        interface=".interfaces.IThemeSpecific"
        type="zope.publisher.interfaces.browser.IBrowserSkinType"
        name="test theme"
        />
    <!-- Browser views -->
    <browser:page
        for="*"
        name="audiencenavigation"
        class=".audiences.IAudienceNavigationPortlet"
        layer=".interfaces.IThemeSpecific"
        permission="zope2.View"
        />
    <!-- Viewlets registration -->
    <!-- Zope 3 browser resources -->
</configure>
```

One way to customize this resource is to provide an override for a more specific (or different) context. The `"*"` context is the most general. (Under the hood, this means `zope.interface.Interface`, or everything.) In this case, it means that this is a generic view that can be applied to any interface.

The `browser:page` directive attributes can be explained further:

- `for`: Registers the page for a specific interface
- `name`: This is what your view is called in the URL
- `class`: The Python class that attaches to your page template
- `template`: The page template that renders your view
- `permission`: The permission required to access your view
- `layer`: The layer where the package is registered, usually `IThemeSpecific`

The code also tells us that we are using the `IAudienceNavigationPortlet` class defined in our `audiences.py` file. We could have disambiguated it further by using the `@@` designation before the name, which would have made it clear that we are looking at a view and not, for example, a content item or a skin layer template.

We can either use a skin layer template named `audiences.pt` (not shown here) that traverses to the view as `context/@@audiencenavigation` and then calls methods on it, or we can use a class-based view (`audiences.py`) that pulls in the template via its `render` attribute and refers to the view instance as view.

Lastly, the browser page is made available only to our current theme product via the `IThemeSpecific` layer designation.

Create a page template for our view

Next, we want to create a page template using TAL and HTML (and a tiny snippet of Python) to render these items. We will call it `audiences.pt` and place it in our `browser/` folder. Notice that it iterates over a series of "audience-items" to output an unordered list.

```
<span class="audiences-list">
    <dt class="audiences-header" tal:content="view/header">
                                Information for...</dt>
<ul>
    <li class="audiences-item"
        tal:repeat="audience view/audiences">
        <a tal:attributes="class string:${audience/selected}
                                audience-${audience/id};
                    href audience/url;
                    title audience/description"
        tal:content="audience/title">
        Link Name
    </a>
    </li>
</ul>
</span>
```

Write the GenericSetup steps to create the new CMF action category

Next, we need to create a file called `actions.xml` and place that in our theme product's `profiles/default` folder. We will populate it with the following code:

```
<?xml version="1.0"?>
<object name="portal_actions" meta_type="Plone Actions Tool"
        xmlns:i18n="http://xml.zope.org/namespaces/i18n">

    <object name="audience_navigation" meta_type="CMF Action
                                    Category" purge="False">
        <property name="title">Audience Navigation</property>

        <object name="example" meta_type="CMF Action">
            <property name="title">Example Audience</property>
            <property name="description">
                The description of the audience is available on
                    mouseover in the audience navigation viewlet.
            </property>
            <property name="url_expr">string:${globals_view
                    /navigationRootUrl}/example</property>
            <property name="icon_expr"></property>
            <property name="available_expr"></property>
            <property name="permissions">
             <element value="View"/>
            </property>
            <property name="visible">True</property>
        </object>

    </object>

</object>
```

When we install our theme product, this CMF action category should automatically be created, as well as a sample action that will render.

Register the viewlet in your theme product

In your theme product's `configure.zcml` file, located at `mybuildout/source/plonetheme.test/plonetheme/test/browser/configure.zcml`, we need to add a few lines so that our viewlet is registered with Zope:

```
<!-- Browser views -->
    <browser:page
        for="*"
        name="audiencenavigation"
        class=".audiences.AudienceViewlet"
```

```
template="audiences.pt"
layer=".interfaces.IThemeSpecific"
permission="zope2.View"
/>
```

Then, restart Zope so that it can read those lines of code:

```
./bin/instance fg
```

Enable the browser page

Finally, to expose the viewlet to your Plone site, you should install the theme product. You can then call your view and see the sample action rendered in your web browser by going to the URL: `http://localhost:8080/myplonesite/@@` `audiencenavigation` or `http://localhost:8080/myplonesite/` `audiencenavigation`.

Presto! We now have a custom browser page that outputs the contents of our new CMF action category.

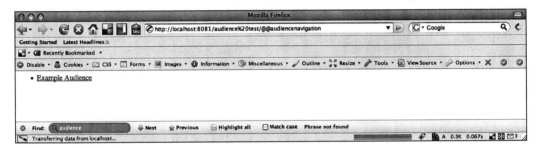

Summary

In this chapter, we have learned:

- What Zope 3 components are involved in filesystem theme development
- About interfaces and adapters
- How to use ZCML code to tie together Zope 3 components
- How to use images and stylesheets and browser resources
- How to write a basic browser page and register it in our theme

In the next chapter, we will look at how to customize viewlets and portlets, the key components that are used when customizing a web site's look and feel.

7
Customizing Viewlets and Portlets

In addition to the Zope 3 resources covered earlier, we have two very special browser resources known as **viewlets** and **portlets**. These components are at the heart of the theming process, and are the most commonly modified elements.

In this chapter, we will explain how to:

- Inspect viewlets using the `@@manage-viewlets` tool
- Modify viewlets and portlets programmatically
- Modify these components through the `portal_view_customizations` tool through the web.

Viewlets

In this section, we will gain an introduction to viewlets, the snippets of reusable functionality that comprise a Plone page. Items such as breadcrumbs, the logo, the personal bar, and many other items visible on a Plone page are viewlets.

In the following screenshot, you will see a number of unique snippets, or viewlets, that have been labeled:

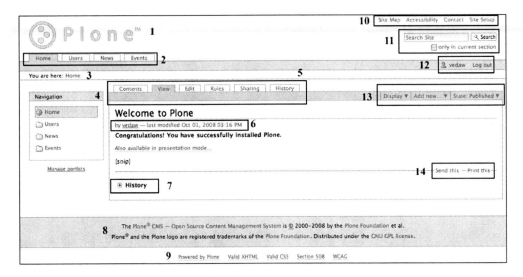

The following is the list of the viewlets displayed in the previous screenshot and their formal names in the Plone namespace. This list is by no means complete, as you may only see certain viewlets in specific situations, such as on a custom page view or the **Contents** tab of a folder.

- Logo (**1**): `plone.logo`
- Global sections (**2**): `plone.global_sections`
- Breadcrumbs (**3**): `plone.path_bar`
- Navigation (**4**): `portlets.Navigation`
- Content views (**5**): `plone.contentviews`
- Byline (**6**): `plone.belowcontenttitle.documentbyline`
- History (**7**): `plone.belowcontentbody.contenthistory`
- Footer (**8**): `plone.footer`
- Colophon (**9**): `plone.colophon`
- Utility navigation/site actions (**10**): `plone.site_actions`
- Searchbox (**11**): `plone.searchbox`
- Personal bar (**12**): `plone.personal_bar`
- Contact actions (**13**): `plone.contentactions`
- Document actions (**14**): `plone.abovecontenttitle.documentactions`

Don't worry too much about what really drives these viewlets; the objective here is to understand where elements can be found and organized, where to put items you are modifying, and patterns to follow to successfully modify your viewlets.

In Plone, viewlets are not looked up directly. In order to be able to organize viewlets with maximum flexibility, they are aggregated using **viewlet managers**. A viewlet manager is also a Zope 3 content provider, and these managers render the viewlets that are registered for them. Viewlet managers are typically given charge of presenting their assigned viewlets in a particular section of a page.

Viewlets are technically considered browser views, but they are more commonly referred to as viewlets, because they encapsulate smaller bits of code. They are a type of content provider, meaning they are components of a page that render small pieces of HTML code.

Most viewlets were formerly implemented in Plone 2.x as page templates (skin layer objects) that needed the boilerplate as well in the form of slots and macros. They are now browser layer resources so that they are more reusable. This means that boilerplate code is needed to hook them up.

In Plone 3, viewlets may be comprised of the following:

- Page templates
- Classes
- Page templates combined with classes

Let's now look at how these viewlets are pulled into Plone's templates. This happens in a file known as `main_template`, located in your buildout in `buildout-cache/eggs/Plone-[version].egg/Products/CMFPlone/skins/plone_templates/`, or in the ZMI inside of your Plone site in `portal_skins/plone_templates/`.

In the past, moving elements around on a page involved making changes to the `main_template.pt` and working with lengthy TAL (templating) statements. This often produced upgrade problems and messy code. In Plone 2.5, for example, the following code controlled the rendering of the `portal_header` section in `main_template.pt`:

```
<div id="portal-top" i18n:domain="plone">
     <div id="portal-header">
       <p class="hiddenStructure">
         <a accesskey="2" tal:attributes="href string:${current_
page_url}#documentContent" i18n:translate="label_skiptocontent">Skip
to content.</a>
         <a accesskey="6" tal:attributes="href string:${current_
page_url}#portlet-navigation-tree" i18n:translate="label_
skiptonavigation">Skip to navigation</a>
```

```
        </p>
            <div metal:use-macro="here/global_siteactions
                                /macros/site_actions">
              Site-wide actions (Contact, Sitemap, Help, Style
                                                Switcher etc)
            </div>
            <div metal:use-macro="here/global_searchbox
                                /macros/quick_search">
              The quicksearch box, normally placed at the top right
            </div>
            <a metal:use-macro="here/global_logo
                            /macros/portal_logo">
              The portal logo, linked to the portal root
            </a>
            <div metal:use-macro="here/global_skinswitcher
                                    /macros/skin_tabs">
              The skin switcher tabs. Based on which role you have,
          you get a selection of skins that you can switch between
            </div>
            <div metal:use-macro="here/global_sections
                                /macros/portal_tabs">
              The global sections tabs. (Welcome, News etc)
            </div>
        </div>
        <div metal:use-macro="here/global_personalbar
                                /macros/personal_bar">
          The personal bar. (log in, logout etc...)
        </div>
        <div metal:use-macro="here/global_pathbar
                                /macros/path_bar">
          The breadcrumb navigation ("you are here")
        </div>
      </div>
```

In Plone 3, if you look at the `main_template.pt` found in your buildout's `buildout-cache/eggs/Plone-[version].egg/Products/CMFPlone/skins/plone_templates/` folder, you will see that the code that controls the `portal_header` mentioned above has now been rewritten to be much slimmer:

```
<div id="portal-top" i18n:domain="plone">
    <div tal:replace="structure provider:plone.portaltop" />
</div>
```

The `main_template.pt` file also contains other similar structures that represent other areas of Plone's layout.

In other words, the `main_template.pt` in Plone 3 does not show the actual viewlets. Rather, the provider TALES expression above is a Zope 3 expression that looks up a content provider from a page template. In this case, the viewlet manager content provider is named `plone.portaltop`.

To see the full list of default viewlets contained within these viewlet managers, open the file named `configure.zcml`, located in your buildout at `buildout-cache/eggs/plone.app.layout [version]/plone/app/layout/configure.zcml`. This file, which is written in ZCML, lists out all of the viewlets and viewlet managers that ship with Plone, along with their formal names.

The code looks something like this:

```
<!-- Register viewlet managers - used in plone's main_template -->
<browser:viewletManager
        name="plone.portaltop"
        provides=".interfaces.IPortalTop"
        permission="zope2.View"
        class="plone.app.viewletmanager.manager.OrderedViewletManager"
        />
<!-- Define some viewlets -->
<!-- The portal header -->
    <browser:viewlet
        name="plone.header"
        manager=".interfaces.IPortalTop"
        template="portal_header.pt"
        permission="zope2.View"
        />
```

Notice the difference between the `browser:viewletManager` and `browser:viewlet` definition and the `OrderedViewletManager` class used by the viewlet managers. In the above example, the `IPortalTop` manager is a viewlet manager that renders the contents of any viewlets controlled by that manager, using the class `OrderedViewletManager`.

It's not really important to understand exactly what `OrderedViewletManager` does, except to realize that it outputs the viewlets contained within a given viewlet manager in a specific order. The `OrderedViewletManager` class is used by all viewlet managers in Plone, therefore all of the viewlet managers behave the same way. They are merely containers that hold the viewlets.

Meanwhile, the `plone.header` viewlet listed above is managed by the viewlet manager that implements the `IPortalTop` interface, outputs the HTML found in `portal_header.pt`, and is available to anyone with the `View` permission.

We can see which viewlets are assigned to which viewlet managers through the web, using a special interface, often referred to as `@@manage-viewlets`. You may see this view in action at: `http://localhost:8080/Plone/@@manage-viewlets` or another URL, where `Plone` is the name of your Plone site. The next screenshot demonstrates what the `@@manage-viewlets` view looks like:

This interface can be used for quickly identifying where a viewlet is assigned, and from a TTW perspective, you can use the **show** and **hide** links to display or suppress certain viewlets, as we'll discuss later. It's cleaner to do this through the filesystem, though. This screen loses value as your theme is built out, because your theme's rendered CSS often obscures the information you are trying to see. The UI issue is likely something that will be fixed in a future version of Plone. Moreover, your theme product's **GenericSetup** may override any changes made through the web.

Now that we understand how viewlets are aggregated and how we can look at this aggregation through the web, let's look at what we need to know in order to modify a viewlet.

Class-based versus template-based viewlets

Think of viewlets and viewlet managers as an organization (your site). Within the organization, there are numerous departments (viewlet managers), and numerous staff members (viewlets) within these departments. For a staff member to be moved from one department (viewlet manager) to another (promoted, or perhaps even fired), paperwork (ZCML, XML, and sometimes Python code) must be filled out.

The first step to modifying viewlets is to locate them and figure out if they are **class-based** or **template-based**. This is a great oversimplification, but will help you get used to the patterns needed to do basic modifications. In reality, all viewlets have classes. If it's not specified in ZCML, it means that it is using the inherited (default) class. It just means that the viewlets don't need any supporting logic from a derived class.

Likewise, a viewlet can have both a class and a template specification. In that case, the specified template is used for rendering, and the template can access the class logic. Browser pages typically work this way.

For shorthand, though, what we are calling class-based viewlets above are simply viewlets that don't have ZCML-specified templates. They may use a template they get from somewhere else, or they may render some other way. Similarly, what we call template-based viewlets are deriving from the inherited class, but there isn't a class defined in `plone.app.layout` for these viewlets.

As explained above, inside of your buildout you should see an `buildout-cache/eggs/` directory. Within that directory, you should find an egg named `plone.app.layout`, with a version number attached. If you drill into that folder, you will find most of the pieces and parts that make up Plone's interface.

Open the default Plone `configure.zcml` file located in `yourbuildout/buildout-cache/eggs/plone.app.layout/plone/app/layout/viewlets`. Here is what the default `configure.zcml` file says about the logo viewlet, for example:

```
<!-- The logo -->
    <browser:viewlet
        name="plone.logo"
        manager=".interfaces.IPortalHeader"
        class=".common.LogoViewlet"
        permission="zope2.View"
        />
```

The code tells us that the Plone logo, formally called `plone.logo`, is managed by the `IPortalHeader` viewlet manager, its class is `LogoViewlet`, and the logo is available to all users with the `View` permission. If we look in the `plone.app.layout.viewlets` directory, we also see a file named `logo.pt`, which is the page template used for rendering the logo. Even though there is the `logo.pt` file involved, because a class is specified in `configure.zcml`, the `plone.logo` viewlet can be thought of as class-based. This is a good example of a viewlet that uses a class and a template, but is still considered class-based because the derived class takes responsibility for the rendering details.

Conversely, if we look at the portal header code, we'll see that it does not have a class declaration, and that it instead specifies a template. This means that all of its logic is contained in that template, and that it can be thought of as template-based. In reality, though, it is using an inherited class.

```
<!-- The portal header -->
    <browser:viewlet
        name="plone.header"
        manager=".interfaces.IPortalTop"
        template="portal_header.pt"
        permission="zope2.View"
        />
```

The important thing to understand here is that when modifying viewlets, we first need to know if they are class-based (using a derived class) or not in order to know how to treat them, and we have to explicitly look at the code in `configure.zcml` to verify if there is an associated page template or not.

Other vital information is found in `common.py`, located in `yourbuildout/buildout-cache/eggs/plone.app.layout [some version number]/plone/app/layout/viewlets/common.py`. This file contains many of the Python classes used by the viewlets with class declarations. (Other viewlets can be found in eggs directories such as `plone.app.content`.) Obviously, viewlets that are template-based do not use this file.

This file is located in your buildout at `buildout-cache/eggs/plone.app.layout/plone/app/layout/viewlets/common.py`. Search the file for the word "logo" and it gives us the following information:

```
class LogoViewlet(ViewletBase):
    render = ViewPageTemplateFile('logo.pt')
    def update(self):
        portal_state = getMultiAdapter((self.context, self.request),
                                        name=u'plone_portal_state')
        self.navigation_root_url = portal_state.navigation_root_url()
        portal = portal_state.portal()
        logoName = portal.restrictedTraverse
                ('base_properties').logoName
        self.logo_tag = portal.restrictedTraverse(logoName).tag()
        self.portal_title = portal_state.portal_title()
```

For many of the default viewlets, we don't want to change the Python code that renders our viewlet; we only want to change the template that outputs the viewlet. Here, we only need to understand that the class name is `LogoViewlet`, and that a page template named `logo.pt` renders the viewlet. It's rare that we'd want to modify the `LogoViewlet` class, especially for non-coders, but it is fairly likely that we'd want to alter what HTML appears in `logo.pt`.

Now that we can distinguish between the types of viewlets, we'll examine how these viewlets are registered in a theme product.

Registering viewlets in a viewlet manager

As we saw earlier, viewlets are aggregated into viewlet managers. We can register viewlets with managers by modifying the `configure.zcml` file located in our theme product, similar to how this happens in the `plone.app.layout configure.zcml` file located at `yourbuildout/buildout-cache/eggs/plone.app.layout/plone/app/layout/viewlets/configure.zcml`.

In our sample theme, we want to register the `plone.personalbar` viewlet with the `plone.portalfooter` viewlet manager in our theme product, so that the login/logout links and other options here are listed at the bottom of the Plone page. The `plone.app.layout configure.zcml` file tells us this:

```
<!-- The personal bar -->
    <browser:viewlet
        name="plone.personal_bar"
        manager=".interfaces.IPortalTop"
        class=".common.PersonalBarViewlet"
        permission="zope2.View"
        />
```

If you look inside the `yourbuildout/buildout-cache/eggs/plone.app.layout/plone/app/layout/viewlets/` directory, you will also see a page template called `personal_bar.pt`. We don't need to modify the output for that page template for now, so we can ignore this for the moment. All we're concerned with here is telling the `plone.portalFooter` to see the personal bar.

We copy-paste the following code into our own theme product's `configure.zcml` file, located at `plonetheme.yourtheme/plonetheme/yourtheme/browser/configure.zcml`, and modify it as shown:

```
<!-- The personal bar -->
    <browser:viewlet
        name="plone.personal_bar"
        manager="plone.app.layout.viewlets.interfaces.IPortalFooter"
        class="plone.app.layout.viewlets.common.PersonalBarViewlet"
        layer=".interfaces.IThemeSpecific"
        permission="zope2.View"
        />
```

Notice the dot-delimited path back to the `plone.app.viewlets IPortalFooter` viewlet manager. We do this because we are not modifying the behavior of the viewlet manager itself, and we're happy to use what the interface provides us by default.

The next line for the class declaration means that the viewlet's class is exactly as before; we're just providing the full dot-delimited path back to the original class.

Finally, we include our layer definition for `IThemeSpecific`, so that our changes only affect the current theme product. Remember, this line is crucial to making sure that your theme product does not step on other themes in the same Zope instance.

As a quick side note, if we opted to subclass the viewlet's Python code, the code might look something like this:

```
<!-- The personal bar -->
    <browser:viewlet
        name="plone.personal_bar"
        manager="plone.app.layout.viewlets.interfaces.IPortalFooter"
        class=".viewlets.PersonalBarViewlet"
        layer=".interfaces.IThemeSpecific"
        permission="zope2.View"
        />
```

This means that our theme will provide a `PersonalBarViewlet` class, probably the one that has been subclassed from `plone.app.layout.viewlets.common.PersonalBarViewlet`, then modified in your theme product's `viewlets.py` file, located in the `browser/` folder. For the purposes of this section, we're not going to worry about this just yet. Here, all we want to do is assign the viewlet to a different viewlet manager, not change the behavior or any template that might be associated with the viewlet.

Also, if you were working with a template-only viewlet here, you could skip the `class` line above. Always rely on what `plone.app.layout`'s `configure.zcml` file gives you to learn what you need to modify.

With this code in place (assuming you did not try to subclass the `PersonalBarViewlet`), the personal bar should appear in the footer once you restart your Zope instance or use the `plone.reload` (http://pypi.python.org/pypi/plone.reload) egg to reload your modified ZCML code. To restart your Zope instance, simply shut it down and restart it in your terminal using the following command:

`./bin/instance fg`

Starting your Zope in the foreground gives you the opportunity to run it in debug mode, so that you can troubleshoot errors, but once you close your terminal, the instance immediately terminates.

It's worth noting that using the `fg` command starts your Zope instance in the foreground. In a production scenario, you would start your Zope instance (and leave it running) by using the following command:

`./bin/plonectl start`

Starting your Zope in the foreground gives you the opportunity to run it in debug mode, so that you can troubleshoot errors, but once you close your terminal, the instance immediately terminates.

Reordering viewlets within a viewlet manager

We already know that Plone orders viewlets within viewlet managers, and we've looked at how we can reassign viewlets to different viewlet managers. Now, we want to look at how we might reorder a viewlet within its current (default) viewlet manager.

You can find Plone's default viewlet ordering mechanism in your buildout in Plone's baseline product, CMFPlone, located in the GenericSetup XML file at `buildout-cache/eggs/Plone-[version].egg/Products/CMFPlone/profiles/default/viewlets.xml`:

```
<?xml version="1.0"?>
<object>
  <order manager="plone.portaltop" skinname="Plone Default">
    <viewlet name="plone.header" />
    <viewlet name="plone.personal_bar" />
    <viewlet name="plone.app.i18n.locales.languageselector" />
    <viewlet name="plone.path_bar" />
  </order>
  <order manager="plone.portalheader" skinname="Plone Default">
```

```
            <viewlet name="plone.skip_links" />
            <viewlet name="plone.site_actions" />
            <viewlet name="plone.searchbox" />
            <viewlet name="plone.logo" />
            <viewlet name="plone.global_sections" />
        </order>
        <order manager="plone.contentviews" skinname="Plone Default">
            <viewlet name="plone.contentviews" />
            <viewlet name="plone.contentactions" />
        </order>
        <order manager="plone.portalfooter" skinname="Plone Default">
            <viewlet name="plone.footer" />
            <viewlet name="plone.colophon" />
        </order>
    </object>
```

As you can see, the viewlets are all grouped by manager; for example,
plone.portaltop, plone.portalheader, plone.contentviews, and
plone.portalfooter. Generally speaking, most Plone 3 themes are based
off of this default configuration, and build onto it or deviate from it, as needed.

It's important to point out that *ordering* a viewlet is not the same thing as *registering*
a viewlet for a viewlet manager. Ordering is handled via a GenericSetup profile,
whereas registering is handled via ZCML configuration. So, by modifying the code
in our theme product's viewlets.xml, we can order the items on a Plone page, but
actual registration of a browser resource happens in configure.zcml, as described
above, and the configure.zcml file is ultimately the file that tells Plone what
viewlet manager a viewlet belongs to.

In this example, we want to move the logo viewlet above the searchbox within the
plone.portalheader viewlet manager. We are not trying to display or order the
logo in a new viewlet manager. CMFPlone's default viewlets.xml configuration
for the portalheader viewlet manager looks like this:

```
    <?xml version="1.0"?>
    <order manager="plone.portalheader" skinname="Plone Default">
        <viewlet name="plone.skip_links" />
        <viewlet name="plone.site_actions" />
        <viewlet name="plone.searchbox" />
        <viewlet name="plone.logo" />
        <viewlet name="plone.global_sections" />
    </order>
    </object>
```

In our own theme product, `plonetheme.yourtheme/profiles/viewlets.xml`, you would insert the following code, where `yourtheme` is your Plone theme product's skin name. It's vital to distinguish it from `Plone Default`.

```
<?xml version="1.0"?>
<object>
<order manager="plone.portalheader" skinname="yourtheme" based-
                                      on="Plone Default">
    <viewlet name="plone.logo" insert-before="plone.searchbox"  />
</object>
```

As you can see, we're not grabbing the entire contents of CMFPlone's `viewlets.xml`, we're only using the parts we need. Optionally, if we wanted an element to appear after a given viewlet, we could specify `insert-after=""` instead.

> Ordering of viewlets can be a touchy thing, so beware.
> Sometimes it works, sometimes it doesn't. Sometimes TTW changes
> to the ordering of viewlets can interfere with our XML. This is a known
> issue that is currently being worked on, and will likely be fixed by the
> time this book is published.

Showing, hiding, and unhiding viewlets within a viewlet manager

Let's now look at how to show viewlets in a different viewlet manager and hide unwanted viewlets that we've overridden.

Let's assume that we're going to move `plone.personal_bar` to the footer area and suppress that viewlet from the `plone.portaltop` viewlet manager. The idea is that if you are going to move a viewlet to a new location, Plone will still think (thanks to the `CMFPlone viewlets.xml` default configuration) that the viewlet is meant to be shown in its original location. Thus, we must issue directives to show the viewlet in one place and suppress it in the first location, or else it will display twice.

CMFPlone's `viewlets.xml` tells us the following:

```
<?xml version="1.0"?>
<order manager="plone.portaltop" skinname="Plone Default">
    <viewlet name="plone.header" />
    <viewlet name="plone.personal_bar" />
    <viewlet name="plone.app.i18n.locales.languageselector" />
    <viewlet name="plone.path_bar" />
  </order>
<order manager="plone.portalfooter" skinname="Plone Default">
    <viewlet name="plone.footer" />
```

```
        <viewlet name="plone.colophon" />
    </order>
</object>
[snip]
```

In our own theme product's `profiles/viewlets.xml`, we would alter the code to look like this, where `yourtheme` is your theme product's skin name, as defined in the `profiles.zcml` file.

```
<?xml version="1.0"?>
<order manager="plone.portalfooter" skinname="yourtheme" based-
                                        on="Plone Default">
    <viewlet name="plone.personal_bar" />
</order>
<hidden manager="plone.portaltop" skinname="yourtheme">
    <viewlet name="plone.personal_bar" />
</hidden>
</object>
```

As you can see, we first want to show the viewlet in the new viewlet manager, using the `order manager` syntax. Then we want to suppress the original viewlet that was registered for `plone.portaltop` through `Plone Default`, using the `hidden manager` syntax.

It's worth stating that unhiding viewlets through GenericSetup is an awkward process, and it's generally easier to just unhide a viewlet using `@@manage-viewlets`. There is GenericSetup code that can allow you to do it via code, and if you have the luxury to work only on the filesystem without using `@@manage-viewlets`, you should.

Next, let's look at how we can override viewlets, both in terms of their behavior and their appearance.

Overriding a viewlet template

As we saw earlier, viewlets can be regarded as either template-based or class-based, although as mentioned, that's really an oversimplification. In this section, we'll look at how we can modify a so-called template-based viewlet that technically inherits from a default class not specified in `plone.app.layout`. We will not be moving the viewlet to a new section; we're only going to modify its appearance.

For example, let's assume that we want to modify the portal header area to include some additional information about our site. If we open `configure.zcml`, located at `yourbuildout/buildout-cache/eggs/plone.app.layout/plone/app/layout/viewlets/configure.zcml`, you can see the following code:

```
<!-- The portal header -->
    <browser:viewlet
        name="plone.header"
        manager=".interfaces.IPortalTop"
        template="portal_header.pt"
        permission="zope2.View"
        />
```

We want to copy this code to our theme product's `configure.zcml`, located at `plonetheme.yourtheme/plonetheme/yourtheme/browser/configure.zcml`. Next, we modify it to indicate that we want to apply changes to a new page template (this is optional), and that we want these changes to only affect our current theme product:

```
<!-- The portal header -->
    <browser:viewlet
        name="plone.header"
        manager="plone.app.layout.viewlets.interfaces.IPortalTop"
        template="mynewportal_header.pt"
        layer=".interfaces.IThemeSpecific"
        permission="zope2.View"
        />
```

Note that we've also given the full dot-delimited path to `IPortalTop`, because w're not in the same Python package.

Next, we need to locate the `portal_header.pt` page template in `yourbuildout/buildout-cache/eggs/plone.app.layout/plone/app/layout/viewlets/` and copy it into our theme product's `browser/` folder.

Then, we rename the page template to call it `mynewportal_header.pt`, if you changed its name in your theme product's `configure.zcml` file. Generally, you only need to rename your page template if the actual behavior of the template changes in a way that implies that its functionality has changed significantly, if, for instance, you alter your logo viewlet to include additional, unrelated pieces of functionality.

In this case, we will alter the page template code only slightly, to include some code that pulls in the name of your web site, such as the portal title (rendered via a viewlet manager):

```
<h1 tal:content="view/portal_title">
    Title of the portal
</h1>
<div id="portal-header">
    <div tal:replace="structure provider:plone.portalheader" />
</div>
```

We have not moved or reordered this viewlet, so there is no need to touch our theme product's `viewlets.xml` file. If you restart your Zope instance, the viewlet should now show the title of your web site in the portal header area.

Next, we look at how to modify a class-based viewlet (technically a viewlet that derives from a subclass located in `plone.app.layout`).

Overriding a non-template-based viewlet

Modifying viewlets that use a derived class involves some extra manipulation of code, because here we are also looking at how we might modify the behavior of a viewlet, as defined in its derived Python class. In this section, we'll look at modifying the breadcrumbs so that they use a different divider between the crumbs.

If we open the `configure.zcml` file in `yourbuildout/buildout-cache/eggs/` `plone.app.layout/plone/app/layout/viewlets/`, you can see the following code:

```
<!-- The breadcrumbs -->
    <browser:viewlet
        name="plone.path_bar"
        manager=".interfaces.IPortalTop"
        class=".common.PathBarViewlet"
        permission="zope2.View"
        />
```

The class declaration here is what tells us that we are working with a template that is defined within a class. We want to copy-paste this code into our theme product's `configure.zcml` file, located at `plonetheme.yourtheme/plonetheme/yourtheme/` `browser/configure.zcml`, and modify it as follows:

```
<!-- The breadcrumbs -->
    <browser:viewlet
        name="plone.path_bar"
        manager="plone.app.layout.viewlets.interfaces.IPortalTop"
        class=".viewlets.PathBarViewlet"
        layer=".interfaces.IThemeSpecific"
        permission="zope2.View"
        />
```

Optionally, you could name your viewlet something like:

```
name="mytheme.path_bar"
```

This can often help if you know that you will have project managers or other administrative types modifying viewlets through `portal_view_customizations` in the ZMI, as it makes it easy to spot the viewlet, but it's also a good thing to do because once you've modified it, it's no longer the original `plone.whatever` viewlet. Changing the name means that you will have to perform an extra step, which we will cover at the end of this section. For the purposes of this example, we will change the name of the viewlet to `mytheme.path_bar`.

Notice that in the above code, we provided a dot-delimited path back to the original viewlet manager's interface. Also, we specify the `IThemeSpecific` layer in order to keep our changes from affecting any other themes on our Zope instance. Most importantly, we change the class declaration to reference the `viewlets.py` file, located in our theme product at `plonetheme.yourtheme/plonetheme/yourtheme/browser/viewlets.py`.

Before we subclass our viewlet, let's make a small change to the page template that renders the viewlet. The original template, `path_bar.pt`, located in `yourbuildout/buildout-cache/eggs/plone.app.layout/plone/app/layout/viewlets/`, looks like the following:

```
<div id="portal-breadcrumbs" i18n:domain="plone">
    <span id="breadcrumbs-you-are-here" i18n:translate=
                    "you_are_here">You are here:</span>
    <a i18n:translate="tabs_home" tal:attributes="href
                    view/navigation_root_url">Home</a>
    <span tal:condition="view/breadcrumbs"
            class="breadcrumbSeparator">
        <tal:ltr condition="not: view/is_rtl">&rarr;</tal:ltr>
        <tal:rtl condition="view/is_rtl">&raquo;</tal:rtl>
    </span>
    <span tal:repeat="crumb view/breadcrumbs" tal:attributes="dir
                        python:view.is_rtl and 'rtl' or 'ltr'">
        <tal:last tal:define="is_last repeat/crumb/end">
            <a href="#"
                tal:omit-tag="not: crumb/absolute_url"
                tal:condition="python:not is_last"
                tal:attributes="href crumb/absolute_url"
                tal:content="crumb/Title">
                crumb
            </a>
            <span class="breadcrumbSeparator" tal:condition="not:
                                                is_last">
                <tal:ltr condition="not: view/is_rtl">
                                &rarr;</tal:ltr>
```

```
            <tal:rtl condition="view/is_rtl">&raquo;</tal:rtl>
        </span>
        <span tal:condition="is_last"tal:content=
                    "crumb/Title">crumb</span>
    </tal:last>
  </span>
</div>
```

We will replace the Unicode characters → (right arrow) with »
(right angle quote), as follows:

```
<div id="portal-breadcrumbs" i18n:domain="plone">
    <span id="breadcrumbs-you-are-here" i18n:translate=
                "you_are_here">You are here:</span>
    <a i18n:translate="tabs_home" tal:attributes="href
                view/navigation_root_url">Home</a>
    <span tal:condition="view/breadcrumbs"
            class="breadcrumbSeparator">
        &raquo;
    </span>
    <span tal:repeat="crumb view/breadcrumbs"tal:attributes="dir
                    python:view.is_rtl and 'rtl' or 'ltr'">
        <tal:last tal:define="is_last repeat/crumb/end">
            <a href="#"
                tal:omit-tag="not: crumb/absolute_url"
                tal:condition="python:not is_last"
                tal:attributes="href crumb/absolute_url"
                tal:content="crumb/Title">
                crumb
            </a>
    <span class="breadcrumbSeparator" tal:condition="not: is_last">
                <tal:ltr condition="not: view/is_rtl">&rarr;</tal:ltr>
                <tal:rtl condition="view/is_rtl">&raquo;</tal:rtl>
            </span>
    <span tal:condition="is_last" tal:content=
                "crumb/Title">crumb</span>
        </tal:last>
    </span>
</div>
```

Save this page template as path_bar.pt, or perhaps yourtheme_path_bar.pt,
depending on if it's important to you that the name should change.

Then, we want to look at the Python class that controls the path bar. The `common.py` file in the `viewlets` directory, located at `yourbuildout/buildout-cache/eggs/plone.app.layout/plone/app/layout/viewlets/`, gives us the following information:

```
class PathBarViewlet(ViewletBase):
    index = ViewPageTemplateFile('path_bar.pt')

    def update(self):
        portal_state = getMultiAdapter((self.context, self.request),
                                        name=u'plone_portal_state')
        self.navigation_root_url = portal_state.navigation_root_url()
        self.is_rtl = portal_state.is_rtl()
        breadcrumbs_view = getMultiAdapter((self.context,
                self.request), name='breadcrumbs_view')
        self.breadcrumbs = breadcrumbs_view.breadcrumbs()
```

The important piece here is to see that the `PathBarViewlet` is derived from a class called `ViewletBase`, and that it uses a page template named `path_bar.pt`. We are going to subclass it.

Inside of your theme product's `viewlets.py`, located at `yourbuildout/src/plonetheme.yourtheme/plonetheme/yourtheme/browser/viewlets.py`, we will add the following code:

```
from Products.Five.browser.pagetemplatefile import ViewPageTemplateFile
from plone.app.layout.viewlets import common

class PathBarViewlet(common.PathBarViewlet):
    """A custom version of the path bar class
    """
    index = ViewPageTemplateFile('new_path_bar.pt')
```

The first line here is just a bit of boilerplate code that you don't need to memorize; just refer back to it when you need it. The second line, however, is needed to call in the classes that `common.py` provides, including `PathBarViewlet`. If you really want to be Pythonic, instead of importing `common`, you would import only the `PathBarViewlet`, using this line:

```
from plone.app.layout.viewlets import PathBarViewlet
```

Next, we need to subclass the `PathBarViewlet` class from `plone.app.layout.common`. Subclassing means that we inherit all its behavior in our class. We are really just creating a special case of `plone.app.layout`'s `PathBarViewlet` to make a minor behavior change. As a result, the new class declaration becomes:

```
class PathBarViewlet(common.PathBarViewlet):
```

Don't be confused by the fact that both of these viewlet classes have the name `PathBarViewlet`. In fact, the original is `plone.app.layout.common.PathBarViewlet`, and our new derived class is `plonetheme.yourtheme.browser.viewlets.PathBarViewlet`. They occupy different Python name spaces.

As a best practice, it helps to document your change with a `docstring`, in the event that you need to introspect your code later; for example:

```
"""A custom version of the path bar class
"""
```

Finally, we change the name of the page template that the class uses to render the code. In this case, we are pointing to the page template we just modified and renamed—`new_path_bar.pt`.

If you're not accustomed to Python programming, don't worry. This is as complex as most subclassing gets. Follow the pattern, and you will get the same results, over and over again. However, if you are adept at Python programming, you could optionally alter your new Python class to behave differently. This is an advanced topic that will not be covered here.

Lastly, since we have created a new viewlet, we also need to register it in our GenericSetup profile, located in our theme product at `yourbuildout/src/plonetheme.yourtheme/plonetheme/yourtheme/profiles/viewlets.xml`, as follows—where `yourtheme` is the name of your skin, and `mytheme.path_bar` is the name of your viewlet. Notice that we also hide the default Plone path bar so that we do not have two path bars appearing on our site.

```xml
<?xml version="1.0"?>
<object>
<order manager="plone.portaltop" skinname="yourtheme" based-on="Plone
                                                            Default">
    <viewlet name="mytheme.path_bar" />
  </order>
<hidden manager="plone.portaltop" skinname="yourtheme">
    <viewlet name="plone.path_bar" />
  </hidden>
</object>
```

You could even position the elements using `insert-before=""` or `insert-after=""`, if you wanted to.

Since we have modified our ZCML code (`.zcml` files), and we have modified our GenericSetup profiles (`viewlets.xml`), we not only need to restart our Zope instance, but we also need to reinstall our product (okay, but only during early development) or reimport our `viewlets.xml` profile through the ZMI (safer option) because we have changed our XML profile.

To import the profile, log into the ZMI and go to `portal_setup`. Click on the **Import** tab at the top, then choose the name of your theme product. Select the **viewlets** step found on the page, and choose **Import Selected Step**. Your viewlet changes should now be registered and appear if you refresh your page.

Portlets

In this section we will cover some of the basic concepts associated with portlet manipulation. Generally speaking, portlets are similar to viewlets in terms of their basic functionality. They render a portion of a page under control of a manager that maintains order.

As of Plone 3, portlets can be designated to appear in either the left column or the right column, formerly known as `left_slots` and `right_slots`, but they cannot yet display elsewhere in a site's structure without additional code. This is a limitation that Plone hopes to overcome.

You can adjust the portlet settings on a given folder or page using the `@@manage-portlets` page, accessible via the **manage portlets** links in the right or left columns of your site. See the Plone Users Manual (`http://plone.org/documentation/manual/plone-3-user-manual`) for more information on how to configure portlets on your site. Most importantly, you can define portlets at your site root that can cascade throughout your site's structure, or you can block parent portlets for a given section. Optionally, you can also manage portlets by the group that a user falls in or by the content type involved.

There are several key differences between portlets and viewlets. With portlets, a portlet is always registered in ZCML with `renderer=` declaration pointing at a `renderer` class. That class has a `render` method in Python that returns the HTML for the portlet. Frequently, this is just a `ViewPageTemplateFile` that parses a template from the filesystem. For example, the default `News` portlet is described in a package commonly known as `plone.app.portlets`, and found in `yourbuildout/buildout-cache/eggs/plone.app.portlets/plone/app/portlets/portlets/configure.zcml`, as follows:

```
<plone:portlet
        name="portlets.News"
        interface=".news.INewsPortlet"
        assignment=".news.Assignment"
        renderer=".news.Renderer"
        addview=".news.AddForm"
        editview=".news.EditForm"
        />
```

> In addition to a `renderer` class, `add` and `edit` declarations are also specified to support the portlet manager's portlet add/configure functionality.

The `renderer` class code returns the output that comes from `news.pt`, also located in `yourbuildout/buildout-cache/eggs/plone.app.portlets/plone/app/portlets/portlets/configure.zcml`. We can verify that it uses `news.pt` if we look at the `news.py` file located in this folder:

```
class Renderer(base.Renderer):
    _template = ViewPageTemplateFile('news.pt')
```

As you can see, in Plone 3, more than one file is involved in the rendering of a portlet. Usually, it's just a matter of walking around the `plone.app.portlets` tree to find the important pieces that give you the information you need: `configure.zcml`, an associated `.py` file, and occasionally an associated `.pt` file, as defined in the `.py` file.

Modifying Plone 3 portlets in a theme product

If we wish to modify only the rendering (and not the adding or editing) of a Plone 3 portlet, the `portletRenderer` ZCML directive is used to replace the render method on an existing portlet `renderer` class with a `ViewPageTemplateFile` associated with a different template on the filesystem. Portlets are rendered by the `portletRenderer` directive using ZCML, written as `<plone:portletRenderer />`. The `portletRenderer` directive can register either a custom version of the whole `Renderer()` class (with `class=""`) or it can register a custom template only (`template=""`) for a given portlet.

For example, in this theme product's `browser/configure.zcml` file, we see:

```
<configure
    xmlns="http://namespaces.zope.org/zope"
    xmlns:browser="http://namespaces.zope.org/browser"
    xmlns:plone="http://namespaces.plone.org/plone"
    i18n_domain="plonetheme.audubonportland">
    <!-- overriding the portlets -->

    <include package="plone.app.portlets" />

    <plone:portletRenderer
        portlet="plone.app.portlets.portlets.events.IEventsPortlet"
        template="events.pt"
        layer=".interfaces.IThemeSpecific"
        />
```

We must explicitly include the `plone.app.portlets` package in ZCML processing—before we attempt to override any portlets—because we are now using the `portletRenderer` directive.

If we are editing only the rendering of an existing portlet, we use the `<plone:portletRenderer />` syntax, but if we are creating a new portlet, we use the standard `<plone:portlet />` syntax at the beginning of our ZCML declaration.

This code tells us that we are using the `portletRenderer` directive to indicate that we are using the default Python code that renders the portlet (hence the dot-delimited patch back to `IEventsPortlet`), we are altering the portlet to refer to a local template named `events.pt`, and our modifications will only affect the current theme product.

We then need to copy `events.pt` to our filesystem product's `browser/` folder, along with any associated metadata files. You don't need to copy `events.py`, but you will need to subclass it. You could optionally put your portlets in a `portlets/` folder, but that is optional and requires some extra boilerplate. See the `plone.app.portlets` package for more information.

Assuming we want to change the name of the page template to `mytheme_events.pt`, we now define a new portlet renderer for our new layer.

Instead of using a custom template, we could use a whole new renderer class. In this case, we can use identical renderer class code, but change the name of the template it renders. If we refer back to `plone.app.portlets.portlets`, and take the code for the `events.py` renderer and alter it to point to `mytheme_events.pt`, we have the following code:

```
class Renderer(base.Renderer):
    _template = ViewPageTemplateFile('mytheme_events.pt')
    def __init__(self, *args):
        base.Renderer.__init__(self, *args)
        portal_state = getMultiAdapter((self.context, self.request),
                                       name=u'plone_portal_state')
        self.portal_url = portal_state.portal_url()
        self.portal = portal_state.portal()
        self.have_events_folder = 'events' in self.portal.objectIds()
[snip]
```

In our `configure.zcml`, it is also possible to use the `for` attribute to customize for a particular type of context, or the `view` attribute to customize for a particular view, as with viewlets. Note that only `plone:portletRenderer` understands `for` and `view`, `plone:portlet` does not.

From the perspective of a filesystem-based product, if you have created a new Plone 3 portlet (not modified off of a default Plone 3 portlet) and it appears in the `browser` directory for your product, that portlet will automatically be available via the **add new portlet** in the `@@manage-portlets` drop-down list once you refresh your page (or restart your Zope instance if you need to).

Creating a new Zope 3 portlet

Let's look briefly at how to create a new Zope 3 portlet. In the interest of reinforcing concepts and doing a bit of compare/contrast, we're going to recreate the browser page we saw in the previous chapter as a Zope 3 portlet.

First, (in a fresh Plone theme product) we create a new file named `audiences.py` in our `browser/` folder and insert the following code. This code will output text and images from various locations inside of our Plone site, and will use a page template called `audiences.pt`. Notice that it is using the `Renderer` class here, and the `memoize` package to cache the return value of the function:

```
from zope.component import getMultiAdapter
from zope import schema
from zope.formlib import form
from zope.interface import implements

from plone.app.portlets.portlets import base
```

```
from plone.memoize.instance import memoize
from plone.portlets.interfaces import IPortletDataProvider
from Products.Five.browser.pagetemplatefile import
                            ViewPageTemplateFile
class IAudienceNavigationPortlet(IPortletDataProvider):

    portlet_title = schema.TextLine(title=u"Title for the portlet",
                                default=u"Information for:",
                                required=True)

class Assignment(base.Assignment):
    implements(IAudienceNavigationPortlet)

    def __init__(self, portlet_title=""):
        self.portlet_title = portlet_title

    @property
    def title(self):
        return u"Audience Navigation"
class Renderer(base.Renderer):

    render = ViewPageTemplateFile('audiences.pt')

    @property
    def available(self):
        return len(self._data()) > 0

    def audiences(self):
        """Return obj with attributes:
            - id
            - url
            - title
            - description
            - selected (str: 'selected' or 'unselected')
        """
        audiences = []
        current_url = self.context.absolute_url()
        for action in self._data():
            audiences.append({
                "id":    action['id'],
                "url":   action['url'],
                "title": action['title'],
                "selected": current_url.startswith(action['url']) and
                                        'selected' or 'unselected',
                "description": action['description'],
                })
        return audiences

    def header(self):
        return self.data.portlet_title
```

```
    # By using the @memoize decorator, the return value of the
function will
    # be cached. Thus, calling it again does not result in another
query.
    # See the plone.memoize package for more.
    @memoize
    def _data(self):
        context_state = getMultiAdapter((self.context, self.request),
                                    name=u'plone_context_state')
        return context_state.actions().get('audience_navigation',
                                                    None)
class AddForm(base.AddForm):
    form_fields = form.Fields(IAudienceNavigationPortlet)
    label = u"Add Audience Navigation portlet"
    description = u'This portlet displays the audiences that have
                        been entered into the portal_actions tool'
    def create(self, data):
        assignment = Assignment()
        form.applyChanges(assignment, self.form_fields, data)
        return assignment
class EditForm(base.EditForm):
    form_fields = form.Fields(IAudienceNavigationPortlet)
    label = u"Edit Audience Navigation portlet"
    description = u'This portlet displays the audiences that have
                        been entered into the portal_actions tool'
```

Add the interface for our browser page

In our theme product in `browser/interfaces.py`, we need to insert the
following code:

```
from plone.theme.interfaces import IDefaultPloneLayer

class IAudienceNavigationLayer(IDefaultPloneLayer):
    """Marker interface that defines a Zope 3 browser layer.
    """
```

Create a page template for our view

Next, we want to create a page template using TAL and HTML (and a tiny snippet
of Python) to render these items. We will call it `audiences.pt` and place it in our
`browser/` folder. Notice that it iterates over a series of "audience-items" to output
an unordered list.

```
<dl class="portlet portlet-audience-navigation">
    <dt class="portletHeader" tal:content="view/header">Information
                                                for...</dt>
```

```
      <dd class="portletItem"
          tal:repeat="audience view/audiences">
          <a tal:attributes="class string:${audience/selected}
                                          audience-${audience/id};
                              href audience/url;
                              title audience/description"
            tal:content="audience/title">
            Link Name
          </a>
      </dd>
      <dd class="portletFooter">
      </dd>
  </dl>
```

Write the GenericSetup steps to create the new portlet

Next, we need to create a file called `portlets.xml` and place that in our theme product's `profiles/default` folder. We will populate it with the following code:

```xml
<?xml version="1.0"?>
<portlets>

    <portlet
        addview="onenw.audiencenavigation.AudienceNavigation"
        title="Audience Navigation"
        description="This portlet displays the site's audiences."
        />

</portlets>
```

When we install our theme product, this portlet should automatically be available for installation via the `@@manage-portlets` tool.

Write the GenericSetup to create a new CMFAction category and actions

We add the following code to our theme product's `portlets.xml` file:

```xml
<?xml version="1.0"?>
<object name="portal_actions" meta_type="Plone Actions Tool"
    xmlns:i18n="http://xml.zope.org/namespaces/i18n">
    <object name="audience_navigation" meta_type="CMF Action
                                        Category" purge="False">
        <property name="title">Audience Navigation</property>
        <object name="example" meta_type="CMF Action">
```

```
                    <property name="title">Example Audience</property>
                    <property name="description">
                        The description of the audience is available on
                            mouseover in the audience navigation portlet.
                    </property>
                    <property name="url_expr">string:${globals_view/
                            navigationRootUrl}/example</property>
                    <property name="icon_expr"></property>
                    <property name="available_expr"></property>
                    <property name="permissions">
                     <element value="View"/>
                    </property>
                    <property name="visible">True</property>
                </object>
            </object>
        </object>
```

When we install our theme product, this CMF action category should automatically
be created, as well as a sample action.

Register the portlet in your theme product

Next, we register our portlet in our `browser/configure.zcml` file:

```
<configure
    xmlns="http://namespaces.zope.org/zope"
    xmlns:browser=http://namespaces.zope.org/browser
    xmlns:plone="http://namespaces.plone.org/plone"
    i18n_domain="plonetheme.audience">
<include package="plone.browserlayer" />
<genericsetup:registerProfile
        name="default"
        title="Sample Audience Navigation Portlet"
        directory="profiles/default"
        description=Sample Audience Navigation Portlet''
        provides="Products.GenericSetup.interfaces.EXTENSION"
        />
    <interface
        interface=".interfaces.IAudienceNavigationLayer"
        type="zope.publisher.interfaces.browser.IBrowserSkinType"
        name=""
        />
    <include package="plone.app.portlets" />
    <plone:portlet
        name="sample.audiencenavigation.AudienceNavigation"
        interface=".audiences.IAudienceNavigationPortlet"
        assignment=".audiences.Assignment"
```

```
        renderer=".audiences.Renderer"
        addview=".audiences.AddForm"
        editview=".audiences.EditForm"
        />
  </configure>
```

Notice that we have to include the `plone.app.portlets` package in order to create or modify a portlet.

Next, restart Zope so that it can read those lines of code:

`./bin/instance fg`

Enable the portlet

Finally, to expose the portlet to your Plone site, you should install the theme product. You can then verify that it works by going to the following URL: `http://localhost:8080/myplonesite/@@manage-portlets`. In the drop-down list on this view, you should see an **Audiences** portlet listed. Add the new portlet, and when you visit the home page, you should have a new portlet listing the contents of the new CMF action category.

Using Classic portlets in a theme product

Optionally, you can create a **Classic** portlet. Classic portlets can be distinguished from newer portlets by the fact that they are portlets that behave exactly like former Plone 2.x portlets. Thus, they do not require boilerplate code to make them work. In other words, a Classic portlet is typically just a self-contained page template, whereas newer Zope 3-styled portlets contain more hooks that allow you to do more "fancy" stuff, such as live reconfiguration.

If you create a Classic portlet, it will live in your theme product's `skins/templates` directory (not in the browser space). This is optional, of course. To install it on your site, you must add that portlet as a Classic portlet via `@@manage-portlets`. If your portlet is named `my_portlet.pt`, then add it using the syntax `my_portlet` (corresponding to the name of the page template you are using). It is important that you do not add the `.pt` extension when using `@@manage-portlets` to add Classic portlets.

An example of a Classic portlet is the following `we_do.pt`, which calls a `portal_action` CMF category named `we_do` that contains `portal_actions` within it that drive the user to a given URL. (Make sure you create the category and a few actions within it. Also make sure you add a title and description to each `portal_action`.) Here is an example of one of those `portal_actions`:

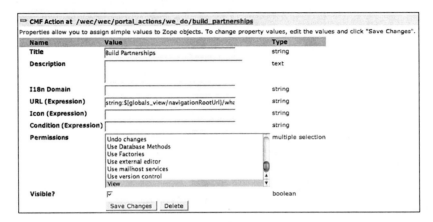

The portlet simply renders these `portal_actions` as a drop-down list, within a basic portlet structure (header, footer, `portletItem` CSS classes).

```
<html xmlns:tal="http://xml.zope.org/namespaces/tal"
      xmlns:metal="http://xml.zope.org/namespaces/metal"
      i18n:domain="plone">

<body>

<tal:portlet
    metal:define-macro="portlet"
    define="actions actions/we_do|nothing;"
    condition="actions">
<dl class="portlet"
    id="portlet-we-do">
    <dt class="portletHeader"><a tal:attributes="href
    string:$portal_url/get-involved">Our Approach</a>
    </dt>

    <dd class="portletItem"
        tal:repeat="action actions">
            <a tal:attributes="href action/url"
               tal:content="action/title">
              [Action Name]
            </a>
            <span class="description"
                  tal:content="action/description">[Action's
```

```
        Description. To be hidden with CSS where unneeded.]</span>
          </dd>
      </dl>
      </tal:portlet>
      </body>
      </html>
```

That's all there is to a Classic portlet!

Don't be afraid of "Classic" portlets just because of the name. They're an entirely appropriate solution for any situation that doesn't require significant Python logic or configurability within the portlet manager interface. Think of them as "simple" or "quick" portlets, if the word "Classic" has a negative connotation.

As a final note, there are two portlet-related packages that were not bundled with Plone 3.0, but as of 3.1 are part of the core. These packages are `plone.portlet. static` and `plone.portlet.collection`. They're configurable portlets that allow for the display of static text or a list of the contents of a collection. Customizing these portlets is the same as customizing any other Zope 3 portlet.

Using portal_view_customizations

Now that we have examined the various Zope 3 components that comprise a theme product, we now need to look at what pieces can be modified through the ZMI. Remember that we are treating stylesheets and images as skin layer objects, so they can be modified the way we discussed in Chapter 5, *Making Manual (TTW) Changes or What Not to Do*.

As for other components, the short answer is that the following can be customized through the ZMI: any templates that come from the `plone.app.layout` and `plone. app.portlets` directories, and any browser layer templates that might be in your theme product.

These templates can be customized through the ZMI using a tool known as `portal_view_customizations`. This tool is accessible using a URL like the following:

```
http://localhost:8080/testsite/portal_view_customizations/
registrations.html
```

Specifically, you will want to scroll down on this page to get to the section called `zope.interface.Interface`.

It is important to note that prior to Plone 3.1.4, the `portal_view_customizations` tool was broken, but can now be used for TTW customizations. Most serious themers do not use `portal_view_customizations`, as it is not easy to extract those changes to the filesystem. It should be regarded as a place for short-term modifications only and avoided at all costs.

You can only modify templates belonging to existing browser resources in this tool; you cannot add new browser resources, nor can you modify the Python classes used by these viewlets. Adding new resources must be done first on the filesystem, so that the appropriate ZCML configurations can be defined. As a result, this tool has limited use.

The `portal.view.customizations` tool was obviously designed by programmers, not skinners, and has a user interface that only a programmer could love. But take a moment to figure it out, and you'll find that it does work.

In the next screenshot, you see all of the browser resources available in a given Zope instance, and the grey text explains which theme product each resource belongs to. This makes it possible for you to know which one you're editing.

```
zope.interface.Interface
    Products.WWRC.global_sections (Products.WWRC.browser.interfaces.IThemeSpecific)
    Products.WWRC.viewlets.content_headers (Products.WWRC.browser.interfaces.IThemeSpecific)
    ace.global_sections (plonetheme.ace.browser.interfaces.IThemeSpecific)
    ace.path_bar (plonetheme.ace.browser.interfaces.IThemeSpecific)
    addform_macros (zope.publisher.interfaces.browser.IDefaultBrowserLayer)
    base-pageform.html (zope.publisher.interfaces.browser.IDefaultBrowserLayer)
    base-subpageform.html (zope.publisher.interfaces.browser.IDefaultBrowserLayer)
    batch_widget (Products.CMFDefault.interfaces.ICMFDefaultSkin)
    bullitt.colophon (plonetheme.bullitt.browser.interfaces.IThemeSpecific)
    bullitt.global_sections (plonetheme.bullitt.browser.interfaces.IThemeSpecific)
    bullitt.path_bar (plonetheme.bullitt.browser.interfaces.IThemeSpecific)
    bullitt.site_actions (plonetheme.bullitt.browser.interfaces.IThemeSpecific)
    calendar.pt (zope.publisher.interfaces.browser.IDefaultBrowserLayer)
    calendar_day.html (Products.CMFDefault.interfaces.ICMFDefaultSkin)
    calendar_widget (Products.CMFDefault.interfaces.ICMFDefaultSkin)
    classic.pt (zope.publisher.interfaces.browser.IDefaultBrowserLayer)
    collection.pt (zope.publisher.interfaces.browser.IDefaultBrowserLayer)
    collection.pt (plonetheme.kswild.browser.interfaces.IThemeSpecific)
    copperriver.logo (plonetheme.copperriver.browser.interfaces.IThemeSpecific)
    customizezpt.html (zope.publisher.interfaces.browser.IDefaultBrowserLayer)
    dogwood.content.storybox_body (dogwood.content.interfaces.IDogwoodContentLayer)
    dogwood.content.storybox_tabs (dogwood.content.interfaces.IDogwoodContentLayer)
    edit-markers.html (zope.publisher.interfaces.browser.IDefaultBrowserLayer)
    events.pt (zope.publisher.interfaces.browser.IDefaultBrowserLayer)
    five_template (zope.publisher.interfaces.browser.IDefaultBrowserLayer)
    folder_contents (zope.publisher.interfaces.browser.IDefaultBrowserLayer)
    folder_factories (zope.publisher.interfaces.browser.IDefaultBrowserLayer)
    form_widget (Products.CMFDefault.interfaces.ICMFDefaultSkin)
    fscvl_static.pt (Products.FSCVLTheme.browser.interfaces.IThemeSpecific)
    full_review_list (zope.publisher.interfaces.browser.IDefaultBrowserLayer)
    keyword_migrator (zope.publisher.interfaces.browser.IDefaultBrowserLayer)
    kss_javascript (zope.publisher.interfaces.browser.IDefaultBrowserLayer)
    kswild.banner (plonetheme.kswild.browser.interfaces.IThemeSpecific)
    language.pt (zope.publisher.interfaces.browser.IDefaultBrowserLayer)
    login.pt (zope.publisher.interfaces.browser.IDefaultBrowserLayer)
    login.pt (zope.publisher.interfaces.browser.IDefaultBrowserLayer)
    manage-portlets-macros (zope.publisher.interfaces.browser.IDefaultBrowserLayer)
    manage-viewlets (zope.publisher.interfaces.browser.IDefaultBrowserLayer)
    manage_interfaces (zope.publisher.interfaces.browser.IDefaultBrowserLayer)
    navigation.pt (Products.FSCVLTheme.browser.interfaces.IThemeSpecific)
    navigation.pt (plonetheme.dogwood.browser.interfaces.IThemeSpecific)
    navigation.pt (zope.publisher.interfaces.browser.IDefaultBrowserLayer)
    navigation.pt (Products.WWRC.browser.interfaces.IThemeSpecific)
```

Some of the elements listed here have customized names, such as `ace.path_bar` or `bullitt.colophon`, which are specific to two themes contained in this particular Zope instance. This naming convention is optional, and can only be done on the filesystem.

If your integrators are making changes using this tool, you should always check this area prior to checking in changes to your filesystem product. To extract code from this section, go to `portal_view_customizations` in the ZMI, and locate the item you wish to extract (look for items highlighted in yellow). Click on the item, and cut-paste it into the appropriate page template in your theme product. If this is a new modification to a page template that is not specifically written for your theme, you'll also need to write the boilerplate to hook the page template up to your theme product.

For now, just understand that this area provides an TTW means by which you can make quick fixes to viewlets and other Zope 3 templates, but it's a fairly limited tool and not all pieces that comprise a theme product are represented here, due to the complexities of Zope. We're not going to cover this specifically, as it'll make sense once you understand the broader scheme of how to do filesystem development.

Summary

In this chapter, we have learned about:

- Viewlets, viewlet managers, and `@@manage-viewlets`
- Portlets and basic portlet customization techniques
- Extracting changes from `portal_view_customizations` to a filesystem product

You should now have all of the major tools that you need to create a theme product. In the next chapter, we'll walk through a real-world theme product to see all of the moving parts in action.

8
Understanding Zope Page Templates and the Template Attribute Language

Plone uses a page templating mechanism known as **Zope Page Templates** (ZPT). ZPT, in turn, uses a language known as the **Template Attribute Language** (TAL). ZPT also uses a language called Macro Extensions, known as METAL, which is outside of the scope of this chapter.

In this chapter, we'll cover the theory of TAL's basic constructs and see how a real Plone site might output dynamic content using these expressions. For the definitive information on Zope Page Templating, please refer to *The Zope Book*:

`http://www.zope.org/Documentation/Books/ZopeBook/2_6Edition/ZPT.stx`.

The objective of using a templating language is to output dynamic content while minimizing the amount of code in page templates. Ideally, templating languages should play nicely with tools that designers might use to theme around a web site. In other words, a tool like Dreamweaver should ignore code, even if it cannot output the dynamic results. An extra benefit is that if some basic best practices are followed, designers should know what output is expected, even if they don't understand the templating language itself.

Plone's page templating language, TAL, does all of these things.

About ZPT

ZPT is an invention of Zope Corporation, and is based on XHTML, which is HTML that conforms to stricter XML standards. XHTML requires code to be well formed (for example, `<img />`, `<span></span>`, and so on), and it requires that code to be properly nested and always in lowercase form. XHTML also allows you to create different sets of markup tags for new purposes. For example, you can create blocks of code, using a syntax such as `<tal:block></tal:block>` or `<metal:block></metal:block>`, to create better structured page templates. **CMFPlone's** `main_template.pt` is a good example of this code in action, though it can also be found in any `.zpt` or `.pt` file.

The goal of TAL is to be a templating language that allows for "round-trip" collaboration by themers and programmers. A designer may create a template, as he/she creates a normal XHTML document, using placeholder text. The designer may then pass it to a programmer or themer who knows TAL attributes and can make it dynamic. Then, the template can go back to the designer for refinement. At every step, it's valid XHTML and plays well with web editors and validators.

XHTML contains tags, including:

- `body`
- `p`
- `div`
- `table`
- `a`
- `img`

Almost all tags in XHTML have attributes, such as `id`, `class`, and `title`. An attribute can be thought of as a characteristic that an object knows about itself. For example, you would never say `<body src="">`, but you would say `<img src="" alt="" />`.

This is where attributes come into play in Zope Page Template. TAL simply allows us to add attributes to XHTML objects, such as those listed above. These attributes are all in a special XML namespace, so they do not interfere with other markup, and are ignored by validators. In order to retain one hundred-percent XML compatibility, you will need to specify the necessary namespaces you need, such as:

```
<html xmlns:tal="http://xml.zope.org/namespaces/tal"
  xmlns:metal="http://xml.zope.org/namespaces/metal">
```

It might be helpful to look at some of the standard Plone page templates to see what other namespaces might come into play, but these are the two main ones you will see.

What does TAL look like in practice?

As mentioned before, TAL is found in any `.zpt` or .pt file, such as in CMFPlone's page templates and in templates associated with viewlets and portlets. The easiest way to understand what TAL looks like is to see an example.

The following expression renders a bit of dynamic content that may not be immediately obvious:

```
<p tal:content="string:Yes, we can!">Barack Obama's campaign
                                                slogan</p>
```

The output becomes:

```
<p>Yes, we can!</p>
```

In other words, "Barack Obama's campaign slogan" is a placeholder for dynamic content—something that you might see if you view this code in Dreamweaver—but the final output is the string expression. Unlike other languages, such as PHP, ColdFusion, or ASP, it's not what's inside of the tag that is important, it's what the tags do that is important.

Let's look at this in the context of Plone. One of the first page templates most themers are confronted with is the `logo.pt` page template. As we discussed in the previous chapters, the logo is a viewlet, found in the `plone.app.layout` package. If we open the `logo.pt` page template found in that package, we see the following code:

```
<a metal:define-macro="portal_logo"
   id="portal-logo"
   accesskey="1"
   tal:attributes="href view/navigation_root_url"
   i18n:domain="plone">
<img src="logo.jpg" alt=""
        tal:replace="structure view/logo_tag" /></a>
```

At first blush, this can be a bit intimidating, but let's break it down. Clearly, we see that there is an `href` tag wrapped around an image. Unlike a standard `a` tag, however, we see:

```
tal:attributes="href view/navigation_root_url"
```

The `tal:` tag indicates that what follows is in the TAL namespace and meant to be handled by the TAL parser. This particular fragment will create or replace the `href` attribute of the current tag with the one pointing to the `navigation_root_url`, or the index page of your site. This `navigation_root_url` is known as an attribute of the `view` object, better understood as a characteristic of a page in the context of the current request. These characteristics might require some experience to divine, but over time, you will become more comfortable finding these attributes and using them in your TAL constructs.

The next piece to look at here is the image `src` attribute. The TAL expression is as follows:

```
tal:replace="structure view/logo_tag"
```

To a user new to Plone, it's not obvious what's happening here. All we know at this point is that the logo gets rendered by completely replacing the current tag. In fact, the view's `logo_tag` comes from the browser view class implementation of `plone.app.layout.viewlets.LogoViewlet`. If we read that viewlet code, we'd discover that it's using the `logoName` property from our `base_properties.props` stylesheet:

```
logoName:string=logo.jpg
```

Clearly, this is a pretty indirect way of rendering a logo. The purpose of all this indirection is to make it possible for you to change the logo graphic via a property sheet. In later chapters we'll look at other options available to you to customize your logo.

For now, just understand that the Python class that controls the logo is what tells the `logo.pt` page template what object to render, and that we are using TAL to pull in that object.

Since the logo isn't necessarily the easiest place to start in terms of understanding TAL constructs, let's look at some of the more basic ways in which TAL might be used.

About the Template Attribute Language

TAL is a concise language, and is not hard to follow once you understand the basic statements and what they do:

- `tal:attributes`—dynamically change element attributes
- `tal:define`—define variables
- `tal:condition`—test conditions
- `tal:content`—replace the content of an element

- `tal:repeat` — iterate over a sequence
- `tal:replace` — replace the content of an element, and remove the element leaving the content
- `tal:omit-tag` — the same as `tal:content`, but also removes the wrapping tag on which the statement is applied
- `tal:on-error` — handle errors

We will walk through these expressions in greater detail, and also look at how the `structure` expression syntax (**TALES**) can be used.

tal:attributes statement

First, let's look at an example of a `tal:attributes` expression that is used for `img` `src` or `href` to change a class:

```
<img src="doesn't matter because it will be subbed out dynamically"
          tal:attributes="src string:http://google.com/logo.jpg"
/>
```

In this example, the `src` attribute is being assigned the string `http://google.com/logo.jpg`, which is the image that will render.

Multiple attributes

In this example, we have more than one attribute and separate them via semi-colons:

```
<img src="doesn't matter because it will be subbed out
                                        dynamically"
      tal:attributes="src string:http://google.com/logo.jpg;
                      alt string:Google's Logo;
                      width string:40px;" />
```

Not including the semi-colons will cause a traceback error and the page will not render.

Nothing dynamic is really happening in these examples; we're just pulling in an image `src` that is explicitly defined right in our page template.

tal:define statement

This type of expression defines a variable that we can use later in our page templates. If you recall, we mentioned that XHTML forces us to use well-formed pages with correct nesting. Using `tal:define`, we can define a variable that is within the scope specific to a part of a page, but not usable outside of that scope.

For example, here we see a simple variable definition:

```
<p tal:define="myvariable string:hello world!">This text is just a
                                            placeholder.</p>
```

We're not doing anything with `myvariable`, but note that it is only in-scope within the `<p>...</p>` tags.

Compare this to the following `tal:define` expressions:

```
<p tal:define="myvariable string:hello">This text is just a
                                            placeholder.</p>
<p tal:attributes="class myvariable">We want this to show up. Will
                                            it?</p>
```

In this second example, it is not possible to assign the class named `myvariable` to `myvariable` defined in the first `<p>...</p>` tag, as `myvariable` is only within scope in the first paragraph (unless it is defined elsewhere in the XHTML tree hierarchy). An error would occur in this case.

How this works in Plone

If you are going to use `tal:define`, you need to make sure you use it in your page template in a way that respects the scope of a defined variable. For example, the following is a sample "testimonial" portlet that defines a variable named `source` at the top that can be used throughout the entire page template, if desired:

```
<dl class="portlet portletTestimonial"
    i18n:domain="plone"
    tal:define="source view/getSource">
    <dt class="portletHeader">
        <span class="portletTopLeft"/>
        <span class="portletTopRight"/>
    </dt>
    <dd class="portletItem">
        <span tal:replace="source/getText">Text</span>
            Testimonial Body
        </tal:body>
    </dd>
    ...
</dl>
```

If this variable was defined in the `<dt>` tag, it would not be usable inside `<dd class="portletItem">`, as it would be out of scope and only available inside the `<dt>...</dt>` tags.

tal:condition statement

A conditional is one of the first concepts you learn in programming. It allows you to test if something is, or is not, true, and act upon the result of that condition. For example, "If it's hot out, we'll go swimming. If it's not, we'll stay home." We use the `tal:define` expression as follows to tell us if the condition will be true or false.

```
<div tal:define="blazing_hot python:False">
    <p tal:condition="blazing_hot">We'll go swimming</p>
    <p tal:condition="not:blazing_hot">We'll stay home.</p>
</div>
```

In this example, the variable `blazing_hot` will evaluate as false, because we are expressly setting the Python Boolean value for false. In Python, any string that's not empty, such as "", will evaluate to true! Empty tuples, lists, and dictionaries (as well as strings − (,), [], {}), the number 0, the Boolean `False`, and the value `None`, all will resolve to false. As a result, the final output is `We'll stay home.`.

In the following statement, the `tal:define` sets the variable `blazing_hot` to resolve as true:

```
<div tal:define="blazing_hot python:True">
    <p tal:condition="blazing_hot">We'll go swimming</p>
    <p tal:condition="not:blazing_hot">We'll stay home.</p>
</div>
```

Hence, the statement resolves to `We'll go swimming`.

In the following variation, the `tal:define` statement has set the variable to evaluate to `nothing`.

```
<div tal:define="blazing_hot nothing">
    <p tal:condition="blazing_hot">We'll go swimming</p>
    <p tal:condition="not:blazing_hot">We'll stay home.</p>
</div>
```

In TALES, `nothing` is a reserved word for `null`, which is always false. It's the same as `None` in Python.

How this works in Plone

An easy example of how a conditional works in Plone is in `path_bar.pt`, located in `plone.app.viewlets`:

```
<span tal:condition="view/breadcrumbs" class="breadcrumbSeparator">
        <tal:ltr condition="not: view/is_rtl">&rarr;</tal:ltr>
        <tal:rtl condition="view/is_rtl">&raquo;</tal:rtl>
    </span>
```

This conditional states that, depending on if you are reading right to left or left to right, you will get a different type of arrow indicator.

Another example of how a conditional might be used in Plone is in `site_actions. pt`, which is also found in `plone.app.layout`. This page template has a condition that states that if any `site_actions` (defined in `portal_actions` through the ZMI) are visible, it will render them in an unordered list and assign attributes (`id`, `i18n` hooks, `href` attribute) to each `site_action`'s list item anchor tag.

```
<ul id="portal-siteactions"
    tal:define="accesskeys python: {'sitemap' : '3', 'accessibility'
                                    : '0', 'contact' : '9'};"
    tal:condition="view/site_actions"
    i18n:domain="plone">

    <li tal:repeat="saction view/site_actions"
        tal:attributes="id string:siteaction-${saction/id}"><a
            href=""
            tal:define="title saction/title;
                        id saction/id;
                        accesskey python: accesskeys.get(id, '');"
            i18n:attributes="title"
            i18n:translate=""
            tal:content="title"
            tal:attributes="href saction/url;
                            title title;
                            accesskey accesskey;"
            >Site action</a></li>
</ul>
```

If there are no visible `site_actions` defined in the ZMI in `portal_actions`, nothing will render, as the condition resolves to false.

tal:content statement

Next, we look at the `tal:content` expression. In our first example, we see that our `tal:content` expression outputs the value of the variable `myvariable` inside the current tag, replacing the current contents. Let's take this expression:

```
<p tal:define="myvariable string:hello world!">This text will render
        <strong tal:content="myvariable">This is invisible!</strong>
</p>
```

It, in turn, becomes:

```
<p>This text will render <strong>hello world!</strong></p>
```

How this works in Plone

A simple example of a `tal:content` expression would also be:

```
<title tal:content="here/title">Page Title</title>
```

Where `here/title` is grabbing the `Title` attribute off of the object you are currently on and populating the `<title />` tag with that value dynamically. The actual words "Page Title" will not render—it's just a placeholder. This would be a useful construct in cases like the `navigation.pt` (navigation portlet) file, found in `plone.app.portlets`, where we want to be able to specify the title of the navigation portlet in our theme product in a way that it could be customized by the end user:

```
<a href="#"
        class="tile"
        tal:condition="view/title"
        tal:attributes="href string:${root/absolute_url}/sitemap"
        tal:content="view/title">Navigation</a>
```

This code ensures that if we manage our portlet via `http://www.mysite.com/@@manage-portlets`, we can specify a title on the fly.

tal:repeat statement

In the case of `tal:repeat`, the code is looped through and an action is performed on each object within the repeat sequence.

```
<ul tal:define="staffers python:('jonb','david','veda','josh',)">
        <li tal:content="staffer" tal:repeat="staffer staffers">
            Staffer
        </li>
</ul>
```

The above `tal:repeat` statement loops over all staffers defined within a Python tuple, and creates an `<li>...</li>` tag for each staffer. The repeat continues until no more objects are found within the Python list, at which point we close the unordered list.

How this works in Plone

The page template `sections.pt` (found in `plone.app.viewlets`) attaches a unique id to each item found in the `portal_actions/portal_tabs` CMF action category in the ZMI. Additionally, depending on if the tab is selected or not, it will apply a CSS class of `selected` or `plain`. For this example, the code has been modified slightly to render in a table instead of as an unordered list:

```
<tal:tabs tal:condition="view/portal_tabs"
          i18n:domain="plone">
    <h5 class="hiddenStructure" i18n:translate="heading_sections">
                                                    Sections</h5>
        <div id="tabWrapper">
            <table id="portal-globalnav-table">
              <tr>
                <tal:tabs tal:repeat="tab view/portal_tabs">
                <td tal:attributes="id string:portaltab-${tab/id}-
                                                        table;
                    class python:view.selected_portal_tab==tab['id']
                                        and 'selected' or 'plain'">
                  <a href=""
                     tal:content="tab/name"
                     tal:attributes="href tab/url;
                             title tab/description|nothing">
                    Tab Name
                  </a>
                </td>
                </tal:tabs>
              </tr>
            </table>
        </div>
</tal:tabs>
```

The rendered code would look something like the following, depending on the ids of the `portal_tabs`:

```
<div id="tabWrapper">
    <table id="portal-globalnav-table">
        <tr>
            <td id="portaltab-climate-and-energy-table"
                                class="selected">
            <a href="http://akcenter.org/climate-energy"
                        title="">Climate and Energy</a>
            </td>
            <td id="portaltab-wildlands-and-rivers-table"
              class="plain">
              <a href="http://akcenter.org/wildland-rivers"
                        title="">Wildland and Rivers</a>
            </td>
            <td id="portaltab-oceans-and-marine-life-table"
              class="plain">
              <a href="http://akcenter.org/oceans-marine"
                        title="">Oceans and Marine Life</a>
            </td>
        </tr>
    </table>
</div>
```

As you can see, it's rendered as a series of `<td></td>` tags with unique IDs that can be styled using CSS. Notice that the `Climate and Energy` tab is marked as selected, as it is the tab we are currently on. That class allows us to style that tab differently, if desired. We often use `tal:repeat` for generating unordered or ordered lists, but certainly, it could be used in other scenarios. It's not uncommon to see it used in conjunction with built-in methods to specify odd, even, start, and end states to aid in styling.

Did you notice the `<tal:tabs ...>` ... `</tal:tabs>` tag in the example above? When you use a `<tal:block>` or `<tal:anything>` tag, the tag itself, along with the closing tag, will be completely removed in the output. You may use this type of construct for defines and repeats if it clarifies your code, as explained earlier.

tal:replace Statement

Typically, this expression is used when you don't want the whole tag and its contents—not just the contents—to be replaced. A basic example is here:

```
<p tal:define="myvariable string:hello world!">Spacestation here...
        <span tal:replace="myvariable">This is invisible!</span>
</p>
```

When this code renders, it becomes:

```
<p> Spacestation here... hello world!</p>
```

In other words, the `tal:replace` expression supplants the entire `<span></span>` statement and fills it in with the value assigned to `myvariable`. This helps you avoid cluttering your output with semantically meaningless tags that you've used just to mark dynamic replacements.

How this works in Plone

An example of when this might be used in Plone is in `CMFPlone/skins/plone_templates/main_template.pt`. In this template, you will find several lines like this:

```
<div id="portal-top" i18n:domain="plone">
        <div tal:replace="structure provider:plone.portaltop" />
</div>
```

This code states that within the id named `#portal-top`, we want to replace a `<div />` with the contents of whatever `provider:plone.portaltop` gives us. This provider is actually the viewlet manager that controls the area known as `plone.portaltop` (more on this in a bit). If we look at our `viewlets.xml` (located in `CMFPlone/profiles/default`) file, we will see that, in a default Plone site, the above statement in `main_template.pt` will replace the entire `<div />` with the rendered contents of the viewlets that are specified in the setup profile for `plone.portaltop`, specifically:

```
<order manager="plone.portaltop" skinname="Plone Default">
    <viewlet name="plone.header" />
    <viewlet name="plone.personal_bar" />
    <viewlet name="plone.app.i18n.locales.languageselector" />
    <viewlet name="plone.path_bar" />
</order>
```

The `tal:replace` expression is used because we don't have a need to retain the `<div />` wrapper in order to see the output of these viewlets.

tal:omit-tag statement

To leave the contents of a tag in place while omitting the surrounding start and end tag, we can use the `omit-tag` statement. If its expression evaluates to a false value, then normal processing of the element continues. If the expression evaluates to a true value, or there is no expression, the statement tag is replaced with its contents. For these purposes, the value `nothing` is false, which has the same effect as returning a false value.

For example:

```
<b tal:omit-tag="python:True">Omit expression is True</b>
<b tal:omit-tag="python:False">Omit expression is False</b>
<b tal:omit-tag="">Omit expression is BLANK</b>
```

The first line of code would render the first statement without bold tags, the second would render with bold tags, and the third would render without bold tags.

How this works in Plone

In Plone, you will often see the `tal:omit-tag` statement used in i18n scenarios (internationalization), but you can also see it in the breadcrumbs viewlet:

```
<span tal:repeat="crumb view/breadcrumbs"
        tal:attributes="dir python:view.is_rtl and 'rtl' or 'ltr'">
    <tal:last tal:define="is_last repeat/crumb/end">
        <a href="#"
            tal:omit-tag="not: crumb/absolute_url"
            tal:condition="python:not is_last"
            tal:attributes="href crumb/absolute_url"
            tal:content="crumb/Title">
            crumb
        </a>
        ...
    </tal:last>
</span>
```

This code basically tells us that a breadcrumb's `Title` will be wrapped with an `href` tag if an URL exists, assuming that it's not the last item in the list of breadcrumbs. If there is no URL, then it will be rendered without the `href` tag.

tal:on-error statement

You can provide error handling for your document using the `tal:on-error` statement. When a TAL statement produces an error, the TAL interpreter searches for an `on-error` statement on the same element, then on the enclosing element, and so forth. The first `on-error` found is invoked. It is treated as a content statement, because it causes the content of the tag to be replaced, but it's triggered only when an error occurs. In this example, if the following `tal:content` statement fails, the words `This is not the homepage` will be rendered:

```
<p tal:content="here/homepage"
   tal:on-error="string:This is not the homepage">This is the
                                          homepage</p>
```

How this works in Plone

While it isn't used often, `tal:on-error` can be used to great advantage. In `portlets_fetcher.pt`, found in 3.x versions of the CMFPlone product, it is used to alert Plone users to problems with portlets:

```
<metal:block tal:repeat="slot sl">
        <tal:dontcrash tal:on-error="structure python:context.plone_
log('Error %s on %s while rendering portlet %s'%(error.type, error.
value, slot[0])) or
                                    '&lt;div class=\'error\
'&gt;Error %s on %s: %s&lt;/div&gt;' % (error.type, slot[0], error.
value)"
                    tal:define="pathexpr python:slot[0];
                                usemacro python:slot[1];">
[snip]
        </tal:dontcrash>
    </metal:block>
```

If Plone attempts to render portlets and there is a problem, it will output the text "Error while rendering portlet". This means that Plone swallows the error gracefully, instead of rendering a traceback error.

TAL "structure" expression syntax

As we saw earlier, when all of the `tal:content` and `tal:replace` expressions above were interpreted and turned into output, something extra was happening. The TALES engine was scanning strings for HTML's reserved characters (such as <, > and &) and replacing them with HTML entities. This is great for two reasons:

- It makes it easier for you to not have to worry about it yourself
- It gives you a safety net against certain kinds of cross-site scripting attacks

But, what if you want to insert some actual HTML code? The escaping would defeat you.

If we use the `structure` keyword in a TALES expression, it will render written HTML as actual HTML. (Note that `structure` is not the same as a TAL attribute, it's actually part of the TAL syntax.) For example:

```
<p tal:content="structure string:<strong>hello</strong>" />
```

Becomes:

```
<p><strong>hello</strong></p>
```

This may even be a bit trickier. You may use the following to get the same result:

```
<p tal:content="structure string:&lt;strong&gt;hello&lt;/strong&gt;" />
```

TAL will translate the key HTML entities in a `structure` expression. Why bother? Because the first version will confuse many HTML editors and validators.

How this works in Plone

The `structure` expression syntax can be very useful when we attempt to control image display. One example of how we use the `structure` expression is inside of our `newsitem_view.pt` page template, located in `CMFPlone/skins/plone_content`:

```
<div class="newsImageContainer"
          tal:condition="here/image_mini|nothing">
        <a href="#"
           tal:attributes="href string:$here_url/image/
                                    image_view_fullscreen"
           id="parent-fieldname-image">
           <img tal:replace="structure python: here.tag(scale=
               'mini', css_class='newsImage')" src="" alt="" />
        </a>
</div>
```

The `python:here.tag(...)` fragment will render an entire image tag, complete with width and height attributes. The `structure` syntax allows us to insert it without having it HTML escaped.

Order of operations

In TAL, the logic in which operations occur is fairly intuitive. It generally occurs in the following order:

- `define`
- `condition`
- `repeat`
- `content` or `replace`
- `attributes`
- `omit-tag`

Think of it this way: you can't attach an attribute value that hasn't yet been defined or proven to exist. As you get used to how page templates are constructed, you'll see that they follow this general order of operations.

Built-in names in TALES

The following is a list of the names that are always available to TALES expressions in Zope, and which you may often see in your page templates. These are considered reserved words. You can read more about these here: `http://wiki.zope.org/ZPT/TALESSpecification13`.

- `nothing` — a special value used to represent a non-value (for example, `void`, `None`, `Nil`, `NULL`).
- `default` — a special name for the contents (data) of a tag. This is usually only used in tricky bits of code.
- `options` — the keyword arguments passed to a template. These are generally available when a template is called from methods and scripts, rather than from the Web.
- `repeat` — the repeat variables. See the `tal:repeat` documentation.
- `attrs` — a dictionary containing the initial values of the attributes of the current statement tag. This is Uncommon.
- `here` or `context` — the object to which the template is being applied.
- `container` — the folder in which the template is located.
- `template` — the template itself.
- `request` — the publishing request object, which includes form data, query strings, and typical web server HTTP variables.

- `user`—the authenticated user object.
- `modules`—a collection through which Python modules and packages can be accessed. Only modules that are approved by the Zope security policy can be accessed.

The names `root`, `here`, `container`, `template`, `request`, `user`, and `modules` are optional names supported by Zope, but are not required by the TALES standard. This list is presented with the purpose of not diving in too deep, but with the objective of showing where some of these words fit in if you happen to see them in your page templates. Most of these, with the exception of `here` and `request`, should be used only lightly in your templates.

It's possible to write extremely complex logic in TAL/TALES—but it's a bad idea. Remember that the purpose of a templating language is to separate logic from presentation. Use TAL and TALES to set conditions for presentation and for dynamic replacement. Move your programming and logic into Python and Python scripts so that you can keep your templates simple and readable/maintainable by designers. After all, if you're intermixing complex logic and presentation, you're going to get a kind of spidery mess that's typical of PHP or ASP.

Summary

In this chapter, we have learned:

- What the Zope Page Templating system is
- That the Templating Attribute Language (TAL) is used by Zope and follows the rules of XHTML
- What the common TAL expressions are
- How these TAL expressions manifest themselves in CMFPlone's page templates and in templates that render viewlets and portlets

As we move forward, we will take these lessons and apply them to an actual theme product. Let's take a closer look at a real-world theme product now.

9
Creating, Installing, and Tweaking our Theme

Now that we have a basic introduction to the machinery that makes themes possible, we are going to use these concepts to dissect an actual theme product.

We will first inspect a few structural changes and install them, and then finally examine the various components and skin layer items that have been changed, one at a time. Where restarting Zope or rerunning your buildout would be required, this will be noted.

About the theme

This theme and its design are available for personal and professional use to anyone, and can be freely modified. You can (and should) download the files from `https://svn.plone.org/svn/collective/plonetheme.guria/trunk` using the following command:

```
svn co https://svn.plone.org/svn/collective/plonetheme.guria/trunk
plonetheme.guria
```

Note the space between the words `trunk` and `plonetheme.guria`. This theme is intended for installation on Plone 3 web sites. The finished theme should look like the following, but we have work to do to make this happen:

This theme was created by me, for use by a charity group in India, called *Guria* (http://www.guriaindia.org), dedicated to ending human trafficking and prostitution. The finished site is currently in development, and is generously hosted free of charge by the talented folks at *Six Feet Up* (sixfeetup.com). Additionally, most of the code and lessons learned come courtesy of similar themes created by the staff at ONE/Northwest in Seattle, Washington.

The design for this theme was created with the assumption that most of the tasks described in previous chapters would need to be present in this theme. In fact, the only task not covered here is the creation of a new viewlet manager. Creation of viewlet managers is discussed at http://plone.org/documentation/how-to/adding-portlet-managers and http://plone.org/documentation/manual/theme-reference/elements/viewletmanager/override.

Creating a theme product

Using the lessons learned from Chapter 3, *Setting up Your Development Environment*, I created a theme product named plonetheme.guria, using the command line syntax paster create -t plone3_theme, while we were located in the src/ directory of our buildout, as seen next:

```
[bash: /opt/mybuildout/src] paster create -t plone3_theme
                                    plonetheme.guria
Selected and implied templates:
  ZopeSkel#basic_namespace  A project with a namespace package
  ZopeSkel#plone            A Plone project
  ZopeSkel#plone3_theme     A Theme for Plone 3.0
Variables:
  egg:      plonetheme.guria
  package:  plonethemeguria
  project:  plonetheme.guria
Enter namespace_package (Namespace package (like plonetheme))
                                            ['plonetheme']:
Enter package (The package contained namespace package (like
                        example)) ['example']: guria
Enter skinname (The skin selection to be added to 'portal_skins' (like
'My Theme')) ['']: Guria Theme for the Plone Theming Book
Enter skinbase (Name of the skin selection from which the new one
                        will be copied) ['Plone Default']:
Enter empty_styles (Override default public stylesheets with empty
                                        ones?) [True]: False
Enter include_doc (Include in-line documentation in generated code?)
                                                        [False]:
Enter zope2product (Are you creating a Zope 2 Product?) [True]:
Enter version (Version) ['0.1']:
```

```
Enter description (One-line description of the package) ['An
                        installable theme for Plone 3.0']:
Enter long_description (Multi-line description (in reST)) ['']:
Enter author (Author name) ['Plone Collective']: Veda Williams
Enter author_email (Author email) ['product-developers@lists.
                        plone.org']: email@email.com
Enter keywords (Space-separated keywords/tags) ['web zope plone
                                                theme']:
Enter url (URL of homepage) ['http://svn.plone.org/svn/collective/']:
Enter license_name (License name) ['GPL']:
Enter zip_safe (True/False: if the package can be distributed as a
                        .zip file) [False]:
Creating template basic_namespace
Creating directory ./plonetheme.guria
[snip]
```

You may wish to generate a new Plone theme product yourself, so that you can compare and contrast the differences between the Guria theme and a vanilla Plone theme.

Notice that the full name of the theme is `plonetheme.guria`, and where an item shows as blank, it defaults to the example value in that step. In other words, the namespace package defaults to `plonetheme`, because there was no reason to change it. The `skinname` is set to a single lowercase word out of stylistic preference. It's important to also note that you should not use hyphens or spaces in your theme names, as they will not be recognized by your buildout.

We've chosen not to override Plone's default stylesheets, and instead, we want to build on top of Plone's default (and excellent!) stylesheets. I prefer this method mostly because the layout needed for Plone's **Contents** view and other complex structural pieces are already taken care of by Plone's base stylesheets. It's easier than trying to rebuild those from scratch every time, but this is merely a personal preference.

Following the creation of the theme, we register the theme product in our `buildout.cfg`, using the following syntax:

```
[buildout]
...
develop =
    src/plonetheme.guria
...
[instance]
eggs =
    plonetheme.guria
...
zcml =
    plonetheme.guria
...
```

If we were using the `eggtractor` egg, there would be no need to add these lines of code to our `buildout.cfg`; all we would need to do is rebuild our buildout and it would automatically recognize the new egg. `eggtractor` can be found at `http://pypi.python.org/pypi/buildout.eggtractor`, and is documented thoroughly.

Assuming we are not using `eggtractor`, we must rebuild our buildout, as we have altered ZCML code and added a new egg:

[bash: /opt/mybuildout/src/] ./bin/buildout

This would be a good time to check your vanilla theme product into Subversion, so that you can track back to the original version, if needed. However, since this is an existing theme, there is no need to do so.

For the purposes of following along, it might be best if you do not yet install the theme. We want to make some changes first. However, we will point out some caveats along the way, in case you installed the theme prematurely.

Altering the theme product's structure

Several modifications have been made to the theme product's structure to shorten folder names and change the default behavior. Again, this is mostly a personal preference. Let's take a look at these changes and how they were achieved.

Renaming the theme

In our theme product, you will see a file named `profiles.zcml`, located at `mybuildout/src/plonetheme.guria/plonetheme/guria/profiles.zcml`. The code looks like this:

```
<configure
    xmlns="http://namespaces.zope.org/zope"
    xmlns:genericsetup="http://namespaces.zope.org/genericsetup"
    i18n_domain="plonetheme.guria">
  <genericsetup:registerProfile
      name="default"
      title="Guria Theme for the Plone Theming Book"
      directory="profiles/default"
      description='Extension profile for the "Guria Theme for the
                          Plone Theming Book" Plone theme.'
      provides="Products.GenericSetup.interfaces.EXTENSION"
      />
</configure>
```

If you named your theme in a way that was less descriptive, you could alter the title. Naming your theme product properly is important, because you may have different types of products used for a given web site—for example, a policy product for content that might be used in tandem with your theme product. This text is what you see in the `portal_quickinstaller` at `http://localhost:8080/mysite/portal_quickinstaller/manage_installProductsForm`, where `mysite` is the name of your Plone site. You can also see this name if you install your theme product via **Site Setup | Add-on Products**, found at `http://localhost:8080/mysite/prefs_install_products_form`.

If you change your XML here, and your theme product is already installed, you'll need to start (or restart) your Zope instance, using:

```
[bash: /opt/mybuildout] ./bin/instance fg
```

Shortening folder names

Next, we look at the folder structure of our theme product. The standard Plone 3 theme produces folders with names like `plonetheme_guria_custom_images`, `plonetheme_guria_custom_templates`, and `plonetheme_guria_styles`. While there is nothing wrong with keeping this structure, it can be cumbersome to type or tab through (especially when checking items into Subversion). However, you might want to keep the existing folder names to help you distinguish which items of base Plone you modified. This can make migrations easier. If you choose this route, you probably want to create additional folders for non-base-Plone items. I personally prefer the shorter folder names and don't worry too much about the migration issues.

In the case of this theme product, I opted to make the folder names shorter. First, I altered the names of the folders in the `skins/` folder to `guria_images`, `guria_styles`, and `guria_templates`.

Then, in the theme, go to `mybuildout/plonetheme.guria/plonetheme/guria/skins.zcml`. The code in this file is altered to appear as follows:

```
<configure
    xmlns="http://namespaces.zope.org/zope"
    xmlns:cmf="http://namespaces.zope.org/cmf"
    i18n_domain="plonetheme.guria">
  <!-- File System Directory Views registration -->
  <cmf:registerDirectory
      name="guria_images"/>
  <cmf:registerDirectory
      name="guria_templates"/>
  <cmf:registerDirectory
      name="guria_styles"/>
</configure>
```

One more step is required here. In `plonetheme.guria/plonetheme/guria/profiles/default/skins.xml`, the code is changed to read as follows:

```
<?xml version="1.0"?>
<object name="portal_skins" allow_any="False"
                    cookie_persistence="False"
    default_skin=" Guria Theme for the Plone Theming Book ">

  <object name="guria_images"
     meta_type="Filesystem Directory View"
     directory="plonetheme.guria:skins/guria_images"/>
  <object name="guria_templates"
     meta_type="Filesystem Directory View"
     directory="plonetheme.guria:skins/guria_templates"/>
  <object name="guria_styles"
      meta_type="Filesystem Directory View"
      directory="plonetheme.guria:skins/guria_styles"/>

  <skin-path name=" Guria Theme for the Plone Theming Book " based-
                                        on="Plone Default">
   <layer name="guria_images"
      insert-after="custom"/>
   <layer name="guria_templates"
      insert-after="guria_images"/>
   <layer name="guria_styles"
      insert-after="guria_templates"/>
  </skin-path>
</object>
```

Basically, the steps are the following:

1. Rename the folders on the filesystem.
2. Modify the `skins.zcml` file to change the name of the filesystem directory view (what you see in the `portal_skins/properties` area of the ZMI).
3. Modify the `skins.xml` file in the `profiles/default` folder to match. This alters the basic profile of your theme product.

If you wanted to add additional folders and filesystem directory views here (a `scripts/` folder, for example), you'd just add code by following the conventions given to you in these files and then create additional folders.

Making changes to the ZCML file means that you would need to do a restart of your Zope instance.

If you installed your theme product before making the changes to the skin layer names, you might want to inspect the skin layers at `http://localhost:8080/mysite/ portal_skins/manage_ propertiesForm`, to make sure that the correct skin layers are listed. You might even need to reimport the "skins tool" step via `portal_setup` at `http://localhost:8080/mysite/portal_setup/manage_ importSteps`. Make sure you choose the correct profile first by choosing your theme product's name from the drop-down list at the top of the **import** page. The theme product's name is the same name as you find in your `profiles.zcml` file.

Adjusting how stylesheets and images are used

Next, we remove some of the default behavior given to us by the `plone3_theme` recipe. In a vanilla theme product, folders named `images/` and `stylesheets/` are inserted into the `plonetheme.guria/plonetheme/guria/browser/` directory. Additionally, a file named `main.css` is included in the `stylesheets/` directory.

I chose not to place the theme's images or stylesheets in the `browser/` directory, as this is generally unnecessary for most themes. Advanced programmers may wish to expose these items to the browser layer, but this is generally a personal choice and carries with it additional consequences as described in Chapter 6, *Working with Zope 3 Components.*

I deleted the folders mentioned above, as well as the `main.css` file. Then, I opened the file named `configure.zcml`, located at `plonetheme.guria/plonetheme/guria/ browser/`, and removed all of the following boilerplate text:

```
<!-- Viewlets registration -->
  <!-- Zope 3 browser resources -->
  <!-- Resource directory for images -->
  <browser:resourceDirectory
      name="plonetheme.guria.images"
      directory="images"
      layer=".interfaces.IThemeSpecific"
      />
  <!-- Resource directory for stylesheets -->
  <browser:resourceDirectory
      name="plonetheme.guria.stylesheets"
      directory="stylesheets"
      layer=".interfaces.IThemeSpecific"
      />
```

I then removed the highlighted code below from `plonetheme.guria/plonetheme/ guria/profiles/default/cssregistry.xml`:

```
<stylesheet title=""
    id="++resource++plonetheme.guria.stylesheets/main.css"
    media="screen" rel="stylesheet" rendering="import"
    cacheable="True" compression="safe" cookable="True"
    enabled="1" expression=""/>
```

And replaced it with the following:

```
<stylesheet title=""
    id="guria.css"
    media="screen" rel="stylesheet" rendering="import"
    cacheable="True" compression="safe" cookable="True"
    enabled="1" expression=""/>
```

This, in effect, tells our theme product that we will be using a stylesheet named `guria.css` (or more correctly, `guria.css.dtml`, as we'll see in a moment). This stylesheet does not yet exist, so we have to create it.

I wanted the option of making use of the **DTML** behavior provided by Plone, so that I could use certain base properties provided to us via the `base_properties.props` file (also located in our `skins/guria_styles/` folder). DTML essentially allows us to use property-sheet variables and apply changes on a more global scale. The easiest way to create this new stylesheet is to go to your `mybuildout/buildout-cache/ eggs/Plone[some version number]/Products/CMFPlone/skins/plone_styles/ ploneCustom.css` and copy the contents of that file into a new stylesheet (named `guria.css.dtml`) in your theme's `guria_styles/` folder (located in the `skins/` directory at `mybuildout/plonetheme.guria/plonetheme/guria/skins/guria_ styles`). The important bits of code you want are as follows:

```
/* <dtml-with base_properties> (do not remove this :) */
/* <dtml-call "REQUEST.set('portal_url', portal_url())"> (not this
                                              either :) */

/* DELETE THIS LINE AND PUT YOUR CUSTOM STUFF HERE */

/* </dtml-with> */
```

Again, we would need to restart our Zope at this point, as we have modified our ZCML.

If we had already installed our theme product, we'd also have to import our `cssregistry.xml` file via `portal_setup` in the ZMI, to capture the new GenericSetup profile settings. However, we have not yet installed the product, so we do not need to worry about this.

Installing the theme product

Now that we've looked a few of the changes we've made to distinguish our theme product from a default Plone theme, let's go ahead and install it. Some of you may already have installed your theme product, and that's okay.

Go to your Zope instance (for example, `http://localhost:8080/manage_main`), and choose **Plone Site** from the drop-down list on the top right. Or, you can go to this URL: `http://localhost:8080/manage_addProduct/CMFPlone/addPloneSite`.

You will then see the following screen. For the purposes of this chapter, we are calling our Plone site **mysite**. Make sure you add a description for your Plone site, as we'll need that later.

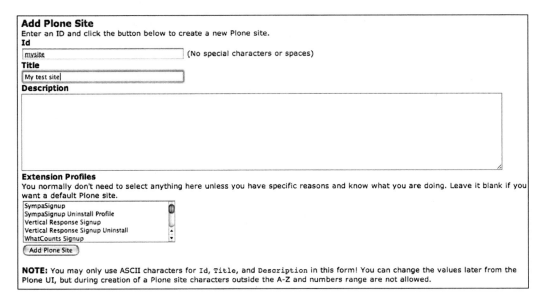

There are three ways to install your theme product:

- You could optionally choose the theme product from the **Extension Profiles** list (as seen in the previous screenshot)

- We could proceed to the `portal_quickinstaller` tool, located in the ZMI at `http://localhost:8080/mysite/portal_quickinstaller/manage_installProductsForm`

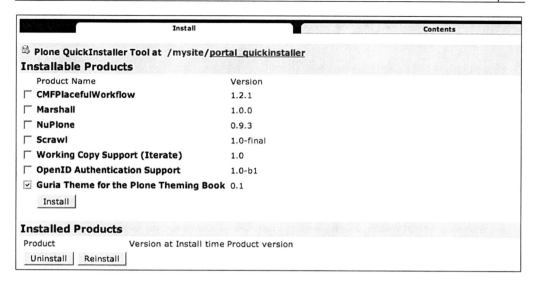

- We could go to **Site Setup | Add-on Products** at
  `http://localhost:8080/mysite/prefs_install_products_form`

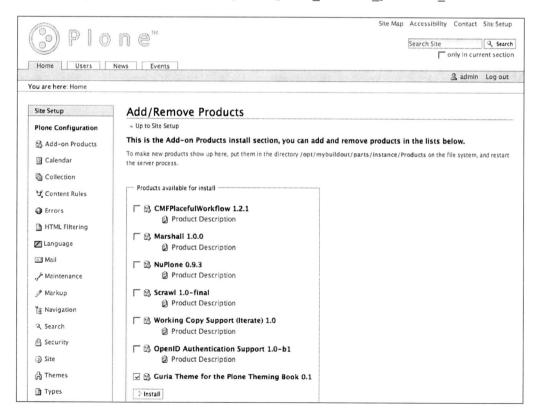

Let's select the extension profile named **Guria Theme for the Plone Theming Book** and click the **Install** button.

At this point, we should also put our site's `portal_css` in **debug mode,** so that we can see any CSS changes instantly. You should not leave a production site in debug mode, as it can negatively impact performance. You can reach the `portal_css` area at `http://localhost:8080/mysite/portal_css/manage_cssForm`. Simply select the **Debug/development mode** checkbox and press **Save**. The **Save** button may appear at the bottom of the page:

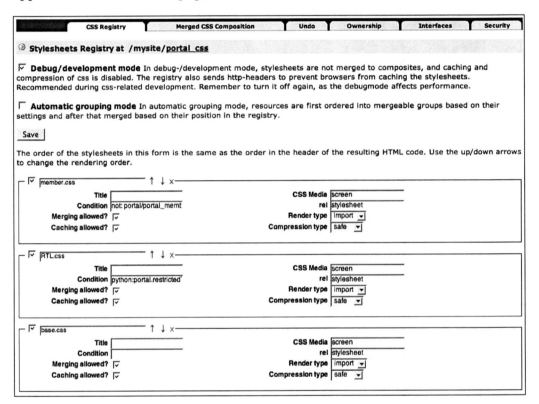

Now, if you visit your site's home page, you should see the installed product as seen next, but we need to do a few things to make it look fully formed.

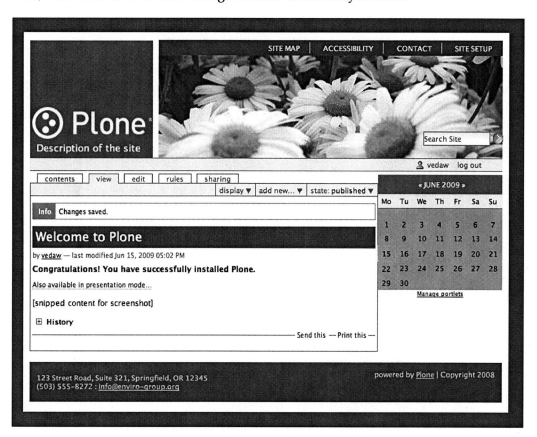

Adjusting web site content to support the design

As we can see, the installed theme does not exactly match the look of the first screenshot of this chapter. Many CSS styles are in place, but the searchbox is in the wrong location, and there is a calendar portlet present. You may also notice that breadcrumbs are not present, as they are suppressed using CSS styles. Additionally, the center page content is not yet populated.

To make the site look more realistic, we need to adjust our viewlets, as well as add and suppress some content and portlets on the web site to support the design.

First, let's adjust the viewlets on the site by going to `http://localhost:8081/mysite/@@manage-viewlets`. We have to do this because the Guria theme does not use ordering to organize the viewlets. At the time that the theme was created, ordering was not functional, but should be now. Using the up arrow, next to the searchbox with the orange "Go" button, you can move the viewlet directly below the viewlet called `ViewletManager: plone.portaltop (plone.app.layout.viewlets.interfaces.IPortalTop)`:

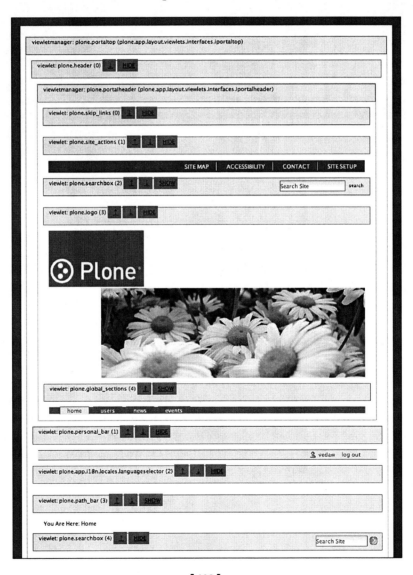

This should move the searchbox into the proper location.

Next, we want to add five new folders. To do so, use the **Add** menu located on the home page, and choose the **Folder** option. You should create some sub-navigation items (pages or folders are easiest) for at least one of these sections to see the styling of sub-navigation items. Make sure you publish each of these items.

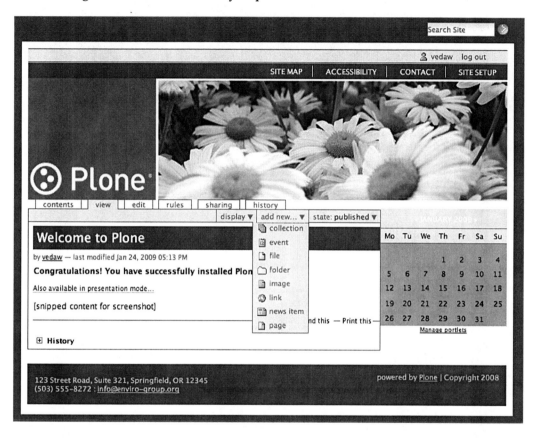

Once we have added a few folders, we need to adjust the settings of the navigation portlet. Click on the **Manage portlets** link on the bottom-right of the screen while on the home page, or go to `http://localhost:8080/mysite/@@manage-portlets`.

The navigation portlet has been added to the site by default. Click on the **Navigation portlet** link. You will see the following screen:

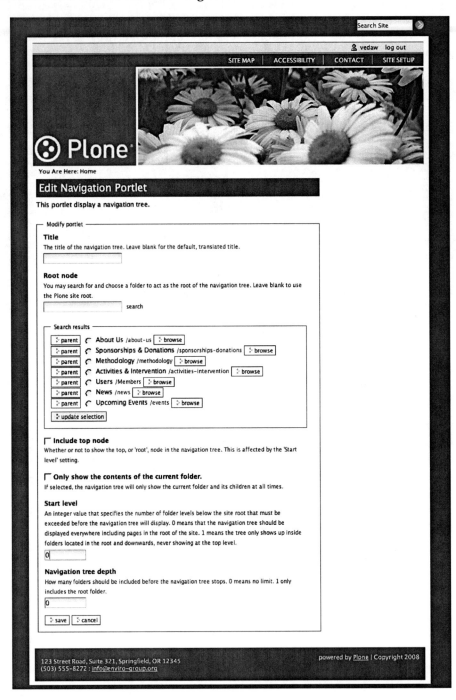

Give the portlet a name and set the start level to **0**. This will allow the navigation portlet to show on the home page. Choose **Save**, and then on the main `@@manage-portlets` screen, we want to remove the right-hand portlets. As you can see, these include **review List**, **News**, **Events**, and **calendar**:

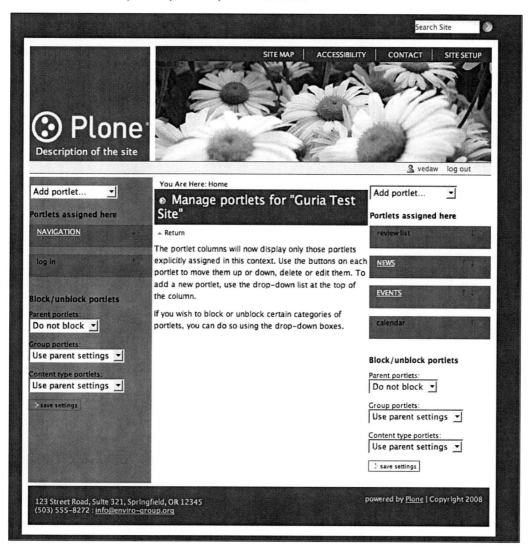

Click on the **X** next to each item to remove each portlet, then click on the Plone logo to return to the home page. You should see the left-hand navigation portlet and no portlets on the right-hand side of the page. This gives us what we need to finish building out our design.

The Guria theme was intended to use the `homepage_view` page template, as seen in the theme product's `skins/guria_templates` folder. This view requires the creation of a folder in the root of the site, called `homepage`, plus several pages (or collections) named `slot1`, `slot2`, and `slot3`. You can optionally create these too if you want to use this particular view.

The alternate view, `homepage2_view`, also located in the `skins/guria_templates` folder, requires the creation of a folder named `homesection` (slightly different from the `homepage_view` example, just to show the difference between the two views), plus the creation of several pages (not collections) named `r1c1` and `r1c2`. Make sure these names are the shortnames, not just the title of the pages.

Summary

In this chapter, we have learned how to:

- Create a custom theme product
- Modify the file structure
- Set up a Plone theme to use mostly skin layers for images and stylesheets
- Install the theme product
- Customize the content of your site to support the design

Next, we will look at how to do basic CSS styling, alter the logo, modify `portal_actions`, and work with viewlets and portlets.

10
General Styling and Templating Changes

Now that our theme product is installed, and we've got our Plone site ready to support the theme, we'll start looking at how the various components and skin layer items were changed, one at a time. Specifically, we'll look at basic styling and modification of viewlets and portlets.

Modifying the various sections of the page

In order to make many of the changes to our themes take effect, we should make sure that our theme product's `configure.zcml` file (not the `browser/configure.zcml` file) contains the following lines:

```
<include package=".browser" />
<include file="skins.zcml" />
<include file="profiles.zcml" />
```

These lines tell our theme product that it should respect any changes made to our `profiles.zcml` file (where our theme product's profile is registered with Zope), and also within the `browser/` folder, where many of our viewlets and page template changes will occur. These lines are added to the theme product by paster by default. It also tells our theme product to respect any filesystem directory views defined in `skins.zcml`.

Basic styling

As you can see by installing the theme, there is already some basic styling in place. Let's take a look at this styling. First, I set a few base properties in our theme product's `base_properties.props` file, located at `mybuildout/plonetheme.guria/plonetheme/guria/skins/guria_styles`:

```
title:string=guria's color, font, logo and border defaults

plone_skin:string=guria

logoName:string=logo.gif

fontFamily:string="Lucida Grande", Verdana, Lucida, Helvetica, Arial,
                                                          sans-serif

fontBaseSize:string=69%
fontColor:string=Black
fontSmallSize:string=85%

backgroundColor:string=#56492e

linkColor:string=#2e5256
linkActiveColor:string=Red
linkVisitedColor:string=Purple

borderWidth:string=1px
borderStyle:string=solid
borderStyleAnnotations:string=dashed

globalBorderColor:string=#79715f
globalBackgroundColor:string=#ffefca
globalFontColor:string=#79715f

headingFontFamily:string="Lucida Grande", Verdana, Lucida, Helvetica,
                                                 Arial, sans-serif

contentViewBorderColor:string=#79715f
contentViewBackgroundColor:string=#ffefca
contentViewFontColor:string=#79715f

inputFontColor:string=Black

textTransform:string=lowercase

evenRowBackgroundColor:string=transparent
oddRowBackgroundColor:string=transparent

notifyBorderColor:string=#ffa500
notifyBackgroundColor:string=#ffce7b

discreetColor:string=#76797c
helpBackgroundColor:string=#ffffe1

portalMinWidth:string=70em
columnOneWidth:string= 195px
columnTwoWidth:string=195px
```

If you compare this against a fresh `base_properties.props` file (found in `mybuildout/parts/plone/CMFPlone/plone_styles/` folder), you'll notice that the logo here points to a `.gif` file and a few backgrounds, border colors, and link colors have been adjusted, the background color has been adjusted, and column widths have been specified. This gives us some global settings to start with.

Then, I made a few changes in the `guria.css.dtml` stylesheet to control the basic framework of the page, using DTML syntax, as needed:

```
/*
   This file is based on the ploneCustom.css.dtml file shipped with
                                                              Plone.

   <dtml-with base_properties> (do not remove this)
   <dtml-call "REQUEST.set('portal_url', portal_url())"> (not this
                                                              either)
*/

/* YOUR CSS RULES START HERE */
#visual-portal-wrapper {
   width:733px;
   padding:10px;
   background-color:#fff;
   margin:60px auto auto auto;
}

h1 {
   background: &dtml-backgroundColor;;
   color:#fff;
   padding:5px;
}

h2 {
   border-bottom:1px dotted #56492e;
}

.documentContent {
   padding:0em .25em .25em .25em !important;
   background-color:#fff;
}

.documentActions li {
   background-color:#fff;
}

legend {
   background-color:transparent;
}
```

We have a brown background for our site, but not because we have defined it in our stylesheet. Instead, we are relying on Plone's default styling found in **CMFPlone's** `base.css` and `base_properties.props` files:

```
body {
    font: &dtml-fontBaseSize; <dtml-var fontFamily>;
    background-color: &dtml-backgroundColor;;
    color: &dtml-fontColor;;
    margin: 0;
    padding: 0;
}
```

The code that we did add in our stylesheet above sets the width of the wrapper around the content of the site and gives it some basic padding and margin settings. The `auto` settings for the `margin-left` and `margin-right` properties center the web site in the browser.

I also did some minor styling to the `h1` header to give it a brown background color and white text, plus some padding. I added a dotted border below the `h2` heading, and lastly, I added some padding around the content in the center of the page and a white background color. I use the `!important` declaration to override the `!important` declaration found in Plone's default `public.css` stylesheet located at `mybuildout/parts/plone/CMFPlone/skins/plone_styles`. I made the background color behind the document actions (print, email) white as well, and disabled the background color for "legend" areas, because they were picking up the dark brown color of the background.

I then adjusted the columns a bit to control the padding, margins, and background colors for `#portal-column-one` (the left column), `#portal-column-two` (the right column), and `#portal-column-content` (the middle column). `#portal-column-one` and `#portal-column-two` both pick up the widths defined in `base_properties.props`:

```
/****** COLUMNS *******/
#portal-columns {
    margin-top:5px;
    padding:5px;
    background-color:#fff;
}
#portal-column-one {
    background-color:#9d8d6b;
}
#portal-column-one .visualPadding {
    padding:0em 0em 0em 0em;
```

```
    }
    #portal-column-two {
        background-color:#fff;
    }
    #portal-column-two .visualPadding {
        padding:0em;
    }
    #portal-column-content {
        padding:0em;
    }
```

Here we are just establishing some basic padding, background-colors, and default widths.

The first column should be the width of the logo, or 195 pixels. Although we do not have a second column visible, because we removed the right-hand column in the previous chapter, we can set a default width in case we choose to add right-hand portlets at a later time. Rather than doing this in our stylesheet, we can do this in our base properties file, as seen here:

```
    columnOneWidth:string=195px
    columnTwoWidth:string=195px
```

This design does not lend itself well to having right-hand portlets, as it is quite skinny and specifically designed for a 600x800 aspect ratio (appropriate for web sites in countries where viewers may not have newer monitors). If you want to add right-hand portlets, you might want to consider increasing the width of the #visual-portal-wrapper, the header image, and the images that will appear in the center of the page).

We now have some basic styling in place, and it's time to move onto the other visual elements on the page.

Changing the logo

One of the most common tasks users want to accomplish is changing the logo on their site. In this case, we want to alter the logo image and also add the description of our site to the viewlet.

First, to alter the logo image, I took the simplest approach and modified base_ properties.props to look for a file named logo.gif located at mybuildout/ plonetheme.guria/plonetheme/guria/skins/guria_images. If the image exists, we're good to go.

However, it's worth knowing how the logo machinery works, because it can be a bit intimidating. If we look at the viewlet's class that renders the logo (located in `mybuildout/buildout-cache/eggs/plone.app.layout [some version number]/plone/app/layout/common.py`), it reads as follows:

```
class LogoViewlet(ViewletBase):
    index = ViewPageTemplateFile('logo.pt')
    def update(self):
        super(LogoViewlet, self).update()
        self.navigation_root_url = self.portal_state.navigation_
                                                      root_url()

        portal = self.portal_state.portal()
        logoName = portal.restrictedTraverse('base_properties').
                                                         logoName
        self.logo_tag = portal.restrictedTraverse(logoName).tag()
        self.portal_title = self.portal_state.portal_title()
```

This code tells us that Plone is looking at a page template named `logo.pt`, which in turn fetches `logoName` from the `base_properties.props` file. Based on that information, it looks up `logoName` in the object database and generates something called a `logoName` and a `logo_tag` attribute that will contain the actual `img` tag for the image, complete with `height` and `width` attributes. The actual image file is found through `restrictedTraverse`, which is a security-conscious (that is, restricted) way of finding something in the object database. When you encounter this in code, you may generally assume that the object is being sought in a skin layer, which is indeed where the image belongs.

If we then look at the `logo.pt` file shipped with `plone.app.layout`, we see that it reads as follows:

```
<a metal:define-macro="portal_logo"
    id="portal-logo"
    accesskey="1"
    tal:attributes="href view/navigation_root_url"
    i18n:domain="plone">
     <img src="logo.jpg" alt=""
          tal:replace="structure view/logo_tag" /></a>
```

At first blush, it looks as though it's actually looking for a file named `logo.jpg`, but that's not the case. Instead, the TAL statement here is doing a `tal:replace` and rendering the view's `logo_tag` attribute. We know from the above code that this contains the `img` tag for the image. In other words, it's looking for whatever image is specified in `base_properties.props`. In our case, this is `logo.gif`, and that `logo.gif` lives in our theme product at `mybuildout/plonetheme.guria/plonetheme/guria/skins/guria_images`.

If we look even deeper at the CMFPlone product, at `mybuildout/parts/plone/`
`CMFPlone/skins/plone_images`, you'll see that there is already a `logo.jpg` in our
skin layer. This means that all we need to do is have a correctly sized `logo.gif` in
our theme product's `guria_images/` folder to override that image, and we're done.

In order to add the description of our site to the logo viewlet, however, we need
to customize the viewlet. Based on our investigation above, we know that we are
working with a class-based viewlet. If we look in `configure.zcml`, located at
`mybuildout/buildout-cache/eggs/plone.app.layout[some version number]/`
`plone/app/layout/viewlets`, and search for "logo", we find the following code:

```
<!-- The logo -->
    <browser:viewlet
        name="plone.logo"
        manager=".interfaces.IPortalHeader"
        class=".common.LogoViewlet"
        permission="zope2.View"
        />
```

The most important thing to note is that no template is specified in the ZCML. We
are working with a class-based viewlet, and we'll need to override the class itself to
change the way it's rendered.

Next, we take the above code and insert it into our theme product's `configure.zcml`
file, located at `mybuildout/src/plonetheme.guria/plonetheme/guria/browser`,
below the viewlets registration. We adjust the code like this:

```
<!-- Viewlets registration -->

    <!-- The logo -->
    <browser:viewlet
        name="plone.logo"
        manager="plone.app.layout.viewlets.interfaces.IPortalHeader"
        class=".viewlets.LogoViewlet"
        permission="zope2.View"
        layer=".interfaces.IThemeSpecific"
        />
```

In this case, we are providing a dot-delimited path back to the original
`IPortalHeader` viewlet manager provided by `plone.app.layout`. We do this
because we are not moving anything, and the default behavior suits us.

> You could rename the viewlet here to something like `mytheme.logo`,
> if you wanted to be very explicit about indicating that the viewlet
> is now different from the original viewlet, but that's ultimately a
> personal preference.

Next, we adjust the `class` path so that it points to a Python class in our own `viewlets.py` file, here designated as `.viewlets.LogoViewlet`. Note that since this starts with a dot, it's relative to the directory containing the ZCML file. We have not yet added this class to our theme product (subclassed it from the original, actually), so let's do that now.

In `common.py`, which we opened above, search for "logo". We want to borrow only the first two lines of the code, which tell us the name of the `LogoViewlet` class and the page template we want to use:

```
class LogoViewlet(ViewletBase):
    index = ViewPageTemplateFile('logo.pt')
```

We will paste this into our `viewlets.py` file and make a few alterations. First, it's important to realize that our theme product doesn't know anything about something called `ViewletBase`, but that's okay, because we will be changing that.

We then make sure the following two lines are present at the top of our `viewlets.py` file:

```
from Products.Five.browser.pagetemplatefile import
                            ViewPageTemplateFile
from plone.app.layout.viewlets import common
```

The first line is already provided, but the second line we need to add. This line tells our theme product that it knows about the file named `common.py` that ships with `plone.app.viewlets`. We could be more Pythonic and just import the `LogoViewlet` from `common`, but since we'll be making other viewlet changes in our theme product, it's just as easy to import all of `common`.

Now, we adjust the code for our `LogoViewlet` class to look like this:

```
from Products.Five.browser.pagetemplatefile import
ViewPageTemplateFile
from plone.app.layout.viewlets import common

class LogoViewlet(common.LogoViewlet):
    """Alter the logo to include the description of our website
    """
    def render(self):
        return self.index()
    index = ViewPageTemplateFile('logo.pt')
```

By doing this, we are subclassing the `LogoViewlet` class defined in `common.py`. Our subclass will automatically do everything the `LogoViewlet` parent class does, except where we override the parent by telling it to look for a page template known as `logo.pt`. You may remember that the original `LogoViewlet` class also used `logo.pt` — but there's a big difference this time. Because the new class is inside our theme product, it will find our version of `logo.pt`, rather than the template in `plone.app.layout`. We also include a docstring here to explain what we're trying to achieve.

> This documentation on `plone.org` shows slightly different syntax when subclassing a viewlet: `http://plone.org/documentation/tutorial/customizing-main-template-viewlets/overriding-a-class-viewlet`. We've used the code seen above to ensure backwards compatibility with all 3.x Plone sites, but you could use the simplified code if you're not concerned with backwards compatibility.

Based on our modifications to `configure.zcml`, our theme product knows to look in our `browser/` directory for this `logo.pt` file.

Next, we copy the `logo.pt` file from `plone.app.layout` into our theme product's `browser/` folder. We want to modify this `logo.pt` file slightly to add an extra HTML tag that will contain the description of our web site, as seen here:

```
<a metal:define-macro="portal_logo"
   id="portal-logo"
   accesskey="1"
   tal:attributes="href view/navigation_root_url"
   i18n:domain="plone">
   <img src="logo.jpg" alt=""
        tal:replace="structure view/logo_tag" /></a>
<span class="description" tal:define="portal context/@@plone_portal_
state/portal" tal:content="portal/Description" />
```

So now, if we restart our Zope to make our ZCML changes take effect and look at the code on our home page using Firebug, we can see that the logo viewlet now displays the description of our web site (assuming one has been specified), in addition to the logo image. We can then position it as follows:

```
.description {
   color:#fff;
   position:absolute;
   top:155px;
   left:10px;
   font-size:140%;
}
```

We might as well define some basic styles for the `#portal-logo` id and the image it contains in our `guria_styles/guria.css.dtml` stylesheet:

```
/****** HEADER AREA *******/
#portal-logo {
    height:180px;
    width:190px;
    background-color:#94582e;
    float:left;
}
#portal-logo img {
    margin:115px 0em 0em 0em;
    float:left;
}
```

All we are doing is positioning the image, defining a height, width, and background color for the logo's `<a></a>` tags (see `logo.pt`), and doing some additional positioning.

As we've observed, we can modify the `logo.pt` file to render differently—either to include additional information, or even to modify how the theme product finds the logo image. For example, we could easily modify the `logo.pt` to look specifically in our theme product for an image and bypass the logo image defined in `base_properties.props`. This could be accomplished with the following code:

```
<a metal:define-macro="portal_logo1"
   id="portal-logo1"
   accesskey="1"
   tal:attributes="href view/navigation_root_url"
   i18n:domain="plone">
        <img src="" tal:define="img nocall:context/my_logo.gif"
             tal:attributes="src img/absolute_url"
             tal:on-error="nothing"
             alt="background image"/>
</a>
```

 Be warned that this approach may or may not work in Internet Explorer. I personally have not had issues with it, but there have been reports to the contrary.

Adding a banner image

If you examine the original design, you'll see that we also want to have a header image in the top area of our site (the daisies). An easy way to add a banner is to apply it to an existing data structure. In our case, we're going to apply it to the `#portal-header` id given to us by the `portal_header.pt` viewlet. We can find this CSS hook by viewing the source on our site.

All we need to do is describe the properties that define that id in our `guria_styles/guria.css.dtml` stylesheet:

```
#portal-header {
    background-image:url(&dtml-portal_url;/homepage_banner.jpg);
    background-position:bottom right;
    background-repeat:no-repeat;
    height:176px;
    width:733px;
    position:relative;
    padding-top:3px;
}
```

This code assigns a background image named `homepage_banner.jpg` to the `#portal-header` id (the image can be found in our theme product's `guria_images/` folder), assigns a default width and height, makes sure that the image doesn't repeat, and positions it.

We'll look at how you can assign different header images to different areas of your site in a few moments.

Customizing the portal actions

The portal actions are the links at the top of the page, specifically **Site Map**, **Accessibility**, **Contact**, and **Site Setup**. These links are added to the site via `portal_actions`, found at `http://localhost:8080/mysite/portal_actions/site_actions/manage_main` in the ZMI. Plone already gives you a few of these when a site is created, but you can also control them through the ZMI or through your filesystem-based theme product.

If you wished to make certain that additional items could be added to the `portal_actions` area of the page when a theme is installed, you could add a file named `actions.xml` to the theme product's `profiles/` directory located at `mybuildout/src/plonetheme.guria/plonetheme/guria/profiles/default/`. The code might contain information such as the following:

```
<object name="site_actions" meta_type="CMF Action Category">
    <object name="library" meta_type="CMF Action"
                         i18n:domain="plone">
     <property name="title" i18n:translate="">Library</property>
     <property name="description" i18n:translate=""></property>
     <property
        name="url_expr">string:${portal_url}/library</property>
     <property name="icon_expr"></property>
     <property name="available_expr"></property>
     <property name="permissions">
      <element value="View"/>
     </property>
     <property name="visible">True</property>
    </object>
    <object name="pressroom" meta_type="CMF Action"
                          i18n:domain="plone">
     <property name="title" i18n:translate="">Pressroom</property>
     <property name="description" i18n:translate=""></property>
     <property
        name="url_expr">string:${portal_url}/pressroom</property>
     <property name="icon_expr"></property>
     <property name="available_expr"></property>
     <property name="permissions">
      <element value="View"/>
     </property>
     <property name="visible">True</property>
    </object>
</object>
```

If you were uncertain of the format to follow, you can go to the `portal_setup` area, located at `http://localhost:8080/mysite/portal_setup/manage_exportSteps` (available via the **Export** tab at the top). Choose the **Action Providers** option, and click on the **Export** button.

The Guria theme does not use **GenericSetup** to manage the site actions options, as this is a distributed theme. Instead, users are required to manage the items in this area manually via the `portal_actions` area of the ZMI, or to modify the theme product further as described above. Let's style the default site actions that ship with Plone:

```
/**** SITE ACTIONS ****/
#portal-siteactions {
    background-color:#56492e;
    padding:5px 0em;
    text-align:right;
    position:absolute;
    width:534px;
    margin-left:199px;
    margin-top:-1px;
}

* html #portal-siteactions {
    margin-left:5px;
    margin-top:0px;
}

*+html #portal-siteactions {
    margin-left:9px;
    margin-top:0px;
}

#portal-siteactions li {
    border:none;
}

#portal-siteactions li a {
    color:#fff;
    border-width:0px 1px 0px 0px;
    border-style:solid;
    border-color:#fff;
    padding-right:15px;
    padding-left:15px;
    text-transform:uppercase;
}

#portal-siteactions li.last-action a {
    border-width:0;
}

#portal-siteactions li a:hover {
    border-width:0px 1px 0px 0px;
    border-color:#fff;
    background-color:transparent;
}

#portal-siteactions li.last-action a:hover {
    border-width:0;
}
```

The `#portal-siteactions` spans the width of the page, and therefore we need to set a background color for the entire container. Some additional padding is also necessary, and the items are set to align to the right of the page. Each individual list item link is set to have a one-pixel, solid, white border on the right side. They also have padding and are set to display in all uppercase.

To fix an Internet Explorer 6 problem with positioning, we insert this hack:

```
* html #portal-siteactions {
    margin-left:5px;
    margin-top:0px;
}
```

And for IE7, we inserted the following hack:

```
*+html #portal-siteactions {
    margin-left:9px;
    margin-top:0px;
}
```

When the user hovers over each item, the above settings remain, but the color of each link changes. This color is controlled by Plone's `public.css` file, which relies on the use of DTML and base properties:

```
#portal-siteactions li a:hover {
    background-color: &dtml-globalBackgroundColor;;
    color: &dtml-globalFontColor;;
    border: &dtml-borderWidth; &dtml-borderStyle; &dtml-
                                    globalBorderColor;;
}
```

We only override the items we don't want from Plone's `public.css` file, specifically the `background-color` and the `border` properties. We don't need to respecify the pieces we want to keep.

You'll also notice in the Guria theme's CSS that there is a rule that mentions a last action:

```
#portal-siteactions li.last-action a:hover {
    border-width:0;
}
```

Plone, by default, does not provide a hook to sniff out what the last item in the list is. This means that we need to customize the viewlet that renders these site actions.

If you wanted to suppress a border on the last item in the list of site actions using CSS (each list item has a unique CSS id), you could. In sites where some site actions are only visible to logged-in users, when a user logs in, more items are added to the site actions area, and the suppressed right-hand border is often assigned only to the last item in the list that is seen in logged-out state. This can appear sloppy.

It is best to assume that the site actions will be in flux, and that we will never know the CSS id of the last item in the list. However, we will always know that one item will always be the last item with a class of `.last-action`, and can style it appropriately.

To customize the viewlet to make this behavior more bullet-proof, open `common.py` and `configure.zcml` found at `mybuildout/buildout-cache/eggs/plone.app.layout[some version number]/plone/app/layout/viewlets`.

Searching for "siteactions" or "site actions" in `configure.zcml` yields the following code:

```
<!-- The site actions -->
    <browser:viewlet
        name="plone.site_actions"
        manager=".interfaces.IPortalHeader"
        class=".common.SiteActionsViewlet"
        permission="zope2.View"
        />
```

This tells us that we are working with a class-based viewlet. We copy this code into the theme product's `browser/configure.zcml` file located at `mybuildout/plonetheme.guria/plonetheme/guria/browser/`. We then modify it like this:

```
<!-- The site actions -->
    <browser:viewlet
        name="plone.site_actions"
        manager="plone.app.layout.viewlets.interfaces.IPortalHeader"
        class=".viewlets.SiteActionsViewlet"
        template="site_actions.pt"
        layer=".interfaces.IThemeSpecific"
        permission="zope2.View"
        />
```

This code provides a dot-delimited path back to the original viewlet manager provided by `plone.app.layout`, because we don't want to move it on the page. It looks at `plone.app.viewlet`'s original `SiteActionsViewlet` class, and at a locally-defined `site_actions.pt`. It is specific to the current theme via the `IThemeSpecific` declaration.

Again, you could rename the viewlet to something like `mytheme.site_actions` if you wanted to, just make sure that all of your code matches up to that name and modify `viewlets.xml` if you need to.

If we open the original `site_actions.pt` file, found in the `plone.app.layout` package, we can see the following code:

```
<ul id="portal-siteactions"
    tal:define="accesskeys python: {'sitemap' : '3', 'accessibility'
                                     : '0', 'contact' : '9'};"
    tal:condition="view/site_actions"
    i18n:domain="plone">

    <li tal:repeat="saction view/site_actions"
        tal:attributes="id string:siteaction-${saction/id}"><a
            href=""
            tal:define="title saction/title;
                        id saction/id;
                        accesskey python: accesskeys.get(id, '');"
            i18n:attributes="title"
            i18n:translate=""
            tal:content="title"
            tal:attributes="href saction/url;
                            title title;
                            accesskey accesskey;"
        >Site action</a></li>

</ul>
```

As you can see, there is no code here that assigns a CSS selector to the last item in the list. We therefore need to copy this template to our `browser/` folder and modify the code as follows:

```
<ul id="portal-siteactions"
    tal:define="accesskeys python: {'sitemap' : '3', 'accessibility'
                                     : '0', 'contact' : '9'};"
    tal:condition="view/site_actions"
    i18n:domain="plone">

    <tal:loop tal:repeat="saction view/site_actions">
    <li tal:define="first python: repeat['saction'].start and 'first-
                                                           action' or '';
                    last python: repeat['saction'].end and 'last-
                                                           action' or '';
                    position python: first or last or 'plain';"
        tal:attributes="id string:siteaction-${saction/id};
```

```
                              class position">
    <a href=""
          tal:define="title saction/title;
                      id saction/id;
                      accesskey python: accesskeys.get(id, '');"
          i18n:attributes="title"
          i18n:translate=""
          tal:content="title"
          tal:attributes="href saction/url;
                          title title;
                          accesskey accesskey;"
          >Site action</a></li>
    </tal:loop>
</ul>
```

This code gives us class selector hooks for the first or the last item in the list, and allows us to declare CSS to not show a border on the right side of the last item, like this:

```
#portal-siteactions li.last-action a:hover {
   border-width:0;
}
```

The rendered HTML will look something like this, with the CSS selectors in place:

```
<ul id="portal-siteactions">

   <li id="siteaction-sitemap" class="first-action"><a
   href="http://localhost:8081/themingbook/sitemap"
   accesskey="3" title="Site Map">Site Map</a></li>

   <li id="siteaction-accessibility" class="plain"><a
   href="http://localhost:8081/themingbook/accessibility-info"
   accesskey="0" title="Accessibility">Accessibility</a></li>

   <li id="siteaction-contact" class="plain"><a
   href="http://localhost:8081/themingbook/contact-info"
   accesskey="9" title="Contact">Contact</a></li>

   <li id="siteaction-plone_setup" class="last-action"><a
   href="http://localhost:8081/themingbook/plone_control_panel"
   accesskey="" title="Site Setup">Site Setup</a></li>

</ul>
```

Even if the first/last/plain code seems a bit tricky, it establishes a pattern that you'll find very useful any time you need CSS selectors applied to the beginning and/or end of a set of repeated elements. You may want to read the template code again to see how this might be applied in other scenarios.

Adjusting the searchbox display

Next, we want to adjust the look and feel of the searchbox. Plone, by default, gives us a "search only in this section" option that is useful but may not lend itself well to a design. We provide some basic styling and positioning to the searchbox and also suppress the "search by section" feature:

```
/****** SEARCHBOX ******/

#portal-searchbox {
    position:relative;
    z-index:20;
    opacity:1;
    padding:0px 0px 0px 5px;
    margin-right:0px;
    margin-top:-40px;
    float:right;
}
.searchSection {
    display:none;
}
input.searchButton {
    background-color:transparent;
    background-image:none;
    border:0;
    padding:1px;
}
#searchGadget {
    padding:3px 0px;
}
```

We then apply some light styling to the livesearch drop-down menu to give it a white background color and no borders:

```
.LSIEFix {
    background-color:#fff;
}
.LSRow {
    border:0px;
}
legend#livesearchLegend {
    background-color:#fff;
}
```

As seen above, we also disabled the background "magnifying glass" image on the search button that Plone usually gives us (`input.searchButton`), and instead do not use a background image at all. Additionally, we removed the background color and the border around that button, plus a little padding. We want to render an actual image as the search button. To do so, we must modify the viewlet that renders the searchbox. By now, you should be beginning to get familiar with the procedure: find the ZCML for the viewlet and find the Python class code and template. Then, copy them to our theme product, and modify each to fit our requirements.

Open `configure.zcml` and `common.py` found in `mybuildout/buildout-cache/` `eggs/plone.app.layout`[some version number]`/plone/app/layout/`. The `configure.zcml` file gives us the following code:

```
<!-- The search box -->
    <browser:viewlet
        name="plone.searchbox"
        manager=".interfaces.IPortalHeader"
        class=".common.SearchBoxViewlet"
        permission="zope2.View"
        />
```

Again, this tells us that we are working with a class-based viewlet. We copy this text into our theme product's `browser/configure.zcml` file, located at `plonetheme.` `guria/plonetheme/guria/browser/`, and modify it as follows:

```
<!-- The search box -->
    <browser:viewlet
        name="plone.searchbox"
        manager="plone.app.layout.viewlets.interfaces.IPortalTop"
        class=".viewlets.SearchBoxViewlet"
        permission="zope2.View"
        layer=".interfaces.IThemeSpecific"
        />
```

This modified markup for the template provides a dot-delimited path back to a different viewlet manager so that we can move the viewlet. It looks at our theme product's `viewlets.py` file and is specific to the current theme product.

Next, we copy the first two lines of the code for `plone.searchbox` from `common.py` into our theme product's `viewlets.py`:

```
class SearchBoxViewlet(ViewletBase):
    index = ViewPageTemplateFile('searchbox.pt')

    def update(self):
        super(SearchBoxViewlet, self).update()
```

```
context_state = getMultiAdapter((self.context, self.request),
                                name=u'plone_context_state')

props = getToolByName(self.context, 'portal_properties')
livesearch = props.site_properties.getProperty
                    ('enable_livesearch', False)
if livesearch:
    self.search_input_id = "searchGadget"
else:
    self.search_input_id = ""

folder = context_state.folder()
self.folder_path = '/'.join(folder.getPhysicalPath())
```

We then adjust the code in our `viewlets.py` file as follows:

```
class SearchBoxViewlet(common.SearchBoxViewlet):
    """Customizing the searchbox to use the locally defined page
                                                    template
    """
    def render(self):
        return self.index()
    index = ViewPageTemplateFile('searchbox.pt')
```

Again, we are merely subclassing the viewlet and telling it to look at our locally-defined `searchbox.pt`, found in the theme product's `browser/` folder.

The modified markup for the template is as follows:

```
<div id="portal-searchbox"
    i18n:domain="plone">
  <form name="searchform"
        action="search"
        tal:attributes="action string:${view/site_url}/search">
      <label for="searchGadget" class="hiddenStructure"
              i18n:translate="text_search">Search Site</label>
      <div class="LSBox">
  <!-- shorten the width of the search box -->
      <input name="SearchableText"
            type="text"
            size="14"
            value=""
            title="Search Site"
            accesskey="4"
            i18n:attributes="title title_search_site;"
            tal:attributes="value request/SearchableText|nothing;
```

```
                               id view/search_input_id"
                    class="inputLabel" />
    <!-- use an actual search button instead of an input field -->

    <!--        <input class="searchButton"
                type="submit"
                value="Search"
                i18n:attributes="value label_search;" /> -->

            <input type="image"
                class="searchButton"
                name="submit"
                alt="submit"
                value="Search"
                tal:attributes="src string:${view/portal_url}
                                    /search_btn.gif;" />

<!-- this bit will be hidden with CSS -->
        <div class="searchSection">
            <input id="searchbox_currentfolder_only"
                class="noborder"
                type="checkbox"
                name="path"
                tal:attributes="value view/folder_path"
                />
            <label for="searchbox_currentfolder_only"
                i18n:translate="label_searchbox_currentfolder_only"
                style="cursor: pointer">
                only in current section
            </label>
        </div>
<!-- end hiding -->
        <div class="LSResult" id="LSResult" style=""><div
            class="LSShadow" id="LSShadow"></div></div>
        </div>
    </form>

    <div id="portal-advanced-search"
        class="hiddenStructure">
        <a href="#"
            tal:attributes="href string:${view/site_url}/search_form"
            i18n:translate="label_advanced_search"
            accesskey="5">
            Advanced Search&hellip;
        </a>
    </div>
</div>
```

In other words, we are removing the default behavior that renders an `input` field and are instead rendering an actual search button named `search_btn.gif`. This image is located in our theme product's `skins/guria_images` folder.

Moving the searchbox

But wait! There's more. If we double back to our theme product's `configure.zcml` and look at the viewlet manager specified, we see that the searchbox is now assigned to the `IPortalTop` viewlet manager:

```
<!-- The search box -->
    <browser:viewlet
        name="plone.searchbox"
        manager="plone.app.layout.viewlets.interfaces.IPortalTop"
        class=".viewlets.SearchBoxViewlet"
        permission="zope2.View"
        layer=".interfaces.IThemeSpecific"
        />
```

Default Plone renders the search button in the `IPortalHeader` viewlet manager, but we want the search button slightly higher than normal. Perhaps we could accomplish this with pure CSS, but it's just as easy to move the viewlet to a different manager. This means that we must now move the existing `plone.searchbox` viewlet within our theme product's `viewlets.xml` file located at `mybuildout/plonetheme.guria/plonetheme/guria/profiles/default`:

```
<?xml version="1.0"?>
<object>
  <order manager="plone.portaltop" skinname="Guria Theme for the
                    Plone Theming Book" based-on="Plone Default">
   <viewlet name="plone.searchbox" />
   <viewlet name="plone.personal_bar" />
  </order>
  <order manager="plone.contentviews" skinname="Guria Theme for the
                    Plone Theming Book" based-on="Plone Default">
   <viewlet name="plone.path_bar" />
  </order>
  <hidden manager="plone.portaltop" skinname="Guria Theme for the
                                              Plone Theming Book">
   <viewlet name="plone.path_bar" />
  </hidden>
  <hidden manager="plone.portalheader" skinname="Guria Theme for the
                                              Plone Theming Book">
    <viewlet name="plone.searchbox" />
    <viewlet name="plone.global_sections" />
  </hidden>
</object>
```

At the same time, we must also hide the default searchbox viewlet provided by Plone. Notice how the new viewlet is assigned to the skinname `Guria Theme for the Plone Theming Book` and the hidden viewlet is hidden also from the `Guria Theme for the Plone Theming Book` skinname. This `skinname` comes from the `profiles.zcml` file in our theme. The format is like this because we are extending base Plone, and we don't want to remove any of the power from `Plone Default`.

There are other viewlets that have been manipulated here in `viewlets.xml`, and we'll get to those momentarily.

It's worth noting that "insert-before" or "insert-after" syntax may not work (this is fixed in later versions of Plone 3.x), and you might have to reorder the viewlets by hand using the `@@manage-viewlets` tool: `http://localhost:8081/mysite/@@manage-viewlets`. We're not going to worry about ordering of viewlets in this case.

Moreover, there is some jeopardy in moving viewlets into the `IPortalTop` viewlet manager. The point of keeping viewlets in `IPortalHeader` is that we have "Skip to Content" and "Skip to Navigation" links that have to be at the top of the page when viewed in a text or voice browser, for accessibility reasons. If we move any viewlet to `IPortalTop` and place it above `IPortalHeader`, those useful links are not at the topmost part of the page. This, in turn, weakens the accessibility of the Plone site. It might make more sense to create a new viewlet manager directly below `IPortalTop`.

If we want to see our changes take effect, we must either install the theme on a fresh Plone site, or we can import the `viewlets.xml` GenericSetup step via `portal_setup` in the ZMI, making sure we select our theme as the profile: `http://localhost:8081/mysite/portal_setup/manage_importSteps`. We'll also need to restart our Zope instance because we altered `configure.zcml`. Reinstalling the theme product is not advised.

Adjusting the personal bar

Next, we look at the personal bar. This is the bar that lists the **login/logout** links and also displays the user icon with a link to a **Preferences** panel. We want to adjust the location of this bar. We don't really need to move it to a new viewlet manager; we only want to move it so that it appears below the searchbox.

Again, due to accessibility reasons, this may not be the best thing to do. It might make more sense to move the personal bar to the footer area where it is less likely to interfere with the look and feel of the site, but that's a task for another day.

To do so, we make a quick adjustment in our theme product's `profiles/default/ viewlets.xml` file:

```
<?xml version="1.0"?>
<object>
  <order manager="plone.portaltop" skinname="Guria Theme for the
                  Plone Theming Book" based-on="Plone Default">
   <viewlet name="plone.searchbox" />
   <viewlet name="plone.personal_bar" />
  </order>
...
</object>
```

All we do is tell our viewlet to appear after the searchbox. We would then import our `viewlets.xml` file in `site_setup` in the ZMI after making this change.

Additionally, we add a bit of CSS code to support the layout of the personal bar:

```
/**** PERSONAL TOOLS ****/
#portal-personaltools {
    clear:both;
}
```

All we want is to make sure that the personal bar continues to stretch across the width of the page and does not get stepped on by other elements on the page. A visual "clear" gives us this.

Suppressing the top navigation

Now we want to examine the top navigation. Normally on a Plone site, you see top-level tabs that can be used to focus the navigation. Additionally, installing a product called `webcouturier.dropdownmenu` (`http://plone.org/products/ webcouturier-dropdownmenu/`) can enhance this navigation code. Installing it immediately provides drop-down navigation that can be styled via CSS. If you have already customized the global navigation viewlet, this may not work out of the box, and you'll have to subclass from the `webcouturier.dropdownmenu` viewlet.

In our case, we want to suppress the top navigation entirely. We could do this via CSS, or we could remove it entirely by suppressing the viewlet itself. In the Guria theme product, we suppress it via our `viewlets.xml` file located at `mybuildout/ src/plonetheme.guria/plonetheme/guria/profiles.zcml`:

```
<?xml version="1.0"?>
<object>
...

  <hidden manager="plone.portalheader" skinname="Guria Theme for the
                  Plone Theming Book" >
```

```
      <viewlet name="plone.searchbox" />
      <viewlet name="plone.global_sections" />
    </hidden>
  </object>
```

Again, this change would require importing the "viewlets" **GenericSetup** step via `portal_setup`.

Moving and styling the breadcrumbs

Next, let's look at the breadcrumbs. By default, Plone displays the breadcrumbs above the three columns that comprise the left, right, and middle content areas. In our case, we want to move these breadcrumbs directly above the center content, above the tabs available for logged-in and permissioned users for managing content (**Contents**, **Edit**, and so on.).

We know that we need to move the viewlet in our `viewlets.xml` file:

```
  <?xml version="1.0"?>
  <object>
  ...
    <order manager="plone.contentviews" skinname=" Guria Theme for the
                        Plone Theming Book" based-on="Plone Default">
    <viewlet name="plone.path_bar" />
    </order>
    <hidden manager="plone.portaltop" skinname="Guria Theme for the
                                        Plone Theming Book" >
    <viewlet name="plone.path_bar" />
    </hidden>
  ...
  </object>
```

The viewlet manager known as `plone.contentviews` displays directly above the center content. We can use `@@manage-viewlets` to verify this, if necessary: `http://localhost:8080/mysite/@@manage-viewlets`.

Next, we need to see if we are dealing with a class-based or template-based viewlet. Open `common.py` and `configure.zcml` file in `plone.app.layout`, located at `mybuildout/buildout-cache/eggs/plone.app.layout[some version number]/plone/app/layout/`. Searching for "pathbar" in `configure.zcml` gives us:

```
  <!-- The breadcrumbs -->
    <browser:viewlet
        name="plone.path_bar"
        manager=".interfaces.IPortalTop"
        class=".common.PathBarViewlet"
        permission="zope2.View"
        />
```

This tells us that we are working with a class-based viewlet. We copy this code into our theme product's `browser/configure.zcml` file and modify it as follows:

```
<!-- The breadcrumbs -->
    <browser:viewlet
        name="plone.path_bar"
        manager="plone.app.layout.viewlets.interfaces.IContentViews"
        class=".viewlets.PathBarViewlet"
        permission="zope2.View"
        layer=".interfaces.IThemeSpecific"
        />
```

Notice that we are providing a dot-delimited path back to the `IContentViews` manager (not to the `IPortalTop` viewlet manager normally used in base Plone). Additionally, we want to subclass the `PathBarViewlet` class, because we want to alter the divider normally seen between breadcrumbs to make them more visually appealing.

We copy the following two lines from `plone.app.layout`'s `common.py` into our theme product's `browser/viewlets.py` file:

```
class PathBarViewlet(ViewletBase):
    index = ViewPageTemplateFile('path_bar.pt')
```

We then modify the lines as follows:

```
class PathBarViewlet(common.PathBarViewlet):
    """Moving to a new viewlet manager and adjusting the dividers
    """
    def render(self):
        return self.index()
    index = ViewPageTemplateFile('path_bar.pt')
```

Next, we copy the `path_bar.pt` file, found in `plone.app.layout`, to our `browser/` folder and alter it to use `&raquo;` instead of `&rarr;` and `&laquo;` instead of `&larr;`.

```
<div id="portal-breadcrumbs"
    i18n:domain="plone">

    <span id="breadcrumbs-you-are-here" i18n:translate=
                "you_are_here">You are here:</span>
    <a i18n:translate="tabs_home" tal:attributes="href
                view/navigation_root_url">Home</a>
    <span tal:condition="view/breadcrumbs"
            class="breadcrumbSeparator">
        <tal:ltr condition="not: view/is_rtl">&raquo;</tal:ltr>
```

```
    <tal:rtl condition="view/is_rtl">&laquo;</tal:rtl>
</span>
<span tal:repeat="crumb view/breadcrumbs"
      tal:attributes="dir python:view.is_rtl and 'rtl' or 'ltr'">
    <tal:last tal:define="is_last repeat/crumb/end">
        <a href="#"
           tal:omit-tag="not: crumb/absolute_url"
           tal:condition="python:not is_last"
           tal:attributes="href crumb/absolute_url"
           tal:content="crumb/Title">
            crumb
        </a>
        <span class="breadcrumbSeparator" tal:condition="not:
                                                         is_last">
            <tal:ltr condition="not: view/is_rtl">
                              &raquo;</tal:ltr>
            <tal:rtl condition="view/is_rtl">&laquo;</tal:rtl>
        </span>
        <span tal:condition="is_last"
              tal:content="crumb/Title">crumb</span>
    </tal:last>
</span>
</div>
```

We then need to do some basic styling of the breadcrumbs:

```
/**** BREADCRUMBS ****/
#portal-breadcrumbs {
    border-bottom:none;
    text-transform:capitalize;
    padding-left:1em;
}
.section-front-page #portal-breadcrumbs {
    display:none;
}
```

We remove the border that normally displays below the breadcrumbs, capitalize
them, and add a little padding. We also suppress them from the home page using the
hook that Plone gives us using the shortname of the page. In this case, the CSS hook
is .section-front-page. While this shortname can be a little brittle, most Plone sites use
front-page as the default home page shortname. It's generally sufficient to advise
site administrators not to change this shortname in order to keep the CSS styling
intact. For more information on this, you can look at the discussion on sectional
styling in the next chapter.

Because we changed ZCML, we need to restart Plone, and because we altered the
viewlets.xml file, we also need to import the "viewlets" step using portal_setup
in the ZMI.

Base portlet styling

Now we need to look at what a portlet might look like. We can add a couple of test portlets to the left column using `http://localhost:8080/mysite/@@ manage-portlets`. Most portlets in Plone follow some basic styling—they have a `.portletHeader`, a `.portletItem`, a `.portletFooter`, and so on. This means that we can write some basic CSS to handle the display of these items:

```css
/**** BASE PORTLET STYLES ****/
.portlet {
    border:none;
    background-color:#bcb29c;
    margin-bottom:0em;
    margin-top:0px;
}
.portlet a {
    color:#fff !important;
}
.portletHeader {
    background-color:#807554 !important;
    border:none;
    text-transform:uppercase;
    color:#fff;
    padding:.5em .5em .5em 1em;
}
.portletHeader a {
    background-color:#807554;
    border:none;
    text-transform:uppercase;
    color:#fff;
}
.managedPortlet .portletHeader, .managedPortlet .portletHeader a {
    color:#000;
}
.portletHeader a {
    color:#fff;
}
.portletFooter {
    border:none;
}
.portletItem {
    background-color:none;
    border:none;
}
```

Much of this code can be grabbed from CMFPlone's `portlets.css` stylesheet, located at `mybuildout/buildout-cache/eggs/Plone[some version number]/Products/CMFPlone/skins/plone_styles`. We only override some of the borders, adjust some background colors and font colors, and adjust the padding. We also have to force the link color in order to override an `!important` declaration in Plone's `portlets.css` file. Similarly, we have to force the color of the header to override another `!important` declaration on the `.portletHeader`.

The most important thing to be aware of here is that some `.portletHeader` elements have an anchor tag contained within them, and those anchor tags might accidentally pick up a font color defined by base properties. It's important to write code to support that possible scenario, as we've done here.

Adjusting the footer and the colophon

Now we can also do some basic adjustment to the footer and the colophon. Based on the design, we see that the footer and the colophon are contained within a box with a brown background-color, and that the elements are in approximately the same location as they would be in a default Plone site. We need to add a wrapper around these elements to create that brown container.

One of the easiest ways to accomplish this is to modify the `main_template.pt` found in CMFPlone at `mybuildout/buildout-cache/eggs/Plone[some version number]/Products/CMFPlone/skins/plone_templates`. You could certainly create a new viewlet manager if you wished, and thereby minimize upgrade issues that might involve changes to the `main_template.pt`, but you should not be afraid of modifying `main_template.pt`.

 Viewlet managers are explained at `http://plone.org/documentation/how-to/adding-portlet-managers` and `http://plone.org/documentation/manual/theme-reference/elements/viewletmanager/override`.

For now, we're just going to modify `main_template.pt` by adding the wrapper. First, we need to copy the file from CMFPlone and put it into our theme product's `skins/guria_templates` folder:

```
<!-- wrapping the footer and colophon so we can apply a bg color they
                                                   will share -->

<div id="footer-colophon-wrapper">
        <div tal:replace="structure provider:plone.portalfooter" />
</div>
```

The world doesn't revolve around viewlets, but it's certainly the core of theming. In the past, most changes to web sites involved modifying `main_template.pt` or templates such as `document_view.pt`, and that's still perfectly legal. Hypothetically, though, we could insert anything into the `main_template.pt`, including TAL statements or basic XHTML, as we've done here.

We next need to do a bit of CSS styling, taking care to make sure the anchor tags also receive some special attention:

```
/**** FOOTER AND COLOPHON AREA ****/
#footer-colophon-wrapper {
    background-color:#56492e;
    width:733px;
    height:60px;
    margin-top:5px;
}

#portal-footer {
    color:#cccc99;
    width:40%;
    text-align:left;
    float:left;
    background-color:transparent;
    border:0;
    padding-left:1em;
    margin-top:1em;
}

#portal-footer a {
    color:#cccc99 !important;
    text-decoration:underline;
}

#portal-colophon {
    color:#cccc99;
    text-align:right;
    width:40%;
    float:right;
    padding-right:1em;
    margin-top:1em;
}

#portal-colophon a {
    color:#cccc99 !important;
    text-decoration:underline;
}
```

This code defines a background color for the wrapper element, plus a width, height, and some padding. Then, we alter some of the Plone's default styling of the footer and colophon to remove background colors and borders, then define widths for each of those items and position them next to each other. Finally, they are assigned colors and underlines for anchor tags.

However, there is more to be done. We want to customize the footer and colophon to contain some custom text. Open the `configure.zcml` file, located in `plone.app.layout` at `mybuildout/buildout-cache/eggs/plone.app.layout` [some version number] `/plone/app/layout/`, and search for "footer" and "colophon". The code is as follows:

```
<!-- Footer -->
    <browser:viewlet
        name="plone.footer"
        for="*"
        manager=".interfaces.IPortalFooter"
        template="footer.pt"
        permission="zope.Public"
        />

    <!-- Colophon -->
    <browser:viewlet
        name="plone.colophon"
        for="*"
        manager=".interfaces.IPortalFooter"
        template="colophon.pt"
        permission="zope.Public"
        />
```

We copy this code into our theme product's `browser/configure.zcml` file, located at `plonetheme.guria/plonetheme/guria/browser/`, and modify it as follows:

```
<browser:viewlet
        name="plone.footer"
        manager="plone.app.layout.viewlets.interfaces.IPortalFooter"
        layer=".interfaces.IThemeSpecific"
        template="footer.pt"
        permission="zope2.View"
        />
    <browser:viewlet
        name="plone.colophon"
        manager="plone.app.layout.viewlets.interfaces.IPortalFooter"
        layer=".interfaces.IThemeSpecific"
        template="colophon.pt"
        permission="zope2.View"
        />
```

For both of these elements, we provide a dot-delimited path back to the `IPortalFooter` viewlet manager. We don't need to move these items, so it's fine to leave them assigned to `IPortalFooter`. We also notice that neither of these viewlets is class-based, and hence they list the `footer.pt` and `colophon.pt` page templates. That means we don't need to do anything to `viewlets.py`. We also use the `IThemeSpecific` designation here to apply our changes to this theme product only.

Next, we copy the `footer.pt` and `colophon.pt` files, found in `plone.app.layout`, into our theme product's `browser/` folder. We then modify the `footer.pt` as follows:

```
<div class="vcard"
    id="portal-footer"
    metal:define-macro="portal_footer"
    i18n:domain="plone">

        <tal:comment tal:condition="nothing">
            Use hCard formatting for contact info.
        </tal:comment>

    <div class="fn org hiddenStructure"
        i18n:translate="footer_txt_org_name">
        ORGANIZATION'S NAME GOES HERE!!!  It will be hidden by CSS;
                                        we need it
        only for hCard compliance. This should be filled in if you
                                use this theme for your site.
    </div>

    <div class="adr">
        <span class="street-address"
            i18n:translate="footer_txt_addr">123 Street
                                        Road</span>,
        <span class="extended-address"
            i18n:translate="footer_txt_ext_addr">Suite 321</span>,
        <span class="locality"
            i18n:translate="footer_txt_city">Springfield</span>,
        <span class="region"
            i18n:translate="footer_txt_province">OR</span>
        <span class="postal-code"
            i18n:translate="footer_txt_postal_code">12345</span>
    </div>

    <span class="tel"
        i18n:translate="footer_txt_phone">(503) 555-8272</span> :
    <span class="email"><span tal:replace="structure python:here.
                        spamProtect('info@enviro-group.org')">
        [spam protected email addr]
    </span></span>
</div>
```

There's a lot of geek-speak in the original template, so we want to reduce both that and some of the visual noise.

As for the colophon, we modify it as follows:

```
<tal:comment tal:condition="nothing">
    Removing everything to tone down the nerdyness a notch. Altered
                            the colophon to also show a copyright.
</tal:comment>
<div id="portal-colophon" metal:define-macro="colophon"
                    i18n:domain="onenorthwest">
    <span i18n:translate="txt_powered_by_plone" id="powered-by-
                                            plone">
        powered by
        <span i18n:name="plone_org_link">
            <a href="http://plone.org"
                i18n:attributes="title title_this_site_is_plone"
                title="This website is built on the Plone Content
            Management System. Click to learn more.">Plone</a>
        </span>
    </span>
    <span i18n:translate="txt_copyright" id="copyright">
        <span i18n:name="bef_link">
            Copyright 2009
        </span>
    </span>
</div>
```

It's considered good to the Plone open source community to keep the Plone branding for viral marketing of Plone, and we also keep the copyright.

That's all we need to do here. We've changed ZCML, so we need to restart our Zope instance after this step.

Altering the navigation

Next we need to do some basic styling of the navigation. It's wise at this point to drill down a bit into the navigation on the site so that we can see how the sub navigation will appear. We don't need to modify the behavior of the navigation, so we'll focus only on the CSS styling. Most of this styling can be grabbed from CMFPlone's `navtree.css`, located at `mybuildout/part/plone/CMFPlone/skins/plone_styles`, and adjusted as necessary.

1. First, we apply a background color that is different from what is specified in the base portlet styling, and we suppress the portlet header:

```
.portletNavigationTree {
    padding: 0;
```

```
        background-color:#9d8d6b;
    }
    .portletNavigationTree .portletHeader {
        display:none;
    }
```

2. Next, we focus on the individual items in the menu and alter the padding and margins. We also remove all but the bottom border and apply a color to the hyperlinks using an `!important` declaration. Then, we make all of the hyperlinks uppercase.

```
    .navTreeItem {
        padding: 0;
        margin: 0;
    }

    .navTreeItem a,
    dd.portletItem .navTreeItem a {
        border-width:0px 0px 1px 0px;
        border-bottom: 1px solid #bbaf98;
        padding-top: 0.25em;
        padding-bottom: 0.25em;
        color:#fff6ab !important;
        text-transform:uppercase;
    }
```

3. For the hover states, we want the links to turn white. We also have to remove borders around the hyperlinks, as Plone applies these by default. If you see your text jumping around when you drag mouse over it, and you can't figure out where that jumping is coming from, it's usually related to borders that are the same color as the background color.

```
    .navTreeItem a:hover,
    dd.portletItem .navTreeItem a:hover {
        background-color:transparent;
        color: #fff !important;
        border-width:0px 0px 1px 0px;
        border-bottom: 1px solid #bbaf98;
    }
```

4. Next, we look at the currently selected item styling. We don't want a background color, so we remove that. We again remove the borders that are given to us by base Plone, and we want the hyperlinks to be white:

```
    li.navTreeItem a.navTreeCurrentItem {
        background-color: transparent;
        border-width:0px 0px 1px 0px !important;
```

```
    border-bottom: 1px solid #bbaf98 !important;
    color:#fff !important;
}
```

5. Finally, we look at the sub navigation and make those items uppercase:

```
ul.navTree .navTreeLevel1 a {
    text-transform:uppercase !important;
}
```

Looking at the `navtree.css` file provided by CMFPlone will give you a sense of all of the different things that could be styled. Generally, this boils down to the overall portlet styling (header, footer, and so on), individual link items, link items in hover state, and sub navigation. The CSS here can be a little convoluted, so you may find yourself fighting with it.

At this point, if you install the theme, it should look something like this (don't forget to reorder your viewlets by hand if you need to). However, since we disabled the right-hand portlets earlier in the chapter, what you see might be slightly different:

Summary

In this chapter, we have learned how to:

- Change the logo
- Modify the `portal_actions` on a site
- Modify various viewlets and portlets and the templates that are used to render a Plone site
- Do basic CSS styling

You should now have a real-world understanding of viewlets, portlets, and CSS and how they tie together. Next, we will look at how we can make even deeper changes to the structure of a page using sectional styling, page template adjustments, and more.

11
Custom Page Views and Sectional Styling

Now that we have seen how basic theming is accomplished, we'll take a closer look at how we can adjust the look and feel of a home page view. This can be accomplished in a variety of ways, some of which involve simple CSS and others which require more knowledge of page templating and Python code. We'll also look at sectional styling and wrap up our theme's development with some browser testing.

Changing the default home page display

The Guria theme product ships with a few different examples of how you could modify your home page layout. It is important to note that not all of the CSS has been written to support all of these different views. The intention for final implementation was to use the `homepage_view` method (not `homepage2_view`), and styling for the former's look and feel is completely in place. The `homepage2_view` styling is only partially complete. Look in the theme product's `guria_templates` folder to see these two templates.

Using CSS styles and the visual editor

Let us look first at the simplest way to customize your home page: using CSS styles inside of the visual editor to create a different look and feel. We can accomplish this either by doing some small, simple coding in our CSS stylesheets, or we can add this code to our theme product via a `kupu.xml` (or similar) **GenericSetup** file in our theme product's `profiles/` directory. Kupu is the current visual editor for Plone, and may be replaced by another editor in the future. The principles here should be the same, even if the official editor changes.

If you want to see a GenericSetup implementation in action, download Denys Mishunov's excellent `webcouturier.hosting.theme` at: `http://plone.org/ products/webcouturier-hosting-theme/`. This theme is also a great example of the Plone 3 theming best practices.

In our case, we're going to go the simpler, more manual route and not use the GenericSetup method. We're also going to repurpose some of the CSS from the `webcouturier` theme.

1. First, we want to insert some CSS into our theme product's `guria.css` to create additional styles that can be inserted into a Plone page:

```css
/**** KUPU STYLES FOR HOMEPAGE TABLE ****/
/** we also need to configure kupu in the site setup area **/
.homeTable {
    width: 100%;
    margin-bottom: 0.5em;
    border-spacing: 5px;
    border-collapse: separate;
}
.homeTable th {
    padding: 0.7em 0.8em;
    font-size: 1.2em;
    color: #fff;
    text-align: left;
    background-color: #7d7564;
}
.homeTable th a {
    color: #fff;
}
.homeTable td {
    padding: 0.5em 0 0;
    border-top: 3px solid #ccc;
    font-size: 0.9em;
    vertical-align:top;
}
.homeTable td a {
    text-decoration: underline;
    border: 0;
}
.homeTable ul {
    padding: 0.5em 0.7em 1em 1em;
}
.homeTable tbody tr td ul li {
    margin:0;
}
.homeTable ul li a,
.homeTable ul li a:hover,
```

```
.homeTable ul li a:visited {
    color: &dtml-fontColor;;
}
.homeTable p {
    margin: 0;
    padding: 0.5em 0.3em 0.3em 2.5em;
}

p.orangeText {
    color:#cd8c04;
}
```

2. Then, we add these styles to the visual editor. On our web site, go to the visual editor's configlet, found at `http://localhost:8080/mysite/kupu_library_tool/kupu_config`. At the bottom of the page is a **Styles** box where you can insert new styles that you want to provide to your site's content administrators. We will insert the following styles: **homeTable|Table with brown headers** in the **Tables** area and **Orange Text|p|orangeText** in the **Styles** area. Then press **Save**.

Now, if we go to our home page (or any page) and edit it, we'll see the **Orange Text** option available in the **Styles** drop-down list, and if we add a table, the **Table with brown headers** option will also be available. The other styles that have been defined will also be exposed to our theme as children of the `.homeTable` style, but those items do not need to be added to the visual editor.

In this way, we can alter the default styling of a page's contents and create the illusion that more sophisticated code is at work.

Using a basic page template for a home page view

Now let's look at the page template named `homepage2_view.pt`, located at `mybuildout/plonetheme.guria/plonetheme/guria/skins/guria_templates`. (We'll look at `homepage_view.pt` in a bit.)

We copied two files from `mybuildout/buildout-cache/eggs/Plone[some version number]/Products/CMFPlone/skins/plone_templates` into our theme product to create these new files: `document_view.pt` and `document_view.pt.metadata`. We then renamed them as `homepage2_view.pt` and `homepage2_view.pt.metadata` and altered the name of the title in the `.metadata` file:

```
[default]
title=Second Homepage View
```

To the `homepage2_view.pt` file we then added the following custom code directly below the `plone.belowcontenttitle` provider:

```
<div tal:replace="structure provider:plone.belowcontenttitle" />
<!-- insert some custom code here to pull in the contents of some
                                                        pages -->
<!-- the pages must be have shortnames of r1c1 and r1c2 -->
<tbody>
<table id="homepage-table">
   <tr>
       <td tal:define="r1c1 nocall:portal/homesection/r1c1" tal:on-
                                               error="nothing">
          <th tal:content="structure r1c1/Title">Column One -
                          Change this in homepage2_view</th>
          <div tal:replace="structure r1c1/getText" />
       </td>
       <td tal:define="r1c2 nocall:portal/homesection/r1c2" tal:on-
                                               error="nothing">
          <th tal:content="structure r1c2/Title">Column Two -
                          Change this in homepage2_view</th>
          <div tal:replace="structure r1c2/getText" />
       </td>
   </tr>
</table>
</tbody>
<!-- end custom code -->
```

All this code does is pull in the contents of two pages named `r1c1` (symbolizing row 1, column 1) and `r1c2` (row 1, column 2). These two page objects need to be created in a folder on your Plone site named `homesection`. If an object is not found, an error will not be raised.

In this way, we can do some light customizations to a page to adjust the layout. Additional rows and columns could be added with distinct styles. Just make sure that their shortnames correspond accordingly.

To use this template:

1. We need to go into the ZMI to **portal_types/Document (Page)** and add `homepage2_view` as an available view method for documents: `http://localhost:8080/mysite/portal_types/Document/manage_propertiesForm`.

2. Then, from the home page (or whatever page you want to apply this view to), choose **Second Homepage View** from the **Display** drop-down list. It may be necessary to access the home page by selecting it via the **Contents** tab.

It's also not uncommon to customize the page template that provides the view of a collection. This file is named `atct_topic_view.pt`, and is located at `mybuildout/buildout-cache/eggs/Products.ATContentTypes[some version number]/Products/ATContentTypes/skins/ATContentTypes/`. We will not cover modification of a collection view, as it is very similar to modifying a document view, but you should know that at this point, knowledge of Python and advanced TAL becomes very helpful.

Using Python code to render a home page view

The next example is pretty dense, and is provided only to show an alternate solution. It's similar to the example where you want to pull in the content of a page or other object, but this one also allows you to pull in images and collections and limit the number of items they return. It also uses `memoize`, a Python function decorator for caching the values of functions and methods. This might be of interest to the geeks in the crowd.

It is recommended at this point that if you have not downloaded the theme, you definitely do so and walk through the code yourself. I'll explain in theory how it's hooked up and how it works, but we're not going to go in too deep here.

Like the view described above, we copied CMFPlone's default `document_view.pt` and `document_view.pt.metadata` into our theme product's `skins/guria_templates` folder, renamed them to `homepage_view.pt` and `homepage_view.pt.metadata`, and altered the `.metadata` file to read as follows:

```
[default]
title=Homepage View
```

Next, let's look at some of the code the `homepage_view.pt` contains. This page template contains a table with three columns, each of which is populated with the contents of a page and an image that is pulled in from a specific location. Let's look at part of the first column's XHTML:

```
<td id="home-cell-one"
        tal:define="items hp_view/getSlot1Items"
        tal:condition="items">
        <div class="cell-wrapper">
            <th class="hiddenStructure">Column One</th><span
                                        class="col1"></span>
            <img tal:define="img hp_view/getSlot1Image"
                tal:condition="img"
                tal:attributes="src img"
             class="slot1image"
                height="68"
                width="167" />

            <div class="folder-listing"
                tal:repeat="item items">
    ...
```

We see code like `items hp_view/getSlot1Items`. This implies that there is a view somewhere that has a function named `getSlot1Items`. If we look closer at `interfaces.py`, located at `mybuildout/plonetheme.guria/plonetheme/guria/browser/interfaces.py`, we see that the following code matches up to what we see in the `homepage_view.pt` page template.

```
class IHomepage(Interface):
    """Browser view for homepage logic"""
...

def getSlot1Image(self):
        """Returns an absolute url for the image to appear in the
                                                first slot"""
        return self._getSlotImage(1)

    @memoize
    def getSlot1Items(self):
```

```
        """Return the first 3 content items for the first slot. We're
    assuming that a Collection lives at the path /homepage/slot1; we'll
    return its first three items.
        """
        return self._getSlotItems(1)
```

We still need to figure out where the hp_view is defined and hooked up to our theme. In the same browser/ folder, look at configure.zcml:

```
<!-- Browser views -->
    <browser:page
        for="*"
        name="hp_view"
        class=".homepage.Homepage"
        layer=".interfaces.IThemeSpecific"
        permission="zope2.View"
        />
```

This is where we tell our theme product to use this hp_view in the current theme. We then need to look and see where the logic is for the interface described in interfaces.py. That is contained in the file named homepage.py (see the dot-delimited class mentioned in configure.zcml). Here we see explanation of some basic logic and also the code associated with getSlot1Image and getSlot1Items.

Even if you are not a programmer (and I am not), you can see that the way this code works is that your Plone site needs to have a folder added to it named Homepage. The three slots that are part of the home page return the following items:

- homepage/images/slot1.jpg
- homepage/images/slot2.jpg
- homepage/images/slot3.jpg

And the first three items returned by collections are created at:

- /homepage/slot1
- /homepage/slot2
- /homepage/slot3

Where slot1, slot2, and slot3 are the shortnames of the collections.

As with the previously discussed home page view, to make this available for selection, you must go to the ZMI and add **homepage_view** to the available views for **Document (Page)**: http://localhost:8080/mysite/portal_types/Document/ manage_propertiesForm. Then, from the home page (or whatever page you want to apply this view to), choose **Homepage View** from the **Display** drop-down list. Again, you may have to access the home page's default page via the Contents tab.

Clearly, there are a number of ways in which to modify the look and feel of page, even if you are not a programmer. If you are a programmer, the sky is the limit!

Next, we'll look at how we can change the look and feel of our Plone site from section to section.

Sectional styling

Here we will learn how to do sectional styling using a CSS hook that Plone gives us for free. This type of sectional styling is not used in our theme product, except to suppress the breadcrumbs from the home page, but we discuss it here as a prelude to the advanced topic of sectional banners that follows it.

The `body` tag in **CMFPlone's** `main_template` has an HTML class attribute that allows you to theme different sections of the site with different styles. All you do is use the prefix of `section-` and then the shortname of the item in the root folder. In `main_template.pt` there is a script that generates, on the fly, a class for each section of the site. The script is called `getSectionFromURL`:

```
<body tal:attributes="class string:${here/getSectionFromURL}
                                    template-${template/id};
                    dir python:test(isRTL, 'rtl', 'ltr')">
```

The rendered HTML it creates looks like:

```
<body class="section-news section-news-aggregator template-
                                    folder_summary_view"
        dir="ltr">
    <div id="visual-portal-wrapper">
...
```

What this in effect tells us is that we are in the `news` folder, which contains an object with a shortname of `aggregator` (the default collection object that pulls in news items). Using CSS, we can hook onto the `.section-news` class.

In your stylesheets, prefix the style you want to be different for that section with `.section-foldername`, replacing `foldername` with the id or shortname of the folder in question. For example, this code would change the background image for the **News** section of your site:

```
.section-news {
    background-image: url(&dtml-portal_url;/gradient2.png);
    background-repeat:repeat-x;
}
```

Here are a few additional examples of how it might be used. First, we assign a property to the global elements, such as `body`, and then we assign properties to the section-specific element to differentiate it:

```
body { background-image:
    url(gradient.png);
}
/* this is specific to a section with a shortname of foo */
    body.section-foo {
    background-image: url(gradient2.png);
}
#visual-portal-wrapper {
    background-color:#000;
}
/* this is specific to a section with a shortname of foo */
.section-foo #visual-portal-wrapper {
    background: white;
    margin: auto;
    width: 883px;
    position: relative;
}
#portal-logo {
    margin: 1em;
    background-image: url(logo.jpg);
    background-repeat: no-repeat;
}
/* this is specific to a section with a shortname of foo */
.section-foo #portal-logo {
    margin: 1em;
    background-image: url(logo-foo.gif);
    background-repeat: no-repeat;
}

.section-front-page #portal-breadcrumbs {
    display:none;
}
```

In the code above, we added section-specific code for the `body`, `#visual-portal-wrapper`, and `#portal-logo` areas. This type of pattern can be used in an almost infinite number of ways.

The only issue to consider here is that if you change the shortname of your section, your styling will break. Users should be educated to not change shortnames unless they know what they are doing.

As we've seen, you can write CSS that alters the logo on a section-by-section basis. You might also want to have a different banner image in each section. To do so, you could use TAL instead to alter your page template to look for an image based on your current context:

```
<img width="125"
    tal:replace="structure nocall:context/banner.jpg|default" />
```

In this case, you would not want an image named `banner.jpg` to be inside of your theme product, as it would conflict with the images named `banner.jpg` that you insert into the various sections of your Plone site as content

The disadvantage to this method is that the images will be considered content, and thus will not be cacheable without extra work. However, it would give site maintainers more control over the look and feel of their site.

There are certainly other options available; these two are just the most common.

Applying Internet Explorer fixes

Now that we've wrapped up all of the templating work on our theme and the bulk of our CSS, we should test the site against other browsers.

As a Mac user, my tool of choice is VMWare Fusion (`http://www.vmware.com/download/fusion/`), but Windows users can use Windows Virtual PC (`http://www.microsoft.com/windows/virtual-pc/`). As of this writing, I typically test first against Safari (WebKit), Firefox 2 (Mac and PC), then Firefox 3 (Mac and PC), then Internet Explorer 6, IE7, then IE8, in that order. If I have time, I also test against Opera. If you have multimedia devices, you might wish to test against them as well. This means setting up several virtual machines, which can be very resource intensive.

There are a couple of ways of adding browser-related fixes to your theme product. You could certainly add to the Plone stylesheet (`IEFixes.css`), you could create stylesheets for each individual browser you're patching, or you could do them inline in your theme's main stylesheet. For my purposes, I tend to insert them directly into my main stylesheet so that I don't have to hop between stylesheets. This is just a personal preference.

The CSS for this theme product was pretty solid in Firefox and Safari, so here I am going to focus primarily on IE6 and IE7.

The searchbox frequently shows up with scrollbars around it (and here it does again), as though it doesn't fit quite right. A simple fix to the code addresses that issue in IE6:

```
* html #portal-searchbox {
    overflow:visible !important;
}
```

I also put an `!important` declaration in there, as it didn't want to take effect at first. Other than that and the `#portal-siteactions` fix mentioned earlier, IE6 appears to behave nicely.

IE7 also appears to behave well, and there is no need to adjust the searchbox. However, in the event that we do need to make fixes to the CSS, the syntax for the fix would look like this:

```
*+html #portal-searchbox {
    insert CSS here
}
```

Again, we made a fix to the `#portal-siteactions` for IE7, as seen in the code listed earlier:

```
*+html #portal-siteactions {
    margin-left:9px;
    margin-top:0px;
}
```

It's worth stating that IE8 tends to be pretty standards compliant, so you should try to write your CSS cleanly to appease it. Moreover, there are not CSS hacks available to you, so writing clean code is the best solution. However, if you find that you are having problems (or you have old sites you don't want to spend time reworking with), you may want to tell your sites to behave as though they were being viewed in IE7. This can be done using an Apache tweak, explained here: `http://blogs. msdn.com/hanuk/archive/2008/08/28/apache-httpd-configuration-for-ie7- standard-mode-rendering-in-ie8.aspx`.

At this point, we've covered most of the basics involved in theming a site, and a few extras as well. Now that our site is browser compliant, we're officially done here!

Summary

In this chapter, we have learned how to:

- Create custom home page views, from simple to complex
- Do sectional styling
- Enable and create sectional banners
- Test our site against multiple browsers

Skinning is a complex, but rewarding affair, and understanding the various ways in which you can make changes is the first step towards making educated decisions about how you would implement a design. Next, we will look at additional tools, product, and skinning tricks that can help you be more effective and creative during the skinning process.

12
Add-on Tools and Theming Tips

Now that we've looked at how to build a Plone theme, we'll take a look at some Plone products that can be used to make your web site even more impactful and manageable. We'll also briefly cover some useful tips to be aware of when theming a Plone site.

Popular add-on Plone products

One of the best things about open source development is the proliferation of products to solve common use cases. Plone themers are fortunate to have a solid set of tools available to them to solve these use cases.

Enabling drop downs using webcouturier. dropdownmenu

As most themers know, a lot of clients desire drop-down menus. In the past, this required coding HTML strings and the use of a product by Quintagroup named qPloneDropDownMenu. This product is still the recommended drop-down menu product for Plone 2.5x, but for 3.x, the real star is Denys Mishunov's product, webcouturier.dropdownmenu.

The joy of this product is that you install it, and it works instantly. The product works by subclassing the globalsections viewlet via the following code, found in the browser/configure.zcml file of the webcouturier.dropdownmenu product:

```
<!-- Override global sections viewlet -->
    <browser:viewlet
        name="plone.global_sections"
```

```
manager="plone.app.layout.viewlets.interfaces.IPortalHeader"
class=".dropdown.DropdownMenuViewlet"
layer=".interfaces.IDropdownSpecific"
permission="zope2.View"
/>
```

In the event that you've already customized your `globalsections` viewlet, you will have to subclass the `DropdownMenuViewlet` class in the `webcouturier.dropdownmenu` product.

Unlike older drop-down menu products, `webcouturier.dropdownmenu` does not require any ongoing maintenance or manual adjustment of URLs. It is controlled by the navigation settings found in the **Site Setup** area, so you can control what types of items display in the navigation. The product also provides some basic CSS styling that can be easily adjusted in your own theme product, if desired. It can be downloaded here:

`http://plone.org/products/webcouturier-dropdownmenu/`

Collage

Another helpful Plone product is Malthe Borch's Collage. Collage allows you to create a grid containing rows and columns, and within those columns you can pull in the contents of other objects—a folder, a page, a collection, or even an image. Using this mechanism, you can create a complex page layout without knowing any programming.

Until very recently, Collage did not have hooks that allowed it to be styled using CSS, and it did not respect different views. For example, if you created a special `mysection_view.pt` (same as a `homepage_view`), and you assigned that view to your page, Collage would default to the original `document_view`. This behavior has now been altered so that CSS hooks are available and different views are respected. This is a huge win for sites that are heavily styled and need to maintain consistency.

I suggest that when using Collage, you do not create your objects within the Collage itself; you should instead create the objects in your normal Plone content tree, and pull those items in as aliases. The reason for suggesting this is that it is not possible to access the contents of a Collage via the standard `folder_contents` view that is normally possible in a folder. Hence, if you need to move that content to another area of your site, you cannot. This also invites some jeopardy when migrating to a new version of Plone.

It's worth mentioning that Collage will not become part of core Plone in the future, as the mechanism for organizing blocks of content on a page in the future will be accomplished via a new drag-and-drop mechanism. The lead programmer for Collage has stated, however, that there will be a migration path, but the reality of this is unknown.

Finally, the usability of the Collage product is a bit clunky, but with some common sense, it's easy to use and can be a quite powerful layout tool for Plone 3. It can be downloaded here: `http://plone.org/products/collage`.

Tableless styling using Plone Tableless

A popular product for CSS purists is Simon Kaeser's `plone.tableless`. Plone's default `main_template` is created using tables, which many themers do not wish to use. To get a tableless version of Plone's `main_template`, simply install this product; make sure your site's `portal_css` is in debug mode, and test the following code:

```
#portal-column-one {float:right;}
#portal-column-two {float:left;}
```

If you're able to switch the position of these two columns, the product works and you can style in full tableless mode.

There are a few issues with Plone and tableless layouts that are unrelated to this product, but in general it works. As of this writing, the product was not tested against some of the newer browsers. It can be downloaded here: `http://plone.org/products/plone-tableless/`.

CSSManager

End users often want to have some control over basic modifications to their site—background color, link colors, and so on. The WebLion Group from Penn State University created CSSManager, a product that gives a simple, **through the web** interface to let users change the colors, borders, site logo, and other visual characteristics of their Plone site. Essentially, it uses the DTML variables defined in the `base_properties.props` file available within Plone.

The product can be downloaded here: `http://plone.org/products/cssmanager`. To use it, install the product, go to your site's **Site Setup** area, and find the configlet for this tool, and try changing a few options.

The CSSManager tool will supersede a theme product's `base_properties` if the CSSManager skin layer is above the theme product's skin layers in `portal_skins/ properties` in the ZMI. If uninstalled, your settings can still be found in the `custom` folder for your Plone site via this URL: `http://localhost:8080/mysite/portal_ skins/custom/base_properties/manage_propertiesForm`. So you can feel confident removing it if you no longer need it.

Products.EasyAsPiIE

Until IE7, there was no fully native support for PNG alpha channel transparency in Internet Explorer. However, since IE5.5, there has been some support in the form of a proprietary filter called `AlphaImageLoader`. Internet Explorer filters can be applied directly in your CSS (for both inline and background images), or by setting the same CSS property with JavaScript.

Unfortunately, there's no CSS property called `filter` in the W3C CSS spec. It's a proprietary extension added by Microsoft that could potentially cause other browsers to reject your entire CSS rule.

Also, `AlphaImageLoader` does not magically add full PNG transparency support so that a PNG in the page will just start working. Instead, when applied to an element in the page, it draws a new rendering surface in the same space that element occupies and loads a PNG into it. If that sounds weird, it is. However, by and large the result is that PNGs with an alpha channel can be accommodated.

The WebLion Group's `Products.EasyAsPiIE` product uses this filter approach to handle transparent PNGs with IE6. All it does is enable JavaScript written by Angus Turnbull: `http://www.twinhelix.com`.

You can download it from here: `http://plone.org/products/products- easyaspiie/` and follow the installation instructions.

Optionally, if you choose not to use this product, you can also just export to PNG8 format, instead of PNG24, to get around IE6 problems, and of course there are a lot of alternative solutions out there as well. You can read more about PNGs here: `http://www.sitepoint.com/blogs/2007/09/18/png8-the-clear-winner/`. Both Photoshop and Fireworks can export to PNG8, though other graphical programs may not.

collective.skinny

Another Plone product that has surfaced is Daniel Nouri's `collective.skinny`, which can be downloaded from `http://plone.org/products/collective-skinny/`. This product is an example implementation of a separate, public-facing skin that abstracts away some of the complexity of the theming process. According to the product page, it's been described as being vastly easier than skinning Plone the conventional way, but it also has a few drawbacks. For example, you can't use it for community sites where people other than your site editors log in and modify content. It's also a little confusing from my perspective, but it's a product adventurous themers might pay attention to.

It's probable that **Deliverance** and `collective.xdv` (the future of theming for Plone) will make this product obsolete, as Deliverance removes a lot of complexity and makes theming accessible to individuals who don't even know what Plone is. For more information on Deliverance and `collective.xdv`, please read the final chapter of this book.

FS Dump

For themers who started their skin creation through the web or who have content they wish to extract from the ZMI, FS Dump is an excellent tool. To use it, download the product from `http://www.plone.org/products/fsdump` and follow the installation instructions. This is a product that lives in the Products namespace, so it is not installed like egg-based products. The product page doesn't indicate that it works on Plone 3, but the last time I tried it on a Plone 3 site, it worked.

Once installed, use the **Add** drop-down menu, found at `http://www.mysite.com/manage_main`, and create a `Dumper` instance in a folder (or product) that contains the TTW code to be dumped. This tool appears to work best when trying to dump items from the `custom/` folder, though, hypothetically, it should work for any other folder in the ZMI.

Next, supply an absolute path to a directory on the filesystem in which the dumper is to create the files, for example `/opt`. (Note that the user for whom Zope is running needs *write* access to this directory.)

Click the **Change and Dump** button to do the dump to the indicated directory, and then copy the dumped files into your theme product's `skins/` folder in the appropriate locations.

qPloneSkinDump

Another popular dumper product is known as Plone Skin Dump (qPloneSkinDump) by Quintagroup. Plone Skin Dump allows users to create a Plone product in the Products namespace by exporting the `custom/` folder. It creates an old-school Plone theme product for you, but it does not provide the plonetheme-type of product. The product has not been tested against Plone 3, so it may not be the best option. Moreover, at the time this chapter was written, it was not possible to download the product from its SourceForge repository.

In the event you wish to try this product, you can find it here: `http://plone.org/ products/plone-skin-dump`. Again, it is in the Products namespace, so all you need to do is drop it in your buildout's `products/` folder. You can then follow the directions posted on the product page. It's a bit more complicated than FS Dump, but obviously it does a bit more.

Collection and static portlets

While portlets are not add-on products, they are tools that can greatly enhance the impact of your site and worth mentioning.

Default Plone provides collection and static portlets that can be added on any page by clicking on the **Manage Portlets** link on your site. These portlets provide great power and can be styled using CSS. A collection portlet, for example, can be set to display random contents fitting certain criteria—maybe a randomized spotlight content type tagged with a special keyword. This keeps the look and feel of a site fresh and gives some power to the end user.

These portlets have the same structure as other portlets, so they will use any default styling that may be applied.

Sectional theming

As discussed earlier, a very common need for Plone users is the ability to create sub sites, sectional theming, and URL-based theme switching.

We already looked at how to do sectional theming by using the CSS hooks provided by Plone using shortnames. Another option is sectional theming via the use of Apache's `mod_proxy` and Zope rewrite rules. This approach will not be covered here due to its complexity, but tutorials on how this can be accomplished can be found at `http://www.plone.org/documentation`.

To make sectional theming even easier, a product named `themetweaker. themeswitcher` was written.

themetweaker.themeswitcher

This product is another gem written by the great folks at WebLion. It is described as a product for switching themes on folders (only those with the `IATFolder interface` as of this writing) in Plone. It works only with theme products that are registered as a browser layer, which is not a concept we will cover here. Browser layer declaration is a more programming-oriented process and is described in *"Professional Plone Development", Martin Aspeli, Packt Publishing* and at `http://plone.org/documentation/tutorial/customization-for-developers/browser-layers`.

The `themetweaker.themeswitcher` product has several dependencies that are described in the product's `README` file, along with basic installation instructions. It can be installed using the instructions found here: `https://weblion.psu.edu/trac/weblion/wiki/ThemeSwitcher`.

If you install the product using the ZMI's `portal_quickinstaller`, it gives you an actions tab on your folders in the content area of the page. Assuming you install it via `portal_quickinstaller`, each folder will have a **ThemeSwitcher** tab that will bring up the switcher form. Here you will be able to choose from a list of installed themes that use browser layer to register themselves. To determine if the theme is registered as a browser layer, look to see if the theme contains a `browserlayer.xml` file; if it does, chances are it is registered as a browser layer.

If you do not install the product via `portal_quickinstaller`, you will need to manually type the switcher form path (for example, `http://localhost:8080/plonesite/folder1/switcherform`), because the actions tabs have not been installed. This is likely behavior that will be fixed as the product evolves.

The WebLion team is actively trying to solve issues around sub site theming, as explained here: `https://weblion.psu.edu/trac/weblion/wiki/SubsiteTheming`. Also, be aware that the themes that are installed using this package should have an uninstall routine, as explained here: `https://weblion.psu.edu/trac/weblion/wiki/PloneThreeThemeUninstallProfile`. Otherwise, you will not be able to uninstall your themes.

As a caveat, I have not used this product personally, as I use other methods of doing sectional theming, so any questions should be directed to the WebLion team.

Non-Plone-specific products for theming

Plone theming obviously has some community tools that have been created to make the theming process easier, but it's also possible to incorporate some advanced technologies. The following are a couple of non-Plone-specific products that can be used to alter the look and feel of your site.

sIFR

sIFR (Scalable Inman Flash Replacement) is a technology that allows you to replace text elements on screen with Flash equivalents. It is explained in depth at `http://wiki.novemberborn.net/sifr3/`, and can be seen in action at `http://www.dogwoodinitiative.org` (see the portlet header elements).

The idea is to use fonts that are embedded within a Flash file and render those on a web page instead of standard text. The process is actually quite simple, but has some delicate syntax that can be a bit painful to get right. It's best to follow the source code found in the official demo (`http://dev.novemberborn.net/sifr3/beta2/demo/`), and to refer to the discussion forum if you have questions (`http://discuss.joyent.com/viewforum.php?id=20`).

Rules-based theming

The final chapter of this book will address specifically what rules-based theming is, but what you need to know here is that some flavor of Deliverance or `collective.xdv` will be the de facto standard for theming in the future. In fact, it even works now, with some effort and understanding. `Plone.org` was even redesigned using `collective.xdv`, with obvious success.

Basically, rules-based theming reduces the process of theming to mere CSS—no fancy viewlet work, no understanding of Zope 2 versus Zope 3 technologies, CMF, and so on. It may introduce more complexity in other ways (themers will need to learn XSLT, for instance), but that remains to be seen.

Best of all? It's not just for Plone. It's available to any technologies that use **WSGI (Web Server Gateway Interface)** or have an XSLT processor available. WSGI is a specification for web servers and application servers to communicate with web applications (though it can also be used for more than that). It is a Python standard described in depth at `http://www.python.org/dev/peps/pep-0333/`. You can also read more about Apache's mod_xslt at `http://www.mod-xslt2.com/`.

Read the last chapter to get a better understanding of how this changes the Plone theming landscape.

Debugging tools and tips

While add-on tools are great for enhancing a web site, debugging tools are also very handy. In this section, we'll look at a Plone product that helps with introspection, and we'll also learn about tracebacks and ways to effectively conduct browser testing.

GloWorm

A commonly mentioned Plone add-on is the helpful GloWorm, written by the WebLion team. It can be downloaded from here: `http://plone.org/products/gloworm`. GloWorm is an inspection tool that can be useful when doing theming, because it helps you to sniff out different elements on a page. For newer Plone themers in particular, this is a very handy tool.

It provides information such as:

- Archetypes field information
- TAL statements (`tal:defines`, `tal:attributes`, `tal:content`, `tal:condition`)
- Viewlet registration information
- Inline editing of viewlet templates
- Viewlet manager information
- Reordering of viewlets
- Show/hide viewlets
- Tree-structured view of all viewlet managers and viewlets included in a page

The dependencies are outlined on the product page mentioned before, along with installation instructions.

Once installed, an **inspect this page** link will appear in the document actions section of content objects on your site. Clicking this link will open up a panel at the bottom of the page, which is the **GloWorm Inspector Panel**. (You may also open this inspector by appending `@@inspect` to the current page's URL.)

You can click a viewlet's name to inspect it. From the inspection panel, you can then customize the template by clicking on the **Customize** button. In the viewlet inspection view, you can also click the viewlet manager name to inspect that viewlet manager and to reorder viewlets. Here is a sample screenshot of GloWorm in action:

The only real limitation to this product is that the actions performed using this tool cannot be extracted out to the filesystem. You're essentially making customizations using the `portal_view_customizations` tool and by altering GenericSetup TTW, neither of which are easily extracted out. This is less a limitation of the product, and more due to the nature of Plone. In time, GloWorm may become an integral part of theming, though that remains to be seen. The version current at the time of this writing has some instability, but it's a product worth watching.

For a demo of this product, visit this web page: `http://weblion.psu.edu/news/gloworm-1.0-screencast`. For more information, you may wish to follow the WebLion Group's blog (`http://weblion.psu.edu/news/`), or visit their IRC chatroom (`#weblion`).

About tracebacks and Pdb (the Python debugger)

A Python "traceback" is a detailed error message that is generated when an error occurs in executing Python code. Since Plone, running atop Zope, is a Python application, most Plone errors will generate a Python traceback.

To find the traceback, check your `event.log` log file or go into the error log panel in the ZMI. Alternatively, use the ZMI to check the error log object in your Plone instance. Or, if you're running your Zope instance in foreground mode, you'll see it in your terminal window.

A traceback will be included with nearly all error entries. A traceback will look something like this: `Traceback (innermost last): ... AttributeError: adapters`. They can be very long. The most useful information is generally at the end. In time, you'll learn to read these errors and debug your code accordingly, even though at first they may seem a bit intimidating.

 If you are requesting help on #plone (IRC) or on the plone-users list, you should try to include a traceback log entry with the report. (For #plone, don't forget to always paste your error to `http://paste.plone.org` and *not* into the IRC window.)

For the programmers in the crowd, you may also find it useful to use Pdb to step through your errors, as described here: `http://plone.org/documentation/tutorial/debugging-tips-and-tricks-a-real-life-example/using-pdb/`. Pdb is a Python debugger that allows you to set a trace point in your code, so that you can step through errors. This slideshow by David Glick contains information on Pdb and other troubleshooting methods as well: `http://www.slideshare.net/davisagli/when-good-code-goes-bad-tools-and-techniques-for-troubleshooting-plone-presentation` (see slide 30).

Running more than one operating system at a time

As discussed in the chapter (Chapter 10) on tools for theming, virtual machines have turned out to be rather handy for testing against different versions of Internet Explorer. The two most popular products for doing this on Mac are VMware and Parallels, though there are others available for Mac and PC.

You will need a couple of instances set up with the desired operating system installed. Each instance could have a different version of Internet Explorer installed, and at this point in time, IE6, IE7, and IE8 are the recommended versions to install. For IE6 and IE7, you should also install the IE Developer Toolbar, which can be found at `Microsoft.com`. For IE8, the toolbar is built in. Of course, for Firefox, you should install Firebug (`getfirebug.com`) and the Web Developer Toolbar (`https://addons.mozilla.org/en-US/firefox/addon/60`).

Some minor differences exist between Mac and PC users' versions of Firefox 3, and it's still a good idea to test against Firefox 2, so you may want to install different versions of Firefox as well. Rather than creating new instances for Firefox 2 and 3, it's easier just to piggyback them on top of the existing Internet Explorer instances. You can then tweak your CSS until it works well on Firefox 2 and 3, then Safari, then any other browsers you want to support.

The only downside of using virtual machines is that they can be resource hogs, but they are essential to doing proper testing.

Summary

In this chapter, we have learned about:

- Popular add-on Plone products for changing your site's look and feel
- Possible options for sub site theming
- Non-Plone products that can be used to alter your site's look and feel
- Tools that can be helpful when debugging your themes

You should now have a basic idea of some of the tools that can be used to enhance your site and others that can help you during development. We'll look next at how we can incorporate media into our theme products, both on the theme side and on the end user/site administrator side.

13
Plone and Multimedia

Now that you know how to customize the look and feel of your web site, let's look at the window-dressing that can really make your web site look more professional and more interactive: multimedia.

In this chapter we will show you how to integrate tools such a Flash, slideshows, YouTube videos, and more into your page. We will also explore some Plone-specific products that enhance Plone's handling of audio and video. In this chapter, we will not cover JavaScript or KSS, a client-side framework for implementing rich user interfaces with AJAX functionality, but those with interest in these areas should look into some of the tutorials on `plone.org`.

Flash integration

Incorporating Flash in a Plone site is a not entirely a straightforward process, but is actually quite simple once you know how to do it. There are two options here: embed Flash into your content or embed Flash into a page template.

Embedding Flash and other media in a page

YouTube and other multimedia sites provide the HTML code necessary to embed a video on your own web site. This code can be inserted into the visual editor's HTML view, as seen here:

In this case, we'll look at the code provided by a YouTube video:

The code we're concerned with here is the **Embed** code shown on YouTube:

```
<object width="425" height="344"><param name="movie"
value="http://www.youtube.com/v/-OSd0Rf_yu0&hl=en&fs=1"></
param><param name="allowFullScreen" value="true"></param><param
name="allowscriptaccess" value="always"></param><embed src="http://
www.youtube.com/v/-OSd0Rf_yu0&hl=en&fs=1" type="application/x-
shockwave-flash" allowscriptaccess="always" allowfullscreen="true"
width="425" height="344"></embed></object>
```

To do so:

Inside of this code, you'll see blocks with words such as `object`, `param`, and `embed`. These tags are normally filtered out by safe-html filter inside of Plone, but we can tell Plone to respect those tags and not filter our HTML code.

1. We go to **Site Setup** for our Plone site and click on the **Visual Editor** configlet. Then, click on the **Toolbar** tab and enable the checkbox next to **Embed tab in External link drawer** (not shown in the following screenshot, scroll down to the option):

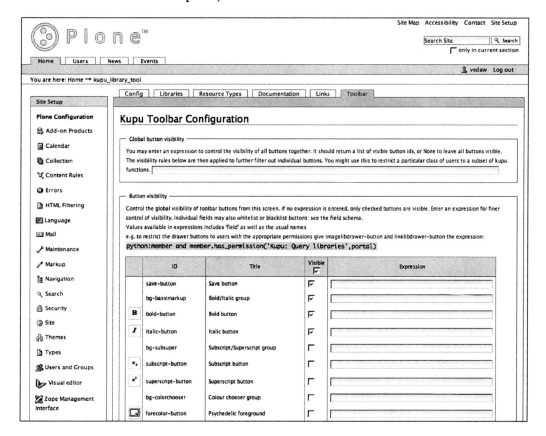

2. Next, scroll down to the bottom of the screen and click **Save**. Then, go to the **Site Setup | HTML Filtering** configlet:

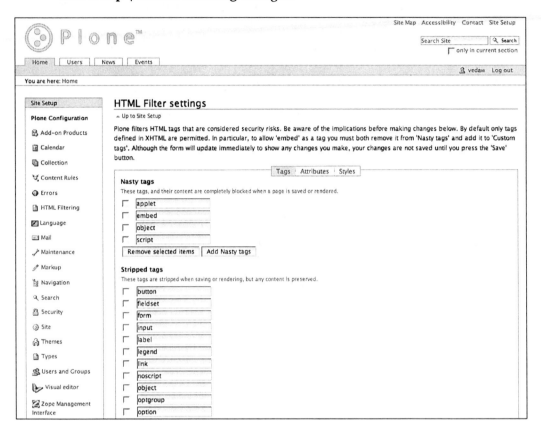

On this panel, remove **object** and **embed** from the **Nasty Tags** list. Also remove **object** and **param** from the **Stripped Tags** list. Finally, add **embed** to the **Custom Tags** list and scroll to the bottom of the screen and click the **Save** button.

3. With these changes made, you should be able to click the **External Link** button on the visual editor while on a page where you wish to embed the video. Then, click on the now-visible **Embed external object** tab. This will let you paste in a chunk of embedding code from YouTube, Flickr, or other services:

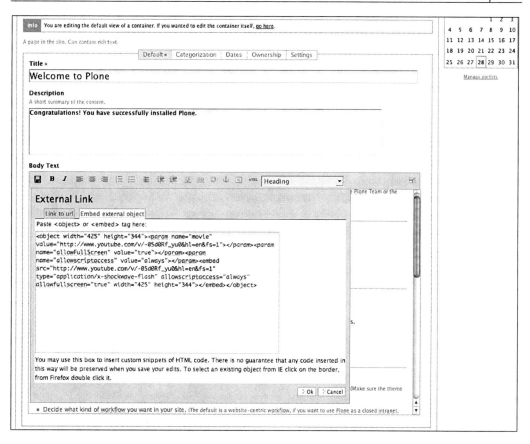

Just that easily, you too can embed multimedia into your pages, and you can disregard the warning at the bottom of the dialog box.

Security Considerations

There is a reason why `object` and `embed` tags are marked by default as "nasty". They may be used to launch attacks on other users, in particular other users that may be logged in and have privileges on your site. If you have untrusted users adding or editing content on your site, you should probably not allow their use.

In the future, it is hoped that transforms will be put into place, which will mean that you do not need to manipulate the visual editor or HTML filter settings in order to insert multimedia—the work is being done in this area.

Embedding Flash in a page template

The second, and more programmatic, way to build media into your web site is to embed it in a page template. This is generally reserved for situations where the media is an integral part of the design—for example a block of Flash that might be embedded into the header of your web site's home page—or cases where security concerns prevent turning off safe-html filtering.

You generally will not want to embed media into your site's `main_template`, as every page uses that `main_template` and the media will be reloaded each time you navigate to a different page. More likely, you will want to embed your media into a `homepage_view.pt` file or some other alternate `document_view`. In the case of this site, `http://www.resource-media.org/`, the `homepage_view.pt` displays a large block of Flash video framed by navigation:

If we then examine the code in its `homepage_view.pt` (based off of **CMFPlone's** default `document_view`, found in `mybuildout/parts/plone/CMFPlone/skins/ plone_content/`), we can see that the Flash is embedded directly into the content area of the view:

```
<html xmlns="http://www.w3.org/1999/xhtml" xml:lang="en"
      xmlns:tal="http://xml.zope.org/namespaces/tal"
      xmlns:metal="http://xml.zope.org/namespaces/metal"
```

```
        xmlns:i18n="http://xml.zope.org/namespaces/i18n"
        lang="en"
        metal:use-macro="here/main_template/macros/master"
        i18n:domain="plone">
<body>

<metal:content fill-slot="content">
    <tal:content-macro metal:define-macro="content"
                       tal:define="dummy python:request.set
                                   ('disable_border',1)">

    <object classid="clsid:d27cdb6e-ae6d-11cf-96b8-444553540000"
codebase="http://download.macromedia.com/pub/shockwave/cabs/flash/
swflash.cab#version=9,0,0,0" width="667" height="451" id="flash-intro"
align="middle">
        <param name="allowScriptAccess" value="sameDomain" />

        <param name="allowFullScreen" value="false" />

        <param name="wmode" value="transparent" />

        <param name="movie" value="intro.swf" /><param name="quality"
value="high" /><param name="bgcolor" value="#a8ac69" /> <embed
src="intro.swf" quality="high" bgcolor="#a8ac69" width="667"
height="451" name="intro" align="middle" allowScriptAccess="sameDo
main" allowFullScreen="false" type="application/x-shockwave-flash"
wmode="transparent" pluginspage="http://www.macromedia.com/go/
getflashplayer" />

    </object>

    <div tal:replace="structure provider:plone.belowcontent" />

    </tal:content-macro>
</metal:content>

</body>
</html>
```

Meanwhile, the `intro.swf` file lives in the `portal_skins/resourcemedia_images` folder, just like any other skin layer element. This means that if you are working on the filesystem, the file would go in `mybuildout/src/plonetheme.mytheme/plonetheme/mytheme/skins/mytheme_images/` or similar.

In this fashion, you can easily insert multimedia into a page template.

Plone add-ons for multimedia

Now that we understand the basics of how to insert multimedia code into our site, let's look at a few add-ons that can be used to add visual interest and extra metadata.

collective.flowplayer

Written by the talented Martin Aspeli, this tool is a lightweight Plone integration layer for Flowplayer, a great, GPL'd Flash-based player for FLV (Flash Video) and MP3 (audio) files. More information on Flowplayer can be found at `http://flowplayer.org/`, and the product can be downloaded from `http://pypi.python.org/pypi/collective.flowplayer`.

The integration is nearly seamless. You can upload a FLV or MP3 file as a standard file object, and from that you get a video player. There's no special content type, and no complex configuration involved:

Other features include the following:

- It works with ZODB blob files
- You get playlists for folders or collections
- You can put videos in portlets
- You can put video content into your content pages, with Kupu integration

Flowplayer is highly configurable. The `collective.flowplayer` package exposes almost its entire configuration through a property sheet in `portal_properties`, allowing you to do things such as applying a custom watermark or a default splash image:

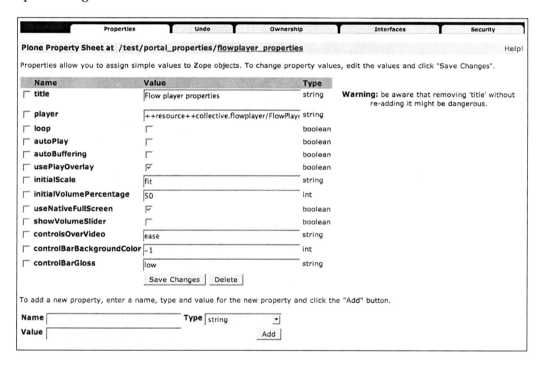

There's also some nice jQuery code available, which means that you can write pretty simple markup and get graceful degradation for your video content.

Slideshow Folder

Slideshow Folder provides a simple, elegant animated slideshow for Plone. It can be downloaded from `http://plone.org/products/slideshowfolder`. Written by Jon Baldivieso, David Glick, and Johnpaul Burbank, it gives integrators an easy-to-use slideshow tool:

Slideshow Folder integrates the Slideshow 2 JavaScript class into Plone, and is a powerful, feature-rich, and easy-to-customize slideshow library.

Slideshow Folder offers the following features:

- Animated slideshows with configurable transitions
- Navigation thumbnails
- Image captions
- Intelligent preloading of images to save bandwidth

- A play/pause/forward/reverse slideshow controller
- Looping and random-order slideshows
- Optional support for "lightbox" style image pop ups
- Look and feel completely customizable via CSS

Once installed, each folder and collection in your site will have a new option in its **Actions** drop-down menu; simply choose the **Make Slideshow** option. That will select a slideshow view for that folder and give you a new **slideshow settings** configuration tab. As soon as there are published images in the folder, you'll see the slideshow.

 Collections rely on the criteria that you put in them to render the images for the slideshow. Non-images are ignored. That means that workflow restrictions are based solely on your collection's criteria.

To change the slideshow's settings, see the new **slideshow settings** tab on the folder:

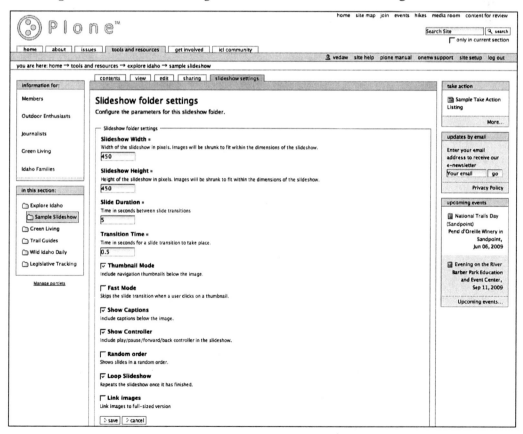

Each image's description will be used for its caption. Additionally, each slideshow will have a **disable slideshow** option in the **Actions** drop-down menu. This will revert it to being a normal folder (or collection), including deleting any slideshow settings. (It will not delete any content, though.)

For information on limitations and ways to customize this add-on, you can visit `http://plone.org/products/slideshowfolder`. You can also view the demo video there.

All in all, it's a lightweight, easy-to-use product that provides an attractive slideshow for end users, and well worth checking out.

Plone4Artists Video

The most commonly recognized Plone multimedia products were created by a team of individuals known as Plone4Artists, specifically by Nate Aune and Rocky Burt. Plone4Artists is described as an initiative to assemble a Plone products bundle with features commonly required for artist community web sites. These features include enhanced audio, video, and other multimedia management.

Plone4Artists Video is an add-on product for Plone that lets you add videos to your Plone site. It supports the uploading of video files, or embedding of videos, that are already hosted on popular video sharing sites, such as YouTube and Google Video.

Essentially, you upload a video file using the default Plone **File** type via the **Add** menu on your Plone site. Plone4Artists Video then subtypes that file in order to display it in ways that are appropriate to video. Because Plone4Artists Video does not add new kinds of content types, it makes it easier to upgrade your Plone site in the future.

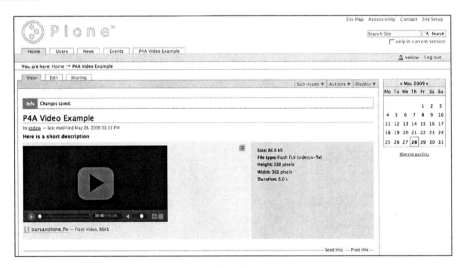

If you edit a video file that has been uploaded to your site, you will see that there are additional fields available to you than you would normally see. You can add formatted text and a thumbnail image that people can see when the video is not playing:

Users can also rate videos via the **Content Ratings** tool that ships with Plone4Artists Video. They can also leave comments, if desired.

Plone4Artists Video turns regular folders into video containers. You can enable this by going to the **Subtypes** drop-down on the folder containing your videos and choose **Video Container**. This, in turn, changes the look and feel of the folder so that it can display multiple video files in a way that is appropriate and can be browsed easily.

Collections can also be turned into video containers. Simply create a collection and specify the criteria to pull in the files of type **File** and any additional criteria, and save it. Then, use the **Subtypes** drop-down list and choose **Video Container**.

Video podcasting is also an option, and is provided with Plone4Artists Video by default. To subscribe to a video podcast, copy the link to the RSS feed that is located on the video container or collection. Go to your preferred music software and choose to subscribe to the podcast, and the latest video is downloaded automatically. Users can even subscribe to a feed of video links using a third-party RSS aggregator, such as Bloglines or Google Reader.

Plone4Artists Video also makes it possible to link to remote files, so that you can reduce the load on your disk space or bandwidth. For example, if you wish to display a video from YouTube, blip.tv, or Google Video on your site, you can! You can copy the URL for that item, create a new "link" object in your Plone site, and paste that URL into the link object. The video displays automatically in the site, along with **Content Ratings** information, the URL, and the author of the video. (The author's name must be added by hand in Plone.)

Plone4ArtistsVideo is supported by Plone 3, and is always evolving. For more information, and to see any dependencies, visit this URL: `http://www.plone.org/products/plone4artistsvideo`.

Other products to watch out for

Developing for an open source means that add-on products are always a moving target as new versions of Plone are released. However, this does not mean that products that don't yet support the latest version do not have value. These products include some of the Plone4Artists offerings, as well as one called Plumi.

Plone4ArtistsAudio

Plone4ArtistsAudio is a product that allows you to upload audio, extract metadata, create podcasts, store the files on the filesystem, and to even assign Creative Commons licenses. In more programmatic terms, what it does is allows you to upload a normal Plone "file" object to your Plone site. Plone4ArtistsAudio will detect it as an MP3 or Ogg file and "decorate" it with metadata.

As of this writing, support for Plone 3 is experimental, but there is word of a buildout-based setup that does work. Interested parties should contact the Plone4Artists team about audio support for Plone 3.

Plone4ArtistsAudio can also sniff out any additional metadata that may already be attached to the MP3 file, such as artist name, album name, or artwork. Once the file is uploaded, it is automatically displayed along with the associated metadata. If we edit the audio file in Plone, any changes are automatically written directly to the audio file.

The audio file can then be listened to right on the page, in a pop-up player. It can be streamed, or it can be downloaded to your hard drive.

Plone4ArtistsAudio also provides functionality similar to the **Video Container** folder, except this time it's an **Audio Container**. Select **Activate Audio** from the **Actions** drop-down menu in your Plone site to see a more informative display. Available on that view is a button that allows you to listen to all of the audio in the folder, as well as a podcasting button.

This same behavior is also available to collections in Plone. Simply create a collection whose criteria pulls in items whose MIME type is `audio/mpeg` and any other desired metadata. Then, activate the audio via the **Actions** drop-down menu.

Plone4ArtistsAudio works together with Plone's blob file product to support external storage of audio data. This keeps your `data.fs` nice and slim. After the blob file product is installed on your site, you add your audio files to your Plone site as blob file objects via the **Add** drop-down menu. Rather than writing those audio files to your `data.fs`, they are instead written to the filesystem.

Plone4ArtistsAudio also works together with the ContentLicensing product to make it easy to add Creative Commons or other licensing to your audio files.

To download Plone4ArtistsAudio, visit `http://www.plone.org/products/plone4artistsaudio`.

The Plone4Artists group has many other add-on products that may be of interest, and you should always check to make sure that they will work with your version of Plone. For more information on their entire suite of products and for screencasts, you can visit `http://plone4artists.org/`.

Plumi

Plumi is a free video-sharing **Content Management System (CMS)** based on Plone and produced by the EngageMedia collective: `http://engagemedia.org/`. Plumi enables you to create your own sophisticated video-sharing site. By adding it to an existing Plone instance, you can quickly have a wide array of functionality to facilitate video distribution and community creation.

As of this writing, Plumi was not yet supported by Plone 3, but for future updates, you may wish to check out `http://blog.plumi.org`.

Summary

In this chapter, we have learned:

- How to embed multimedia into the content of a page
- How to embed multimedia into a page template
- About Plone-specific add-ons that provide multimedia support
- About Plone multimedia products to watch out for

These tools should allow you to easily add some extra "bling" and interactivity to your site. Next, we will look at how to deploy a Plone theme for a client, and how to give back to the Plone theming community.

14
Deploying and Contributing Themes

We have covered most of the major pieces involved in creating a theme product. As we've seen, this can be a complex and delicate process at times, and there are a lot of moving parts involved.

This chapter will cover the steps and best practices involved in deploying your theme on a server as well as the process for releasing your theme "into the wild" for other people to enjoy and install on their Plone web sites.

Deploying your theme on a server

We're not going to cover hosting here, as that falls under the sysadmin umbrella, but refer to `http://www.plone.net`, or `#plone`, for ideas on hosting companies. We're also going to skip over some more system-administration-type tasks and focus instead on the theming aspect of taking a site live.

The typical process for creating a theme involves the following:

1. Create a Subversion repository to hold your theme product.
2. Create a theme product using the paster recipe.
3. Add the theme product to the repository.
4. Add a development site's `data.fs` to your local instance. (This is only for client-specific web sites where the site structure will affect the design implementation. If you can theme a vanilla Plone site while keeping in mind the use cases that need to be solved, you should.)
5. Theme locally and test as you go.

6. Check the theme into Subversion. This is actually an incremental process, something you do as you go from stage to stage during the theming process, while being careful not to check in broken code. The objective here is to be able to roll back to an earlier version, if needed.

7. Install the theme onto the web site and do final configuration.

8. Take the site live.

Let's look now at the work involved in testing and actually deploying the theme.

Maintaining an orderly deployment

Generally speaking, anything we do locally to configure our theme needs to get reproduced on the finished live site.

You could, for example, keep a running list of any manual changes you've made and make the same changes manually twice, which can be a time-consuming process. This typically should only be for the addition of content, manipulation of viewlets, or enabling and applying a custom view. Obviously, it is not ideal to do many manual modifications, but it's good to keep a record of them so that you can apply them when the time is right.

It is generally recommended that all functionality that can be handled within the theme product be done there in order to avoid rework. Your work environment might dictate how appropriate that is, however. For example, in my office, Project Managers typically manage areas such as the `portal_actions` or `site_actions` by hand through the ZMI. So as an implementer, I do not build these areas into my theme product's **GenericSetup**, but I certainly could if I needed to.

One way to keep things in sync is to have a development instance where clients can work on their content and where the theme can be simultaneously deployed and tested. Then, the `data.fs` from that instance can be copied over to the production instance. This ensures that all manual changes made on the development instance get carried over instantly. This process works well, because it means that you can feel certain that everything is ready to go with the theme and the content at the moment the site goes live. You can create a single buildout to achieve this end, containing a base configuration, a development configuration, and a production configuration, for example. This is usually an appropriate solution for clients who already have an existing web site or who are undergoing a migration.

In the event that a client is managing his/her content on the production site and not on the development instance, moving the `data.fs` in this case is not a good idea, as it might result in serious data loss. In this case, minimal manual configuration and a theme product containing all configuration settings via Generic Setup is generally the way to go.

Clearly, there's more than one way to deploy a theme product. And just because everything works on your local site does not mean there will be a smooth transition to the development server. So it's important to be prepared.

Documentation

As part of taking a site live, it's not uncommon that you'll need to do a little documentation, especially with respect to high-end web sites. This might be documentation for you or for your development team, such as any special business rules or custom functionality, that is convoluted enough to warrant writing it down. Also, if the person maintaining the site is not the person who built it, it might not be immediately obvious where the content lives or how to modify it, and it will save time on future refresher trainings to write it down.

Another way to make future maintenance or migration easier for your development team is to document the actual code as you work on it, especially if there is something particularly unusual about it. For example, a docstring in the `viewlets.py` file can help to indicate why a viewlet was modified, or a comment in a page template can explain how that template differs from a default Plone template.

If you're deploying your theme for public consumption, you'll also need to document any dependencies, such as any add-on products, that may have been used during development of your theme (such as the Plone Tableless product). This can also be handled in the `setup.py` file or by configuring a buildout accordingly.

You should also make sure you create an `install.txt` file to distribute along with your theme. You should not assume that anyone downloading your theme product will know how to install a theme, or that he/she will have the `buildout.eggtractor` extension installed to make the process easier. This theme has excellent documentation, and is a good example to follow: `http://plone.org/products/webcouturier-hosting-theme/`.

Configuration

Before doing anything, you should always take a snapshot of the development site using `portal_setup` in the ZMI. This gives you the opportunity to track backwards to a working version if something goes wrong during the go-live process.

The next step, then, is to install the theme product on the instance that will be the production site. Next, you can add any necessary content that is needed to support the design. As part of content creation, you will also have to add any new views to `portal_types`. Once you've added these views, remember to activate those custom views on the development site using the **Display** drop-down menu.

You might need to make changes in the `portal_actions` area as well, depending on your work processes. Typically, you want the `portal_actions` and other similar pieces to be the part of your theme product in order to avoid rework, but you may choose to make these changes manually.

Thanks to a bug in GenericSetup (now fixed), the ordering of viewlets doesn't always happen consistently. A viewlet that is in the wrong place can look like a CSS error. So it helps to compare the order of viewlets on the production site against your local instance, using `@@manage-viewlets`, before attempting any CSS fixes. GenericSetup can be a touchy thing to work with, and sometimes it's just faster to make a few changes by hand, instead of trying to sort through your `viewlets.xml`, and make it work as desired. Or, you can export the `viewlets.xml` step from your working local version and include the relevant bits in your theme product. Ordering of viewlets for themes should be handled through the code as much as possible.

In addition, for publicly available themes, make sure that it is backwards compatible for all versions of Plone 3. This really only affects how you subclass your viewlets in `viewlets.py`, as discussed in Chapter 7, *Customizing Viewlets and Portlets*, and at `http://plone.org/documentation/tutorial/customizing-main-template-viewlets/overriding-a-class-viewlet`.

Another fairly time-consuming task can be portlet configuration. This is technically a content-related issue, but you should verify that all the portlets on the site are styled correctly, and also that static and collection portlets display as expected.

It's not uncommon (especially in a team scenario) for products to be installed after the theme product. This, in turn, can affect how the site displays. In this case, you should always check the order of the skin layers in `portal_skins`. You will generally want to make the theme product's layers appear just below **custom** in the **portal_skins | Properties** tab.

You should also check the order of your JavaScript and CSS files and make sure that they are being found by your theme. Again, this can affect the display of your site. You can check this by visiting the `portal_javascripts` and `portal_css` areas. If a file is not found, a yellow box will display a warning.

Finally, remember to check your theme into Subversion and then clean out the `custom` folder and `portal_view_customizations` in the ZMI, rolling any of those files into your theme product, if necessary. If more than one person is working on the site, or if you're dealing with a migration scenario, you may get a little out of sync here, so it's always best to be careful when rolling these items into your theme product. This may involve doing a "diff" comparison of an item in the `custom` folder to the files in your theme product to see where differences occur. Also, be careful of accidentally rolling older files into the theme product and overwriting your newer code, particularly in the case of migrations.

Quality assurance

Not surprisingly, the most time-consuming part of working on a theme is often the browser testing stage. While it's not possible to test against all browsers, it's good to follow the "A-List" recommendations found here: `http://developer.yahoo.com/yui/articles/gbs/index.html`. The use of VMware or Parallels and the proper browser add-ons (such as YSlow) is essential here. You may also choose to test against new media, such as iPhones and BlackBerries. Emulators (`http://iphonetester.com`) can be used, but they are not nearly as reliable as the real thing. Browser testing is typically done a few days prior to go-live in order to allow enough time to fix errors.

Another aspect of quality assurance involves testing the site's look and feel. This might include:

- Testing the areas of the site you might not visit often
- Testing the section-specific styling
- Verifying that any styles that need to be added to the visual editor are indeed added
- Verifying that viewlets are in the correct order, and that extra viewlets do not bleed through from other themes
- Checking that accessibility is taken into consideration
- Writing and testing the uninstall process

Let's look at these items in more detail.

- The areas of the site where you would not ordinarily look include areas such as the **Site Map**, **Site Setup**, the login page, or `@@manage-viewlets`. These pages are generated differently than most content on a Plone site, and their look and feel may not match the rest of the site, depending on your CSS. Section-specific CSS is also something to watch out for, and you should make sure that shortnames have not been altered, as this might negatively impact section-specific styling. In addition, the **Related Items** pop-up window should be checked to verify that the text is readable. On dark backgrounds, it can be hard to read, so you may wish to style that window to have a lighter background color. This window can be found on the **Categorization** button you see when you edit a piece of content, and the class is `.popup`.

- Another easy-to-forget task is to verify that any styles that need to be added to the visual editor are indeed added via **Site Setup**, or that this is addressed via a `kupu.xml` (or similar) file in your theme's `profiles/default` directory. Feel free to check out this theme for an example on what the `.xml` file might look like: `http://plone.org/products/webcouturier-hosting-theme/`. You may even want to put comments in your CSS file as a reminder to set these styles up for the end user.

- It's not always necessary to test how a web site prints out, as typically Plone defaults to suppressing the left and right columns in print mode. However, if there are viewlets that you want suppressed that Plone doesn't know about by default, you should print out a page and make sure it looks acceptable. In cases where you are working on something like a magazine or newspaper web site, this is especially critical. You can adjust `print.css.dtml` if there are elements that need to be hidden. You may also wish to test the presentation mode that is available in Plone, although it's rarely used.

- After you've finished configuring the ordering of your viewlets, you should also verify that you do not see any stray viewlets when you install your theme product. This may mean visiting other sites on your development instance. If you do see stray viewlets, this is typically related to a Plone theme bleeding into your site due to a missing `IThemeSpecific` designation. You should double-check your theme's `configure.zcml` files to make sure that your theme has `IThemeSpecific` designated where necessary.

- Accessibility is also a concern, and you should test enlarged and decreased fonts to make sure that the site is still readable. This is a tough area, especially with sites that are very delicately constructed, but wherever you can support accessibility, you should.

- Although we haven't covered this, you should probably make sure that your theme product has provided an uninstall routine. These are not widely documented, and depending on your internal processes, this may not even be needed. You can find information on uninstall routines here: `http://plone.org/documentation/tutorial/customizing-main-template-viewlets/reordering-and-hiding-viewlets/` and here: `https://weblion.psu.edu/trac/weblion/wiki/PloneThreeThemeUninstallProfile`.

As you can see, there are a lot of pieces involved in deploying and testing an installed theme, and you should do due diligence during the go-live process.

Deploying a theme for public use

A great number of individuals in the Plone community have graciously created themes for use by other people. The process for distributing these themes is fairly simple. It is important that the quality assurance process described above is followed, especially in terms of documenting dependencies, the installation process, and any content that needs to be created to support a theme.

You should store your theme product in Plone's "collective" SVN repository. To gain access to the repository, visit `http://plone.org/documentation/manual/plone-developer-reference/overview/contributing`. You can also find information on the Subversion commands you will need at `http://plone.org/documentation/how-to/svn-import-to-plone-collective-unix/`. Also, you should upload release versions of your theme product to the Python Package Index, PyPI. See the instructions at `http://pypi.python.org/pypi` for more information.

Then, you'll need to add your product to `http://www.plone.org` by doing the following:

1. Go to `http://plone.org/products`, and make sure you are logged in.
2. Click **Add new project**.
3. Enter the details for your theme, and make sure you select **Visual themes** as your category.
4. Make sure you include screenshots or thumbnails, where requested.
5. Save the form, and submit the project for approval. This is to prevent people from creating bogus projects. You can then add your files once it has been approved.

Plone welcomes any contributions to the theming community, and we hope that you will help other users by creating and adding your own themes to `http://www.plone.org`.

 If you wish to contribute theming work for Plone itself, you'll need to use Plone's SVN repository, and will need to sign the contributor agreement (`http://plone.org/documentation/manual/plone-developer-reference/overview/contributing`) to release rights to the Plone Foundation.

You can find numerous free themes on `oswd.org` or on other free templating sites. Please note that these are just straight CSS templates, they are not Plone themes. You may want to make sure your theme does not already exist on `plone.org` by familiarizing yourself with the currently available themes.

Summary

In this chapter, we have learned:

- About a suggested development environment and a theme deployment workflow
- About last minute configuration concerns
- About the quality assurance process and where to look for potential problems
- How to contribute to the Plone theming community by creating publicly available themes

In the next chapter, Alexander Limi will discuss the future of rules-based theming for Plone.

15
The Future of Theming for Plone

In this chapter, Alexander Limi gives us a sneak peek into the future of rules-based theming for Plone. This chapter will feature a complete walk-through of theming a site using the `collective.xdv` add-on.

Why a new approach?

The current approach to theming (also known as "skinning") the Plone sites (Plone 1.0 to 3.x) has been steadily evolving over a number of years, and is powerful, but somewhat complex.

As with most software, the reason for this complexity is usually a side effect of the evolution of the product—adding more functionality and more flexibility to meet the needs of power users, while still retaining the same approach to the problem space.

For Plone, the current theming approach has served us well for the last 8 years, but we realized it was time to reevaluate how theming was done, as it's such an integral part of managing a Plone site.

The main goals for a new approach were:

- No requirement for the people doing the theming to know anything about Plone or Python.
- Use standard tools and libraries whenever they are available.
- Reduce the number of concepts you have to learn in order to get started.
- When requiring you to learn something new, let it be a standard solution that is useful even outside of the Plone world.

- Try to stay as close to the HTML and CSS mindset as possible, as the people doing theming are usually the same people who write the HTML code for the design.

- Make it possible to apply an existing HTML/CSS design to a Plone site while keeping the original markup, instead of having to redo the design in a way that makes Plone happy.

- Let the theme work standalone, without introducing any additional markup. It should look like a standard HTML page with CSS, JS, and images.

About the future of theming in Plone

For the upcoming versions of Plone, we are ninety-nine percent sure that we'll use a variant of what is described here. It will probably change slightly in how it integrates into the product and what knobs are available to deploy a theme in a standard way, but the fundamental approach will be the same.

What we are offering you with the `collective.xdv` package is a way to make use of the likely future standard of theming today. We'll keep this document updated as Plone progresses with newer versions, and if you're reading this documentation in a book or another printed version, always check at `http://plone.org/theming` to view the latest version of this document.

Is XDV ready for serious deployments?

Currently, the `plone.org` web site itself is using XDV for its theme—so it's battle-tested and ready for serious, high-traffic sites.

Background and history

Before starting, let us explain briefly the history of **XDV**, and the reason it exists.

When people talk about this new approach to theming, they will often refer to the general approach as **Deliverance-based**. The original **Deliverance** project (`http://deliverance.openplans.org`) was started by Paul Everitt (`http://pauleveritt.wordpress.com`) a long time ago, and was further enhanced by Ian Bicking (`http://www.ianbicking.org`), who is its current maintainer.

Along the way, Deliverance got more powerful and expanded beyond the initial goals, and started handling cases that were not included in the original scope.

Long story short, a new implementation of the same basic approach was started, called XDV. This is a stripped-down, pure XSLT implementation of the Deliverance concept, and can be compiled down and used directly inside a web server such as Apache, IIS, or nginx (pronounced "Engine X") as a standard XSLT transform, without any extra software running.

This does not mean that XDV is somehow better than the original Deliverance implementation, or that it makes it obsolete—they are different tools with slightly different goals, sharing the same basic approach. We'll get to an overview of which approach is appropriate for what cases in a moment.

The final piece of this puzzle is the add-on called `collective.xdv` (`http://pypi.python.org/pypi/collective.xdv`), which takes XDV and packages it up to make it very convenient for use with Plone.

> The "collective" namespace is a common pattern in Plone add-ons. It denotes software that is managed collectively by the Plone community, and not necessarily by the Plone Foundation.

Why do you need to know all this? It's useful to keep in mind that you can carry across what you learn in using `collective.xdv` to the Deliverance project, should you need to do that at a later point. The basic syntax and approach is largely the same, although the details of the implementation can differ slightly.

Choosing the appropriate theming approach

You have several alternatives when it comes to theming Plone at this point. Let's look at what makes them different.

Product Package:

- **Pros**:
    - The ultimate in flexibility and control.
    - More flexibility when it comes to theming the select parts of a site or sub sites.

- **Cons**:
    - More complex, requires a passing familiarity with **ZCML** and Python.
    - Less upgrade-resistant, as templates change.
    - Shipping your own templates will get you out of sync with the main product.

collective.xdv

- **Pros:**
  - Can be compiled down to XSLT transforms that run as part of the web server process, so you don't need a separate proxy or WSGI setup (`http://www.wsgi.org/wsgi`). This also means a slight performance advantage over Deliverance.
  - Easy to bootstrap with Plone.

- **Cons:**
  - Uses XPath selectors instead of the more familiar CSS selectors (not a big deal as you may fear, since we can use Firebug to make it create the XPath expressions for us, as we'll see later).

Deliverance

- **Pros compared to XDV:**
  - Standalone, can be used without Plone to theme other sites and systems.
  - Supports a more familiar CSS syntax in addition to XPath.

- **Cons compared to xdv:**
  - Less integrated with Plone, requires you to understand more of the ecosystem and setup.
  - Uses its own non-standard (but CSS-like) syntax, can't be deployed inside a web server process.

Which one should I use?

A general rule-of-thumb to help you decide what approach to choose:

- **Use the add-on/product approach** — when you need extreme granularity of control, and are willing to learn some Python and ZCML to get what you want.
- **Use XDV** — when you'd like to keep the theme separate from the code, and want a reusable theme approach that can potentially be deployed as part of the web server process. And when you don't want to worry about most of the "plumbing", and are comfortable using best practices from the Plone community.

- **Use Deliverance** — when you have advanced theming needs, including the ability to apply the same theme to multiple frameworks/web apps in addition to Plone, and are willing to set up a proxy or WSGI pipeline to make it happen.

Of course, reality is always a bit more complicated — you can apply an XDV-based theme to non-Plone setups too, if you know what you're doing.

The important part to know is that you can move between XDV and Deliverance pretty easily, so starting out with `collective.xdv` is likely to be a great start, even if you end up using Deliverance later.

Tools and prerequisites

Before we get started, make sure you have the following software available:

- The latest version of Plone (Plone 3.3 or newer for the best experience).
- The latest version of Firefox (available for all platforms — `http://www.getfirefox.com/`).
- The Firebug add-on for Firefox (`http://getfirebug.com`).
- Your text editor of choice.
- Access to the terminal or command line on the system you are working on.
- A network connection (to make sure buildout can download its packages) — you can work around this by downloading the packages separately if you don't have a network connection, but it's outside of the scope of this tutorial. Consult the buildout documentation if you need to download offline packages: `http://www.buildout.org`.

And again: if you're reading this in printed form, make sure you check the online version at `http://plone.org/theming` for the latest version recommendations, as versions and buildout dependency URLs may change slightly over time.

Got everything set up? Great, let's get down to business!

Adding XDV to your Plone instance

The first step is to add `collective.xdv` to our Plone setup.

We will assume that you have a passing familiarity with Plone's configuration/build system, buildout (`http://www.buildout.org/`) — if not, don't worry, it should be pretty simple to follow along even if you don't. I also assume that you already have Plone and Firefox with Firebug installed. You may also find this tutorial helpful: `http://plone.org/documentation/tutorial/buildout`.

About the setup: Setting up XDV takes some grunt work, because it has some slightly unusual dependencies. When this solution ships with Plone itself, this will of course already be handled for you. So bear with us through the install instructions, and rest safe in the knowledge that this will be much easier in the future. It's the price you pay for being on the forefront of technology, but we can promise you that it will be worth it!

Platform notes

As we don't know whether you'll be on Linux, Mac OS X, or Windows, we have to assume that you know how to get to the command prompt or the terminal on your platform, and know how to find your Plone instances and its associated files. In the command line examples that follow, we'll use the Linux and Mac OS X convention of slashes (– / –) for directories, and use backslash (– \ –) instead, if you're on Windows. The $ marker indicates the command prompt; if you're on Windows, it'll be a > instead. You're not supposed to type that character; it's just an indicator that there's a new command being entered.

With that out of the way, let's get started!

Adding collective.xdv

1. Locate the file `buildout.cfg` in the root of your Plone instance directory on the file system, and open it in a text editor. Locate the section that looks like this:

    ```
    # extends = http://dist.plone.org/release/3.3/versions.cfg
    extends = versions.cfg
    versions = versions
    ```

    It may also have a URL in the `extends` section, similar to the commented-out first line, depending on whether you pull the Plone configuration from the network or locally.

2. To add `collective.xdv` to our setup, we need some slightly different versions of a couple of the packages, so we extend the base configuration with a version list from the Good-Py service. Change this part of the configuration so that it looks like this:

    ```
    extends = versions.cfg
            http://good-py.appspot.com/release/collective.xdv/1.0
    versions = versions
    ```

Good-Py is a web application hosted on Google App Engine that aims to help manage known-good version sets of Python packages (`http://good-py.appspot.com/`).

What happens here is that the dependency list for `collective.xdv` specifies some new versions for you via the Good-Py URL. This way, you don't have to worry about getting the right versions, as buildout will handle it for you.

3. The next step is to add the actual `collective.xdv` add-on to the `eggs` section of `buildout.cfg`. Look for the section that looks like this:

```
eggs =
    Plone
```

This section might have additional lines if you have other add-ons already installed. Just add the `collective.xdv` on a separate line, like this:

```
eggs =
    Plone
    collective.xdv
```

Running buildout

Once you have added these lines to your configuration file, it's time to run buildout so that the system can add and set up `collective.xdv` for you. Go to the command line, and from the root of your Plone instance (in your `buildout/` directory), run `buildout` like this:

```
$ bin/buildout
```

You will see output similar to this:

```
Getting distribution for 'collective.xdv==1.0'.
Got collective.xdv 1.0.
Getting distribution for 'dv.xdvserver'.
Got dv.xdvserver 1.0b4.
Getting distribution for 'plone.postpublicationhook'.
Got plone.postpublicationhook 1.0rc1.
Getting distribution for 'plone.app.registry'.
Got plone.app.registry 1.0a1.
Getting distribution for 'plone.synchronize'.
Got plone.synchronize 1.0b1.
```

If you get errors when doing this instead of the above output, please contact the Plone support forums to get more help with your specific setup (`http://plone.org/support`). There might be some issues, especially if you're on Mac OS X. We have been working on fixing the Mac situation for a while, and it should be fixed by the time you read this, but if it isn't, let us know!

If everything went according to plan, we now have `collective.xdv` installed. It's time to start Plone and activate it for our site!

Activating XDV

Now that we have added XDV to our setup, it's time to activate it for our specific Plone site.

1. Make sure Plone was (re)started, and log in as an administrator.
2. Go to **Site Setup | Add-On Products** and install `collective.xdv`.
3. Once it is installed, go to **Site Setup** and make sure there is a new control panel called **Theme Transform**.

The **Theme Transform** control panel has a number of settings that we'll make use of in a minute, but first we will create a simple HTML file and some transform rules to get started.

Adding the HTML and rule files

Let's create a dedicated directory in your instance where you can keep your theme files:

1. Navigate to your instance directory.
2. Create a directory called `themes`.

Never put anything in the `parts`, `eggs`, or `develop-eggs` directories, as buildout considers these private, and may potentially wipe them when updating your setup.

3. Inside the `themes/` directory, create the following two files using your text editor:

`theme.html`:

```
<html>
<head>
  <title>xdv example</title>
</head>
<body>

    <h1>The simplest possible example of xdv transforms</h1>
    <p id="my-content-area">This body text will be replaced.</p>

</body>
</html>
```

`rules.xml`:

```
<rules xmlns="http://openplans.org/deliverance">

    <!-- Copy over the contents of the page body -->
    <replace content='//*[@id="content"]'
             theme='//*[@id="my-content-area"]' />

</rules>
```

Believe it or not, that's a complete—although very basic—Plone theme using XDV!

We now have an HTML file that forms the base of our design, as well as a rules file that does the transform. All we have left to do is tell Plone about the paths for the theme and rule files and enable the transform.

Enabling the theme transform

Let's go back to the **Theme Transform** Plone control panel:

The settings you need to care about right now are:

- **Enabled**: Turns the XDV theme transformation on or off. Switch this to "on".
- **Domains**: Specifies which domains get the theme transforms applied. You can view your theme during development via `localhost:8080`. The one thing to note here is that `127.0.0.1` (essentially the same as localhost) will never have a theme applied as a safety net, so you can always get back to your site even if an error while developing your theme transform makes it unusable. There is a default value of `localhost:8080` here; adjust if your setup is different, but usually the default value is fine.

The next two values are where it gets interesting:

- **Theme template**: A file path or URL pointing to the theme file. This is just a static HTML file. Add `theme/theme.html` here. It's relative to your instance directory, no need for the full path.

- **Rules file**: The filesystem path to the rules XML file. Add `theme/rules.xml` here.

Ignore the rest of the form values for now, and press **Save**.

Testing that everything works

Now, let's go to the front page of your Plone site via `localhost:8080/yoursite` and see what happened. Admire your beautiful, un-styled HTML page with the content from Plone inserted into it. It should look something like the following:

> # The simplest possible example of xdv transforms
>
> # Welcome to Plone
>
> Congratulations! You have successfully installed Plone.
>
> Also available in presentation mode...
>
> If you're seeing this instead of the web site you were expecting, the owner of this web site has just installed Plone. Do not contact the Plone Team or the Plone mailing lists about this.

Not particularly *visually* exciting, is it? But what you have just set up is a very, very powerful way to theme Plone sites that makes it possible to use any pre-existing design with a Plone backend. The reason this is exciting is that you're using your own HTML and CSS, not modifying Plone's HTML and CSS.

Next, let's step back a bit and explain how it all fits together.

How it works

Let's look at a high-level overview of what is going on in XDV (and Deliverance).

The way XDV works is simple, but since it might take a little tweaking to the mental model you're used to if you have done theming in Plone (or other systems), it's worth an explanation.

The main difference is that you're not touching the templates and HTML from Plone itself at all. Instead, you create the layout and design you want in standalone HTML and CSS files, and then map parts of the content that comes out of Plone into your existing HTML.

This means that you can create as complex (or simple) designs as you want, and let Plone supply the content.

This also means that you can write your own from-scratch HTML and CSS, but also map various Plone elements to wherever you want in your own design. Plone knows nothing about what happens "on the way out"; it just renders a page as it usually does.

Here is a more visual way to look at it. You can see how the Plone output is mapped into a totally different template and design:

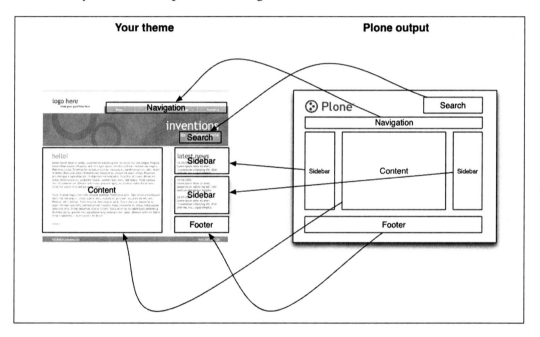

This makes for a much more robust approach to theming, because as long as Plone keeps its HTML classes and IDs the same from one version to the next, your theme will automatically work even in a new version of Plone. And if it has changed, it's a relatively simple operation to update the theme—just locate the new name, and replace it in the rule file.

Let's take a closer look at the rule file.

The rule file

Central to the way content makes its way from your Plone site into your theme is the rule file.

Let's look at your simple `rules.xml` file again:

```
<rules xmlns="http://openplans.org/deliverance">

    <!-- Copy over the contents of the page body -->
    <replace content='//*[@id="content"]'
             theme='//*[@id="my-content-area"]' />

</rules>
```

Ignoring the preamble `<rules>` and the comment, there's one single instruction here. So what does it do?

1. It looks at the Plone side of things ("content"), and locates the part of the HTML that has `id="content"`.

2. It then replaces the part of your theme's HTML that has `id="my-content-area"` with the content it got from Plone.

The syntax (inside the content and the theme attributes) can be a bit intimidating — luckily, we have great tools to make it very easy to get this right. The syntax is called XPath, and is a standard for addressing nodes in the DOM. It's also directly supported in Firebug. A full treatment of how Firebug works is outside the scope of this tutorial, but if you have done any web design in the past, you have probably used it. If not, head over to the Firebug web site (`http://getfirebug.com/`) to learn more — they have documentation and screencasts showing you how to use it.

I will show you a screenshot of the part we're interested in. However, when you're looking at the Plone source code using Firebug, locate the content area as shown next, and right-click the node:

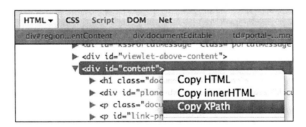

As you can see, there's a way to copy any HTML node and get its XPath expression. When you paste what's now on your clipboard, you will see:

```
//*[@id="content"]
```

…and that's the XPath expression that uniquely identifies that part of the page! You probably recognize this from our original `rules.xml` file. That's the node you're looking for in the Plone source, and you use the same approach to find the node you want to replace in your `theme.html`.

You don't have to teach yourself XPath, just arm yourself with Firebug, and make use of its built-in support for these expressions.

 Deliverance has implemented support for CSS-like syntax — that is, `#content` instead of `//*[@id="content"]` — which is certainly easier to remember. The XPath-based syntax works equally well in both XDV and Deliverance, though.

Let's go over the available rules next.

Rules Overview

Luckily, what goes in the rule file is very simple — there are only four types of rules, and you'll get the hang of them quickly. The rules are:

- Replace
- Append/prepend
- Copy
- Drop

Let's look at what they do and show some real-world examples of how they are used.

<replace>

It replaces an element in the theme with content from the site.

Real-world examples

A useful thing to do is to carry over the `<title>` and `<base>` tags from Plone, so the theme will have the right page titles and work correctly when you do operations on folders:

```
<replace content='/html/head/title'
         theme='/html/head/title' />

<replace content='/html/head/base'
         theme='/html/head/base' />
```

The XPath expressions are actually pretty straightforward when you know exactly where the elements are. You'll get used to the most common variations after using Firebug's **Copy XPath** a few times.

Also note how the entire specified tag is replaced, nothing from the theme file remains.

Another common example is making the content of a page from Plone appear in the theme:

```
<replace content='//*[@id="content"]'
         theme='//*[@id="my-content"]' />
```

<append> and <prepend>

They add the content from the site to the theme, either before or after the specified element.

Real-world examples

Adding the Plone-created CSS and JS in addition to the ones already in the theme:

```
<append content='/html/head/script'
        theme='/html/head' />
<append content='/html/head/style'
        theme='/html/head' />
```

Notice how we take all of the `<script>` and `<style>` tags from Plone, and append them after the current content of the head tag in the theme. This way, you can let Plone manage some of your CSS and JS if you want—useful for conditional `includes`.

Another example is carrying over the `id` and `class` attributes on the `body` tag, since these are useful for styling on a per-page basis, and the visual editor uses them too:

```
<prepend content="/html/body/@class"
         theme="/html/body" />
<prepend content="/html/body/@id"
         theme="/html/body"  />
```

A final example that illustrates the `<append>` usage. Imagine that we only have one sidebar in the Plone site, but have two columns, and we want both to appear inside the sidebar:

```
<append content='//*[@id="portal-column-one"]/div'
        theme='//*[@id="sidebar"]' />
<append content='//*[@id="portal-column-two"]/div'
        theme='//*[@id="sidebar"]' />
```

This way, the second rule doesn't overwrite the first. It *appends* the second column, so both appear inside the `id="sidebar"` node.

<copy>

It copies HTML nodes from the Plone side of things and inserts them inside a tag on the theme side:

```
<copy content='//*[@id="portal-globalnav"]/li'
      theme='//*[@id="main-nav"]' />
```

Notice how this one gets every `<li>` element inside the node with `id="portal-globalnav"` in Plone, and makes a copy inside the node that has `id="main-nav"` in the theme.

<drop>

It removes the specified element if it exists. This one is a bit different than the others, as it only has a `content=` value, and it only makes sense to drop an element from the Plone side.

Real-world example

Getting rid of the icon inside the `"user-name"` node:

```
<drop content='//*[@id="user-name"]/img' />
```

Since there is no id directly on this image, we just drop any `<img>` inside the `"user-name"` id.

That's actually everything you need to know, now the next steps are up to you!

Summary

You now have a new way to make themes for Plone, where do you go from here?

The best way to learn is by doing, so your next step should be to take one of your existing designs and map Plone into it.

If you don't have any themes yourself, a great site for free designs is `oswd.org` (Open Source Web Design). Here are some great themes you can download to get you started:

- Invention (`http://www.oswd.org/design/preview/id/3293`)
- Bitter Sweet (`http://www.oswd.org/design/preview/id/3569`)
- Nonzero (`http://www.oswd.org/design/preview/id/3560`)
- Transparentia (`http://www.oswd.org/design/preview/id/3515`)

Remember that if any of these themes are missing ids for easy mapping in the rule file, just add them in the HTML.

Have fun with your new-found theming superpowers!

Index

Symbols

\<append> rule
about 294
Real-world examples 294
\<copy> rule 295
\<drop> rule
about 295
Real-world example 295
\<prepend> rule
about 294
Real-world examples 294
\<replace> rule
about 293
Real-world examples 293

A

add-on Plone products
about 245
Collage 246
collection portlet 250
collective.skinny 249
CSSManager 247
drop downs, enabling webcouturier.drop-
    downmenu used 245, 246
FS Dump 249
Products.EasyAsPiIE 248
qPloneSkinDump 250
static portlet 250
tableless styling, Plone Tableless used 247
Adobe Fireworks
about 20
features 20
Adobe Photoshop
about 18

features 18, 19
images, slicing 19
layers panel 18
show/hide functionality 18

B

base_properties
about 99
advantage 100
browser layer 113
browser pages
about 113, 121
customizing 121
directive attributes 124
enabling 126
GenericSetup steps, writing 125
new CMF action category, creating 125
page template, creating 124
Python class, creating 122, 123
registering 123
simple browser view, creating 121
viewlet, registering in theme product 125
browser resources
about 118
images, overriding 120
images, using as 118-120
registering, with ZCML 118
stylesheet, customizing 121
stylesheet, declaring 120
stylesheets, using as 120, 121
browsers
about 21
Firefox 24
Internet Explorer 22
Safari tools 36

Packt Open Source Project Royalties

When we sell a book written on an Open Source project, we pay a royalty directly to that project. Therefore by purchasing Plone 3 Theming, Packt will have given some of the money received to the Plone project.

In the long term, we see ourselves and you—customers and readers of our books—as part of the Open Source ecosystem, providing sustainable revenue for the projects we publish on. Our aim at Packt is to establish publishing royalties as an essential part of the service and support a business model that sustains Open Source.

If you're working with an Open Source project that you would like us to publish on, and subsequently pay royalties to, please get in touch with us.

Writing for Packt

We welcome all inquiries from people who are interested in authoring. Book proposals should be sent to author@packtpub.com. If your book idea is still at an early stage and you would like to discuss it first before writing a formal book proposal, contact us; one of our commissioning editors will get in touch with you.

We're not just looking for published authors; if you have strong technical skills but no writing experience, our experienced editors can help you develop a writing career, or simply get some additional reward for your expertise.

About Packt Publishing

Packt, pronounced 'packed', published its first book "Mastering phpMyAdmin for Effective MySQL Management" in April 2004 and subsequently continued to specialize in publishing highly focused books on specific technologies and solutions.

Our books and publications share the experiences of your fellow IT professionals in adapting and customizing today's systems, applications, and frameworks. Our solution-based books give you the knowledge and power to customize the software and technologies you're using to get the job done. Packt books are more specific and less general than the IT books you have seen in the past. Our unique business model allows us to bring you more focused information, giving you more of what you need to know, and less of what you don't.

Packt is a modern, yet unique publishing company, which focuses on producing quality, cutting-edge books for communities of developers, administrators, and newbies alike. For more information, please visit our website: www.PacktPub.com.

Practical Plone 3

ISBN: 978-1-847191-78-6   Paperback: 592 pages

A Beginner's Guide to Building Powerful Websites

1. Get a Plone-based website up and running quickly without dealing with code

2. Beginner's guide with easy-to-follow instructions and screenshots

3. Learn how to make the best use of Plone's out-of-the-box features

4. Customize security, look-and-feel, and many other aspects of Plone

Professional Plone Development

ISBN: 978-1-847191-98-4   Paperback: 420 pages

Building robust, content-centric web applications with Plone 3, an open source Content Management System

1. Plone development fundamentals

2. Customizing Plone

3. Developing new functionality

4. Real-world deployments

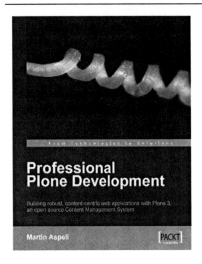

Please check **www.PacktPub.com** for information on our titles

Building Websites with Plone

ISBN: 1-904811-02-7   Paperback: 416 pages

An in-depth and comprehensive guide to the Plone content management system

1. A comprehensive guide for Plone website administrators and developers

2. Design, build, and manage content rich websites using Plone

3. Extend Plone's skins and content types

4. Customize, secure, and optimize Plone websites

Expert Python Programming

ISBN: 978-1-847194-94-7   Paperback: 372 pages

Best practices for designing, coding, and distributing your Python software

1. Learn Python development best practices from an expert, with detailed coverage of naming and coding conventions

2. Apply object-oriented principles, design patterns, and advanced syntax tricks

3. Manage your code with distributed version control

4. Profile and optimize your code

5. Proactive test-driven development and continuous integration

Please check **www.PacktPub.com** for information on our titles

CPSIA information can be obtained at www.ICGtesting.com
Printed in the USA
243751LV00004B/75/P